Joint FAO/WHO Food Standards Programme
CODEX ALIMENTARIUS COMMISSION

CODEX ALIMENTARIUS
VOLUME ONE
GENERAL REQUIREMENTS

**FOOD AND AGRICULTURE ORGANIZATION
OF THE UNITED NATIONS
WORLD HEALTH ORGANIZATION**

Rome 1992

The designations employed and the presentation of material in this publication do not imply the expression of any opinion whatsoever on the part of the Food and Agriculture Organization of the United Nations concerning the legal status of any country, territory, city or area or of its authorities, or concerning the delimitation of its frontiers or boundaries.

M-83

T0534E/1/12.91/3500
ISBN 92-5-103120-7

THE CODEX ALIMENTARIUS

Preface

The Codex Alimentarius Commission is the international body responsible for the execution of the Joint FAO/WHO Food Standards Programme. Created in 1962 by FAO and WHO the Programme is aimed at protecting the health of consumers and facilitating international trade in foods.

The Codex Alimentarius (Latin, meaning Food Law or Code) is a collection of international food standards adopted by the Commission and presented in a uniform manner. It includes standards for all the principal foods, whether processed or semi-processed or raw. Materials for further processing into foods are included to the extent necessary to achieve the purposes of the Codex Alimentarius as defined. The Codex Alimentarius includes provisions in respect of the hygienic and nutritional quality of food, including microbiological norms, provisions for food additives, pesticide residues, contaminants, labelling and presentations, and methods of analysis and sampling. It also includes provisions of an advisory nature in the form of codes of practice, guidelines and other recommended measures.

This is the second publication of the Codex Alimentarius. Prior to 1981 standards adopted by the Codex Alimentarius Commission were published individually as Recommended Standards (CAC/RS series). Following the 14th Session of the Commission in July 1981, all Codex standards were compiled into the first complete version of the Codex Alimentarius, organized into 19 volumes of standards by subject matter, 11 volumes of codes of hygienic practice, and 2 volumes of acceptances. The Codex Alimentarius in this format was available only through the Documents Office of the Joint FAO/WHO Food Standards Programme.

In July 1989 the 18th Session of the Commission endorsed the revised publication of the Codex Alimentarius for distribution and sale through the world-wide networks of FAO and WHO. It is intended to publish the Codex Alimentarius in 14 volumes: the present volume containing general requirements; 9 volumes of standards and codes of practice compiled on a commodity-by-commodity basis; 2 volumes dealing with residues of pesticides and veterinary drugs in foods; a volume containing methods of analysis and sampling; and one on acceptances of standards. The present volume contains all relevant texts adopted by the Commission up to and including those at its 19th Session, July 1991.

An abridged version of the Codex Alimentarius, containing only the food standards adopted by the Commission has also been published as a ready reference and complements the complete version.

CONTENTS OF THE CODEX ALIMENTARIUS

6.   Canned Baby Foods

7.   Processed Cereal-based Foods for Infants and Children

8.   Follow-up Formula

9.   Advisory Lists of Mineral Salts and Vitamin Compounds for Use in Foods for Infants and Children

10.   Code of Hygienic Practice for Foods for Infants and Children (including Microbiological Specifications and Methods for Microbiological Analysis)

VOLUME FIVE

Processed and Quick-Frozen Fruits and Vegetables

1.   Standards

2.   Codes of Hygienic Practice

VOLUME SIX

Fruit Juices

VOLUME SEVEN

Cereals, Pulses (Legumes) and Derived Products

1.   Standards

2.   Codes of Practice

VOLUME EIGHT

Fats and Oils

1.   Standards

2.   Code of Practice

VOLUME NINE

Fish and Fishery Products

1.   Standards

2.   Codes of Practice

VOLUME TEN

Meat and Meat Products; Soups and Broths

1.   Standards

2.   Codes of Practice

INTRODUCTION

STATUTES OF THE CODEX ALIMENTARIUS COMMISSION AND IMPLEMENTATION OF THE FOOD STANDARDS PROGRAMME BY THE COMMISSION

The Codex Alimentarius Commission was established to implement the Joint FAO/WHO Food Standards Programme, the purpose of which is, as set down in the Statutes of the Commission, to protect the health of consumers and to ensure fair practices in the food trade; to promote coordination of all food standards work undertaken by international governmental and non-governmental organizations; to determine priorities and initiate and guide the preparation of draft standards through and with the aid of appropriate organizations; to finalize standards, and, after acceptance by governments, publish them in a Codex Alimentarius either as regional or world-wide standards[1].

The Statutes of the Codex Alimentarius Commission have been approved by the Governing bodies of the FAO and WHO. The Commission is a subsidiary body of these two parent Organizations. The Statutes and Rules of the Commission are to be found in the Procedural Manual of the Commission.

THE CODEX ALIMENTARIUS

Purpose

The Codex Alimentarius is a collection of internationally adopted food standards presented in a uniform manner. These food standards aim at protecting consumers' health and ensuring fair practices in the food trade. The Codex Alimentarius also includes provisions of an advisory nature in the form of codes of practice, guidelines and other recommended measures to assist in achieving the purposes of the Codex Alimentarius. The publication of the Codex Alimentarius is intended to guide and promote the elaboration and establishment of definitions and requirements for foods, to assist in their harmonization and, in doing so, to facilitate international trade.

Scope

The Codex Alimentarius includes standards for all the principal foods, whether processed, semi-processed or raw, for distribution to the consumer. Materials for further processing into foods are included to the extent necessary to achieve the purposes of the Codex Alimentarius as defined. The Codex Alimentarius includes provisions in respect of the hygienic and nutritional quality of food, including microbiological norms, provisions for food additives, pesticide residues, contaminants, labelling and presentation, and methods of analysis and sampling. It also includes provisions of an advisory nature in the form of codes of practice, guidelines and other recommended measures. Codex standards contain requirements for food aimed at ensuring for the consumer a sound, wholesome food product free from adulteration, correctly labelled and presented.

---

[1] The Codex Alimentarius Commission decided, at its 14th Session in July 1981, that its standards, which are sent to all Member States and Associate Members of FAO and/or WHO for acceptance, together with details of notifications received from governments with respect to the acceptance or otherwise of the standards and other relevant information, constitute the Codex Alimentarius.

Acceptance

    The standards and maximum residue limits adopted by the Codex Alimentarius
Commission are intended for formal acceptance by governments in accordance with its
General Principles.

    The standards and maximum limits for pesticide residues, accompanied by an
appropriate communication, are sent for action to Ministries of Agriculture or Ministries
of Foreign Affairs, as appropriate, of Member Nations of FAO and to Ministries of Health
of Member States of WHO. The standards and maximum limits for pesticide residues,
accompanied by the communication referred to, are also sent to national Codex Contact
Points, FAO and WHO Regional Offices, FAO Representatives, Embassies in Rome and Permanent
Missions to the UN in Geneva.

    The standards and maximum limits for pesticide residues, which have taken a number
of years to develop, are the product of a wide measure of international agreement and
cooperation. They are compatible with the norms considered by FAO and WHO as best
guaranteeing the protection of the health of consumers and the facilitation of
international trade in food.

    Volume One, General Requirements, of the Codex Alimentarius contains those
standards, codes and other texts which are generally applicable to all food commodities,
or at least a wide range of them. It is the basic reference document for all other
volumes in the Codex Alimentarius.

CONTENTS

SECTION 1

GENERAL PRINCIPLES OF THE
CODEX ALIMENTARIUS

GENERAL PRINCIPLES OF THE
CODEX ALIMENTARIUS

Purpose of the Codex Alimentarius

1.   The Codex Alimentarius is a collection of internationally adopted food standards presented in a uniform manner. These food standards aim at protecting consumers' health and ensuring fair practices in the food trade. The Codex Alimentarius also includes provisions of an advisory nature in the form of codes of practice, guidelines and other recommended measures intended to assist in achieving the purposes of the Codex Alimentarius. The publication of the Codex Alimentarius is intended to guide and promote the elaboration and establishment of definitions and requirements for foods to assist in their harmonization and in doing so to facilitate international trade.

Scope of the Codex Alimentarius

2.   The Codex Alimentarius includes standards for all the principle foods, whether processed, semi-processed or raw, for distribution to the consumer. Materials for further processing into foods should be included to the extent necessary to achieve the purposes of the Codex Alimentarius as defined. The Codex Alimentarius includes provisions in respect of food hygiene, food additives, pesticide residues, contaminants, labelling and presentation, methods of analysis and sampling. It also includes provisions of an advisory nature in the form of codes of practice, guidelines and other recommended measures.

Nature of Codex Standards

3.   Codex standards contain requirements for food aimed at ensuring for the consumer a sound, wholesome food product free from adulteration, correctly labelled and presented. A Codex standard for any food or foods should be drawn up in accordance with the Format for Codex Commodity Standards and contain, as appropriate, the criteria listed therein.

Acceptance of Codex Commodity Standards

4.A. A Codex standard may be accepted by a country in accordance with its established legal and administrative procedures in respect of distribution of the product concerned, whether imported or home-produced, within its territorial jurisdiction in the following ways:

    (i)   <u>Full acceptance</u>

        (a)   Full acceptance means that the country concerned will ensure that a product to which the standard applies will be permitted to be distributed freely, in accordance with (c) below, within its territorial jurisdiction under the name and description laid down in the standard, provided that it complies with all the relevant requirements of the standard.

        (b)   The country will also ensure that products not complying with the standard will not be permitted to be distributed under the name and description laid down in the standard.

        (c)   The distribution of any sound products conforming with the standard will not be hindered by any legal or administrative provisions in the country concerned relating to the health of the consumer or to other food standard matters except for considerations of human, plant or animal health which are not specifically dealt with in the standard.

(ii)   Target Acceptance

Target acceptance means that the country concerned indicates its intention to accept the standard after a stated number of years and will meanwhile not hinder within its territorial jurisdiction the distribution of any sound products conforming with the standard by any legal or administrative provisions relating to the health of the consumer or to other food standard matters except for considerations of human, plant or animal health which are not specifically dealt with in the standard.

(iii) Acceptance with specified deviations

Acceptance with specified deviations means that the country concerned gives acceptance, as defined in paragraph 4.A(i), to the standard with the exception of such deviations as are specified in detail in its declaration of acceptance; it being understood that a product complying with the standard as qualified by these deviations will be permitted to be distributed freely within the territorial jurisdiction of the country concerned. The country concerned will further include in its declaration of acceptance a statement of the reasons for these deviations, and also indicate:

(a)   whether products fully conforming to the standard may be distributed freely within its territorial jurisdiction in accordance with paragraph 4.A(i);

(b)   whether it expects to be able to give full acceptance to the standard and, if so, when.

4.B.   A country which considers that it cannot accept the standard in any of the ways mentioned above should indicate:

(i)   whether products conforming to the standard may be distributed freely within its territorial jurisdiction;

(ii)   in what ways its present or proposed requirements differ from the standard, and, if possible the reasons for these differences.

4.C.   (i)   A country which accepts a Codex standard according to one of the provisions of 4.A is responsible for the uniform and impartial application of the provisions of the standard as accepted, in respect of all home-produced and imported products distributed within its territorial jurisdiction. In addition, the country should be prepared to offer advice and guidance to exporters and processors of products for export to promote understanding of and compliance with the requirements of importing countries which have accepted a Codex standard according to one of the provisions of 4.A.

(ii)   Where, in an importing country, a product claimed to be in compliance with a Codex standard is found not to be in compliance with that standard, whether in respect of the label accompanying the product or otherwise, the importing country should inform the competent authorities in the exporting country of all the relevant facts and in particular the details of the origin of the product in question (name and address of the exporter), if it is thought that a person in the exporting country is responsible for such non-compliance.

Acceptance of Codex General Standards

5.A.   A Codex general standard may be accepted by a country in accordance with its established legal and administrative procedures in respect of the distribution of products to which the general standard applies, whether imported or home-produced, within its territorial jurisdiction in the following ways:

(i)   Full acceptance

Full acceptance of a general standard means that the country concerned will ensure, within its territorial jurisdiction, that a product to which the general standard applies will comply with all the relevant requirements of the general standard except as otherwise provided in a Codex commodity standard. It also means that the distribution of any sound products conforming with the standard will not be hindered by any legal or administrative provisions in the country concerned, which relate to the health of the consumer or to other food standard matters and which are covered by the requirements of the general standard.

(ii)   Target acceptance

Target acceptance means that the country concerned indicates its intention to accept the general standard after a stated number of years.

(iii) Acceptance with specified deviations

Acceptance with specified deviations means that the country concerned gives acceptance, as defined in paragraph 5.A(i), to the general standard with the exception of such deviations as are specified in detail in its declaration of acceptance. The country concerned will further include in its declaration of acceptance a statement of the reasons for these deviations, and also indicate whether it expects to be able to give full acceptance to the general standard and, if so, when.

5.B.   A country which considers that it cannot accept the general standard in any of the ways mentioned above should indicate in what ways its present or proposed requirements differ from the general standard, and if possible, the reasons for these differences.

5.C.   (i)   A country which accepts a general standard according to one of the provisions of paragraph 5.A is responsible for the uniform and impartial application of the provisions of the standard as accepted, in respect of all home-produced and imported products distributed within its territorial jurisdiction. In addition, the country should be prepared to offer advice and guidance to exporters and processors of products for export to promote understanding of and compliance with the requirements of importing countries which have accepted a general standard according to one of the provisions of paragraph 5.A.

(ii)   Where, in an importing country, a product claimed to be in compliance with a general standard is found not to be in compliance with that standard, whether in respect of the label accompanying the product or otherwise, the importing country should inform the competent authorities in the exporting country of all the relevant facts and in particular the details of the origin of the product in question (name and address of the exporter), if it is thought that a person in the exporting country is responsible for such non-compliance.

Acceptance of Codex Maximum Limits for Residues of Pesticides and Veterinary Drugs in Food

6.A.   A Codex maximum limit for residues of pesticides or veterinary drugs in food may be accepted by a country in accordance with its established legal and administrative procedures in respect of the distribution within its territorial jurisdiction of (a) home-produced and imported food or (b) imported food only, to which the Codex maximum limit applies in the ways set forth below. In addition, where a Codex maximum limit applies to a group of foods not individually named, a country accepting such Codex maximum limit in respect of other than the group of foods, shall specify the foods in respect of which the Codex maximum limit is accepted.

(i)   Full acceptance

Full acceptance of a Codex maximum limit for residues of pesticides or veterinary drugs in food means that the country concerned will ensure, within its territorial jurisdiction, that a food, whether home-produced or imported, to which the Codex maximum limit applies, will comply with that limit. It also means that the distribution of a food conforming with the Codex maximum limit will not be hindered by any legal or administrative provisions in the country concerned which relate to matters covered by the Codex maximum limit.

(ii)   Free distribution

A declaration of free distribution means that the country concerned undertakes that products conforming with the Codex maximum limit for residues of pesticides or veterinary drugs in food may be distributed freely within its territorial jurisdiction insofar as matters covered by the Codex maximum limit are concerned.

6.B.   A country which considers that it cannot accept the Codex maximum limit for residues of pesticides or veterinary drugs in foods in any of the ways mentioned above should indicate in what ways its present or proposed requirements differ from the Codex maximum limit and, if possible, the reasons for these differences.

6.C.   A country which accepts a Codex maximum limit for residues of pesticides or veterinary drugs in food according to one of the provisions of paragraph 6.A should be prepared to offer advice and guidance to exporters and processors of food for export to promote understanding of and compliance with the requirements of importing countries which have accepted a Codex maximum limit according to one of the provisions of paragraph 6.A.

6.D. Where, in an importing country, a food claimed to be in compliance with a Codex maximum limit is found not to be in compliance with the Codex maximum limit, the importing country should inform the competent authorities in the exporting country of all the relevant facts and, in particular, the details of the origin of the food in question (name and address of the exporter), if it is thought that a person in the exporting country is responsible for such non-compliance.

Withdrawal or Amendment of Acceptance

7.   The withdrawal or amendment of acceptance of a Codex standard or a Codex maximum limit for residues of pesticides or veterinary drugs in food by a country shall be notified in writing to the Codex Alimentarius Commission's Secretariat who will inform all Member States and Associate Members of FAO and WHO of the notification and its date of receipt. The country concerned should provide the information required under paragraphs 4.A(iii), 5.A(iii), 4.B, 5.B or 6.B above, whichever is appropriate. It should also give as long a notice of the withdrawal or amendment as is practicable.

SECTION 2

DEFINITIONS FOR THE PURPOSE OF THE
CODEX ALIMENTARIUS

DEFINITIONS FOR THE PURPOSE OF
THE CODEX ALIMENTARIUS

For the purposes of the Codex Alimentarius:

1)   "Food" means any substance, whether processed, semi-processed or raw, which is intended for human consumption, and includes drink, chewing gum and any substance which has been used in the manufacture, preparation or treatment of "food" but does not include cosmetics or tobacco or substances used only as drugs.

2)   "Food hygiene" comprises conditions and measures necessary for the production, processing, storage and distribution of food designed to ensure a safe, sound, wholesome product fit for human consumption.

3)   "Food additive" means any substance not normally consumed as a food by itself and not normally used as a typical ingredient of the food, whether or not it has nutritive value, the intentional addition of which to food for a technological (including organoleptic) purpose in the manufacture, processing, preparation, treatment, packing, packaging, transport or holding of such food results, or may be reasonably expected to result, (directly or indirectly) in it or its by-products becoming a component of or otherwise affecting the characteristics of such foods. The term does not include "contaminants" or substances added to food for maintaining or improving nutritional qualities.

4)   "Contaminant" means any substance not intentionally added to food, which is present in such food as a result of the production (including operations carried out in crop husbandry, animal husbandry and veterinary medicine), manufacture, processing, preparation, treatment, packing, packaging, transport or holding of such food or as a result of environmental contamination. The term does not include insect fragments, rodent hairs and other extraneous matter.

5)   "Pesticide" means any substance intended for preventing, destroying, attracting, repelling, or controlling any pest including unwanted species of plants or animals during the production, storage, transport, distribution and processing of food, agricultural commodities, or animal feeds or which may be administered to animals for the control of ectoparasites. The term includes substances intended for use as a plant-growth regulator, defoliant, desiccant, fruit thinning agent, or sprouting inhibitor and substances applied to crops either before or after harvest to protect the commodity from deterioration during storage and transport. The term normally excludes fertilizers, plant and animal nutrients, food additives, and animal drugs.

6)   "Pesticide Residue" means any specified substance in food, agricultural commodities, or animal feed resulting from the use of a pesticide. The term includes any derivatives of a pesticide, such as conversion products, metabolites, reaction products, and impurities considered to be of toxicological significance.

7)   "Good Agricultural Practice in the Use of Pesticides" (GAP) includes the nationally authorized safe uses of pesticides under actual conditions necessary for effective and reliable pest control. It encompasses a range of levels of pesticide applications up to the highest authorised use, applied in a manner which leaves a residue which is the smallest amount practicable.

Authorized safe uses are determined at the national level and include
nationally registered or recommended uses, which take into account public and
occupational health and environmental safety considerations.

Actual conditions include any stage in the production, storage, transport,
distribution and processing of food commodities and animal feed.

8)   "Codex maximum limit for pesticide residues" (MRLP) is the maximum
        concentration of a pesticide residue (expressed as mg/kg), recommended by the
        Codex Alimentarius Commission to be legally permitted in or on food
        commodities and animal feeds. MRLs are based on GAP data and foods derived
        from commodities that comply with the respective MRLs are intended to be
        toxicologically acceptable.

        Codex MRLs, which are primarily intended to apply in international trade, are
        derived from estimations made by the JMPR following:

        a)   toxicological assessment of the pesticide and its residue; and

        b)   review of residue data from supervised trials and supervised uses
                including those reflecting national good agricultural practices. Data
                from supervised trials conducted at the highest nationally
                recommended, authorized or registered uses are included in the review.
                In order to accommodate variations in national pest control
                requirements, Codex MRLs take into account the higher levels shown to
                arise in such supervised trials, which are considered to represent
                effective pest control practices.

        Consideration of the various dietary residue intake estimates and
        determinations both at the national and international level in comparison
        with the ADI, should indicate that foods complying with Codex MRLs are safe
        for human consumption.

9)   "Veterinary drug" means any substance applied or administered to any
        food-producing animal, such as meat or milk-producing animals, poultry, fish
        or bees, whether used for therapeutic, prophylactic or diagnostic purposes
        or for modification of physiological functions or behaviour.

10)   "Residues of veterinary drugs" include the parent compounds and/or their
        metabolites in any edible portion of the animal product, and include residues
        of associated impurities of the veterinary drug concerned.

11)   "Codex Maximum limit for residues of veterinary drugs" (MRLVD) is the maximum
        concentration of residue resulting from the use of a veterinary drug
        (expressed in mg/kg or µg/kg on a fresh weight basis) that is recommended by
        the Codex Alimentarius Commission to be legally permitted or recognized as
        acceptable in or on a food.

        It is based on the type and amount of residue considered to be without any
        toxicological hazard for human health as expressed by the Acceptable Daily
        Intake (ADI), or on the basis of a temporary ADI that utilizes an additional
        safety factor. It also takes into account other relevant public health risks
        as well as food technological aspects.

        When establishing an MRL, consideration is also given to residues that occur
        in food of plant origin and/or the environment. Furthermore, the MRL may be

reduced to be consistent with good practices in the use of veterinary drugs and to the extent that practical analytical methods are available.

12)   "Good Practice in the Use of Veterinary Drugs" (GPVD) is the official recommended or authorized usage including withdrawal periods, approved by national authorities, of veterinary drugs under practical conditions.

13)   "Processing aid" means any substance or material, not including apparatus or utensils, and not consumed as a food ingredient by itself, intentionally used in the processing of raw materials, foods or its ingredients, to fulfil a certain technological purpose during treatment or processing and which may result in the non-intentional but unavoidable presence of residues or derivatives in the final product.

SECTION 3

CODE OF ETHICS
FOR INTERNATIONAL TRADE IN FOOD

CAC/RCP 20-1979, Rev. 1 (1985)

INTRODUCTION

At its Thirteenth Session, held in December 1979, the Commission adopted the Code of Ethics for International Trade in Food, and decided to send it to all Member Nations and Associate Members of FAO and/or WHO for consideration with a view to implementation. The Code was amended by the Sixteenth Session of the Commission held in July 1985. This Code was developed in the light of the consideration that many countries - particularly developing countries - do not yet have adequate food control infrastructures to protect consumers against possible health hazards in food and against fraud.

Governments are invited to inform the Secretariat of the Codex Alimentarius Commission - Joint FAO/WHO Food Standards Programme, FAO, Rome - of action taken to implement the Code (see Article 10).

CODE OF ETHICS FOR INTERNATIONAL TRADE IN FOOD

CAC/RCP 20-1979, Rev. 1 (1985)

PREAMBLE

THE CODEX ALIMENTARIUS COMMISSION,

RECOGNIZING THAT:

(a)   Adequate, safe, sound and wholesome food is a vital element for the achievement of acceptable standards of living and that the right to a standard of living adequate for the health and wellbeing of the individual and his family is proclaimed in the Universal Declaration of Human Rights of the United Nations;

(b)   Food is a vital and critical item of international trade and its quality is influenced primarily by prevailing commercial practices and such food legislation and food control practices as are in operation in particular countries;

(c)   Food purchases utilize a significant portion of the income of consumers, particularly low-income consumers, who often also represent the most vulnerable group and from whom the ensurance of safe, sound and wholesome food and protection from unfair trade practices is quite critical;

(d)   There is increasingly worldwide concern about food safety, food contamination through environmental pollution, adulteration, unfair trade practices in quality, quantity and presentation of food, food losses and wastage and, generally about the improvement of food quality and nutritional status everywhere;

(e)   Food legislation and food control infrastrucutures are not sufficiently developed in many countries to enable adequate protection of their food imports and prevent the dumping of sub-standard and unsafe foods;

(f)   The GATT Agreement on Technical Barriers to Trade represents an appropriate instrument for the regulation of international trade;

(g)   The International Code of Marketing of Breastmilk Substitutes sets forth principles for the protection and promotion of breast-milk feeding which is an important aspect of primary health care;

AND CONSIDERING THAT:

(a)   The major objectives of the work of the Codex Alimentarius Commission are to protect the health of the consumer and ensure fair practices in the trade in food and to facilitate international trade in food through the elaboration and harmonization of definitions and requirements for food;

(b)   The above stated objectives can best be achieved by each country establishing or strengthening its food legislation and food control infrastrucutures and, where necessary, taking advantage of the work of international organizations competent to advise and provide assistance in these areas and particularly of the recommendations of the Codex Alimentarius Commission;

(c)   A code of ethical conduct for the international trade in food embodying the principles of sound consumer protection can supplement and complement the establishment and strengthening of national food legislation and food control infrastructures and, at the same time, provide an internationally agreed norm and framework for the realization of practical and effective international cooperation,

HEREBY DECIDES TO RECOMMEND THAT ALL THOSE ENGAGING IN THE INTERNATIONAL TRADE IN FOOD COMMIT THEMSELVES MORALLY TO THIS CODE AND UNDERTAKE VOLUNTARILY TO SUPPORT ITS IMPLEMENTATION IN THE LARGER INTEREST OF THE WORLD COMMUNITY

ARTICLE 1 - OBJECTIVE

1.   The objective of this code is to establish standards of ethical conduct for all those engaged in international trade in food or responsible for regulating it and thereby to protect the health of the consumers and promote fair trade practices.

ARTICLE 2 - SCOPE

2.1   This code applies to all food introduced into international trade.[1]

2.2   This code establishes standards of ethical conduct to be applied by all those concerned with international trade in food.

ARTICLE 3 - DEFINITION AND INTERPRETATION

3.1   For the purposes of this code, "food" means any substance, whether processed, semi-processed or raw which is intended for human consumption and includes drink, chewing gum and any substance which has been used in the manufacture, preparation or treatment of "food" but does not include cosmetics or tobacco or substances used only as drugs.

3.2   In their interpretation and application, the provisions of this code are interrelated and each provision shall be construed in the context of the other provisions.

ARTICLE 4 - GENERAL PRINCIPLES

4.1   International trade in food should be conducted on the principle that all consumers are entitled to safe, sound and wholesome food and to protection from unfair trade practices.

4.2   Subject to the provisions of Article 5 below, no food should be in international trade which:

(a)   has in or upon it any substance in an amount which renders it poisonous, harmful or otherwise injurious to health; or

(b)   consists in whole or in part of any filthy, putrid, rotten, decomposed or diseased substance or foreign matter, or is otherwise unfit for human consumption; or

---

[1]   It is understood that the principles of this code should also apply, *mutatis mutandi* to concessional and food aid transactions.

(c)   is adulterated; or

(d)   is labelled, or presented in a manner that is false, misleading or deceptive; or

(e)   is sold, prepared, packaged, stored or transported for sale under unsanitary conditions.

ARTICLE 5 - SPECIFIC REQUIREMENTS

Food Standards

5.1   Appropriate and adequate national food standards should be established and enforced taking into account that uniform consumer protection and the orderly marketing of food can be better achieved through the acceptance of food standards elaborated by the Codex Alimentarius Commission or the adaptation of national standards to such international recommendations.

Food Hygiene

5.2   Food should be subject at all times to sound hygienic practices as set forth in the codes of practice elaborated by the Codex Alimentarius Commission.

Labelling

5.3   All food should be accompanied by accurate and adequate descriptive information particularly:

(a)   in the case of prepackaged food, labelling should be in accordance with provisions and standards elaborated by the Codex Alimentarius Commission; and

(b)   in the case of food in bulk and non-retail containers, labelling should be in accordance with the Codex recommendations for the labelling of non-retail containers of food.

Food Additives

5.4   The use of and the trade in food additives should be in accordance with criteria in the General Principles for the Use of Food Additives adopted by the Codex Alimentarius Commission, taking into account the Codex lists of approved food additives.

Pesticide Residues

5.5   Limits for pesticide residues in food should be subject to control and should take into account the international maximum limits recommended for pesticide residues elaborated by the Codex Alimentarius Commission.

Microbiological Contaminants

5.6   All food should be free from micro-organisms and parasites in amounts harmful to man and should not contain any substance originating from micro-organisms or parasites in an amount which may represent a health hazard.

Other Contaminants

5.7   Levels of other contaminants in food should be subject to control and should take into account the international maximum levels recommended for contaminants elaborated by the Codex Alimentarius Commission.

Irradiated Food

5.8   Irradiated food should be produced and controlled in accordance with provisions and standards of the Codex Alimentarius Commission.

Foods for Infants, Children and other Vulnerable Groups

5.9   Food for infants, children and other vulnerable groups should be in accordance with standards elaborated by the Codex Alimentarius Commission.

Nutritional Aspects concerning in particular Vulnerable Groups and Regions where Malnutrition exists

5.10 (a)   No claims[1] in any form should be made about food - particularly processed food - with minimal nutritive value which implies that the food can make a valuable (significant) contribution to the diet;

(b)   information concerning the nutritional value of food should not mislead the public.

ARTICLE 6 - IMPLEMENTATION

6.1   Food that is exported should conform:

(a)   to such food legislation, regulations, standards, codes of practice and other legal and administrative procedures as may be in force in the importing country;   or

(b)   to the provisions contained in bilateral or multilateral agreements signed by the exporting country and the importing country;   or

(c)   in the absence of such provisions to such standards and requirements as may be agreed upon, with emphasis on the use of Codex Standards wherever possible.

6.2   Where the General Principles stated in Article 4 above, as expanded in specific terms in Article 5, are not covered by appropriate food legislation, regulations, standards, codes of practice and other legal and administrative procedures in the importing country, food that is exported should conform to the General Principles stated in Article 4, taking into account such standards, codes of practice or other guidelines elaborated by the Codex Alimentarius Commission as applicable to the food or practice concerned.

6.3   Where, in an importing country, a food product:

---

[1]   General Guidelines on Claims have been developed by the Codex Committee on Food Labelling and adopted by the Codex Alimentarius Commission (see this Volume of the Codex Alimentarius)

(a)   is found not meeting health and safety considerations, or

(b)   claiming to be in compliance with a standard, code of practice or other generally accepted certification system is found not to be in compliance, whether in respect of the label accompanying the product or otherwise, or

(c)   is the subject of unfair trade practices, or otherwise not conforming to the provisions of this code,

the authorities of the importing country should inform the competent authorities in the exporting country of all the relevant facts of serious cases involving considerations of human health or fraudulent practices and, in particular, the details of the origin of the product in question, and appropriate action should be taken by the exporting country in accordance with its legal and administrative procedures, and a statement concerning the facts of the matter made to the importing country.

ARTICLE 7 - RESPONSIBILITIES FOR IMPLEMENTATION

7.1   The implementation of this code rests with:

(a)   governments of all countries, who should provide adequate food legislation and food control infrastructures, including certification and inspection systems and other legal or administrative procedures that also apply to re-exports of food as appropriate and necessary, and

(b)   more especially governments of exporting countries who should:

(i)   employ as appropriate and practicable, legal or administrative controls aimed at preventing the exportation of shipments of food which does not comply with the provisions of Articles 6.1 or 6.2;

(ii)   promptly notify the importing country of the exportation of shipments of food found not to comply with 6.1 when legal or administrative means of preventing exportation are not available or were unsuccessfully applied or where non-compliance was determined after exportation;

(iii) make available to the importing country upon request appropriate certification, inspection or other procedures as appropriate with the manner of compensation for these services to be agreed upon between the governments.

(c)   all concerned with the international trade in food - particularly in respect of Article 6.1 (c) - who should take into account, as appropriate, the General Principles in Article 4,

and further, will depend on

-   such cooperation and consultative procedures as may be established between governments of importing and exporting countries, and, generally, between all those concerned with international trade, and

- the extent to which international food standards, codes of practice and similar other recommendations, elaborated by the Codex Alimentarius Commission are considered and accepted where relevant and appropriate.

7.2   The code should be promoted by governments in their respective territorial jurisdictions in accordance with their legal and administrative procedures regulating the conduct of exporters and importers.

ARTICLE 8 - EXCEPTIONAL CIRCUMSTANCES

8.   Where special circumstances exist under which it is neither possible nor desirable to apply certain provisions of this code, as in the case of famines and other emergency situations (where the appropriate competent authorities in recipient and donor countries responsible for food control may decide to establish mutually agreed criteria), due regard should always be given to the basic principles of the safety of the food and other provisions of this code as may be applicable under those circumstances.

ARTICLE 9 - EXCHANGE OF INFORMATION

9.   Countries denying entry to food for reasons involving serious considerations of human health or fraud and having reason to believe the food may be offered for sale in other countries should use whatever appropriate facilities exist to warn those countries.

ARTICLE 10 - REVIEW

10.   From time to time, each government will be requested to submit to the Secretariat of the Codex Alimentarius Commission a report on the implementation of this code. Such reports should be compiled and presented to the Codex Alimentarius Commission for its consideration of progress achieved and of any improvement and additions or otherwise which might become necessary, and to enable it to make appropriate recommendations. Such consideration should take into account the evolution of health, safety and trade factors related to the principles upon which this code is based and on its objective.

SECTION 4

CODEX GENERAL STANDARD FOR THE LABELLING OF
PREPACKAGED FOODS
(World-wide Standard)

CODEX STAN 1-1985 (Rev. 1-1991)

INTRODUCTION

The Codex General Standard for the Labelling of Prepackaged Foods was adopted by the Codex Alimentarius Commission at its 14th Session, 1981 and subsequently revised in 1985 and 1991 by the 16th and 19th Sessions. This standard has been submitted to all Member Nations and Associate Members of FAO and WHO for **acceptance** in accordance with the General Principles of the Codex Alimentarius.

CODEX GENERAL STANDARD
FOR THE LABELLING OF PREPACKAGED FOODS
(World-wide Standard)

CODEX STAN 1-1985 (Rev. 1-1991)

1.   SCOPE

This standard applies to the labelling of all prepackaged foods to be offered as such to the consumer or for catering purposes and to certain aspects relating to the presentation thereof.[1]

2.   DEFINITION OF TERMS

For the purpose of this standard:

"Claim" means any representation which states, suggests or implies that a food has particular qualities relating to its origin, nutritional properties, nature, processing, composition or any other quality.

"Consumer" means persons and families purchasing and receiving food in order to meet their personal needs.

"Container" means any packaging of food for delivery as a single item, whether by completely or partially enclosing the food and includes wrappers. A container may enclose several units or types of packages when such is offered to the consumer.

For use in Date Marking of prepackaged food:

"Date of Manufacture" means the date on which the food becomes the product as described.

"Date of Packaging" means the date on which the food is placed in the immediate container in which it will be ultimately sold.

"Sell-by-Date" means the last date of offer for sale to the consumer after which there remains a reasonable storage period in the home.

"Date of Minimum Durability" ("best before") means the date which signifies the end of the period under any stated storage conditions during which the product will remain fully marketable and will retain any specific qualities for which tacit or express claims have been made. However, beyond the date the food may still be perfectly satisfactory.

"Use-by Date" (Recommended Last Consumption Date, Expiration Date) means the date which signifies the end of the estimated period under any stated storage conditions, after which the product probably will not have the quality attributes normally expected by the consumers. After this date, the food should not be regarded as marketable.

---

[1]   When notifying their position on the acceptance of this standard, governments are requested to indicate any provisions concerning the presentation of mandatory information on the label and in labelling, in force in their country which are not covered by this standard.

"Food" means any substance, whether processed, semi-processed or raw, which is intended for human consumption, and includes drinks, chewing gum and any substance which has been used in the manufacture, preparation or treatment of "food" but does not include cosmetics or tobacco or substances used only as drugs.

"Food Additive" means any substance not normally consumed as a food by itself and not normally used as a typical ingredient of the food, whether or not it has nutritive value, the intentional addition of which to food for a technological (including organoleptic) purpose in the manufacture, processing, preparation, treatment, packing, packaging, transport or holding of such food results, or may be reasonably expected to result, (directly or indirectly) in it or its by-products becoming a component of or otherwise affecting the characteristics of such foods. The term does not include "contaminants" or substances added to food for maintaining or improving nutritional qualities.

"Ingredient" means any substance, including a food additive, used in the manufacture or preparation of a food and present in the final product although possibly in a modified form.

"Label" means any tag, brand, mark, pictorial or other descriptive matter, written, printed, stencilled, marked, embossed or impressed on, or attached to, a container of food.

"Labelling" includes any written, printed or graphic matter that is present on the label, accompanies the food, or is displayed near the food, including that for the purpose of promoting its sale or disposal.

"Lot" means a definitive quantity of a commodity produced essentially under the same conditions.

"Prepackaged" means packaged or made up in advance in a container, ready for offer to the consumer, or for catering purposes.

"Processing Aid" means a substance or material, not including apparatus or utensils, and not consumed as a food ingredient by itself, intentionally used in the processing of raw materials, foods or its ingredients, to fulfil a certain technological purpose during treatment or processing and which may result in the non-intentional but unavoidable presence of residues or derivatives in the final product.

"Foods for Catering Purposes" means those foods for use in restaurants, canteens, schools, hospitals and similar institutions where food is offered for immediate consumption.

3.   GENERAL PRINCIPLES

3.1   Prepackaged food shall not be described or presented on any label or in any labelling in a manner that is false, misleading or deceptive or is likely to create an erroneous impression regarding its character in any respect.[1]

3.2   Prepackaged food shall not be described or presented on any label or in any labelling by words, pictorial or other devices which refer to or are

------

[1] Examples of descriptions or presentations to which these General Principles refer are given in the Codex General Guidelines on Claims.

suggestive either directly or indirectly, of any other product with which such food might be confused, or in such a manner as to lead the purchaser or consumer to suppose that the food is connected with such other product.

4.   MANDATORY LABELLING OF PREPACKAGED FOODS

          The following information shall appear on the label of prepackaged foods as applicable to the food being labelled, except to the extent otherwise expressly provided in an individual Codex standard:

4.1   The Name of the Food

4.1.1   The name shall indicate the true nature of the food and normally be specific and not generic:

4.1.1.1   Where a name or names have been established for a food in a Codex standard, at least one of these names shall be used.

4.1.1.2   In other cases, the name prescribed by national legislation shall be used.

4.1.1.3   In the absence of any such name, either a common or usual name existing by common usage as an appropriate descriptive term which was not misleading or confusing to the consumer shall be used.

4.1.1.4   A "coined", "fanciful", "brand" name, or "trade mark" may be used provided it accompanies one of the names provided in Subsections 4.1.1.1 to 4.1.1.3.

4.1.2   There shall appear on the label either in conjunction with, or in close proximity to, the name of the food, such additional words or phrases as necessary to avoid misleading or confusing the consumer in regard to the true nature and physical condition of the food including but not limited to the type of packing medium, style, and the condition or type of treatment it has undergone; for example: dried, concentrated, reconstituted, smoked.

4.2   List of Ingredients

4.2.1   Except for single ingredient foods, a list of ingredients shall be declared on the label.

4.2.1.1   The list of ingredients shall be headed or preceded by an appropriate title which consists of or includes the term 'ingredient'.

4.2.1.2   All ingredients shall be listed in descending order of ingoing weight (m/m) at the time of the manufacture of the food.

4.2.1.3   Where an ingredient is itself the product of two or more ingredients, such a compound ingredient may be declared, as such, in the list of ingredients provided that it is immediately accompanied by a list in brackets of its ingredients in descending order of proportion (m/m). Where a compound ingredient for which a name has been established in a Codex standard or in national legislation constitutes less than 25% of the food, the ingredients other than food additives which serve a technological function in the finished product need not be declared.

4.2.1.4   Added water shall be declared in the list of ingredients except when
the water forms part of an ingredient such as brine, syrup or broth used in a
compound food and declared as such in the list of ingredients. Water or other
volatile ingredients evaporated in the course of manufacture need not be declared.

4.2.1.5   As an alternative to the general provisions of this section, dehydrated
or condensed foods which are intended to be reconstituted by the addition of water
only, the ingredients may be listed in order of proportion (m/m) in the
reconstituted product provided that a statement such as "ingredients of the product
when prepared in accordance with the directions on the label" is included.

4.2.2   A specific name shall be used for ingredients in the list of
ingredients in accordance with the provisions set out in Section 4.1 (Name of the
Food) except that:

4.2.2.1   The following class names may be used for the ingredients falling
within these classes:

Name of Classes	Class Names
Refined oils other than olive	'Oil' together with either the term 'vegetable' or 'animal', qualified by the term 'hydrogenated' or 'partially-hydrogenated', as appropriate.
Refined fats	'Fat' together with either, the term 'vegetable' or 'animal', as appropriate.
Starches, other than chemically modified starches	'Starch'.
All species of fish where the fish constitutes an ingredient of another food and provided that the labelling and presentation of such food does not refer to a specific species of fish.	'Fish'.
All types of poultrymeat where such meat constitutes an ingredient of another food and provided that the labelling and presentation of such a food does not refer to a specific type of poultrymeat.	'Poultrymeat'.
All types of cheese where the cheese or mixture of cheeses constitutes an ingredient of another food and provided that the labelling and presentation of such food does not refer to a specific type of cheese.	'Cheese'.
All spices and spice extracts not exceeding 2% by weight either singly or in combination in the food.	'Spice', 'spices', or 'mixed spices', as appropriate.

All herbs or parts of herbs   'Herbs' or 'mixed herbs',
not exceeding 2% by weight   as appropriate.
either singly or in combination in the food.

All types of gum preparations   'Gum base'.
used in the manufacture of gum base for
chewing gum.

All types of sucrose.   'Sugar'.

Anhydrous dextrose and dextrose   'Dextrose' or 'glucose'.
monohydrate.

All types of caseinates.   'Caseinates'.

Press, expeller or refined   'Cocoa butter'.
cocoa butter.

All crystallized fruit not   'Crystallized fruit'.
exceeding 10% of the weight of the food.

4.2.2.2   Notwithstanding the provision set out in Section 4.2.2.1, pork fat,
lard and beef fat shall always be declared by their specific names.

4.2.2.3   For food additives falling in the respective classes and appearing in
lists of food additives permitted for use in foods generally, the following class
titles shall be used together with the specific name or recognized numerical
identification as required by national legislation.[1]

> Acidity Regulator
> Acids
> Anticaking Agent
> Antifoaming Agent
> Antioxidant
> Bulking Agent
> Colour
> Colour Retention Agent
> Emulsifier
> Emulsifying Salt
> Firming Agent
> Flour Treatment Agent
> Flavour Enhancer
> Foaming Agent
> Gelling Agent
> Glazing Agent
> Humectant
> Preservative
> Propellant
> Raising Agent
> Stabilizer
> Sweetener
> Thickener

---

[1] Governments accepting the standard should indicate the requirements in
force in their countries.

4.2.2.4   The following class titles may be used for food additives falling in the respective classes and appearing in lists of food additives permitted generally for use in foods:

> Flavour(s) and Flavouring(s)
> Modified Starch(es)

The expression "flavours" may be qualified by "natural", "nature identical", "artificial" or a combination of these words as appropriate.

4.2.3   Processing Aids and Carry-Over of Food Additives

4.2.3.1   A food additive carried over into a food in a significant quantity or in an amount sufficient to perform a technological function in that food as a result of the use of raw materials or other ingredients in which the additive was used shall be included in the list of ingredients.

4.2.3.2   A food additive carried over into foods at a level less than that required to achieve a technological function, and processing aids, are exempted from declaration in the list of ingredients.

4.3   Net Contents and Drained Weight

4.3.1   The net contents shall be declared in the metric system ("Système International" units).[1]

4.3.2   The net contents shall be declared in the following manner:

    (i)   for liquid foods, by volume;
    (ii)   for solid foods, by weight;
    (iii) for semi-solid or viscous foods, either by weight or volume.

4.3.3   In addition to the declaration of net contents, a food packed in a liquid medium shall carry a declaration in the metric system of the drained weight of the food. For the purposes of this requirement, liquid medium means water, aqueous solutions of sugar and salt, fruit and vegetable juices in canned fruits and vegetables only, or vinegar, either singly or in combination.[2]

4.4   Name and Address

           The name and address of the manufacturer, packer, distributor, importer, exporter or vendor of the food shall be declared.

4.5   Country of Origin

4.5.1   The country of origin of the food shall be declared if its omission would mislead or deceive the consumer.

---

[1] The declaration of net contents represents the quantity at the time of packaging and is subject to enforcement by reference to an average system of quantity control.

[2] The declaration of drained weight is subject to enforcement by reference to an average system of quantity control.

4.5.2   When a food undergoes processing in a second country which changes its
nature, the country in which the processing is performed shall be considered to be
the country of origin for the purposes of labelling.

4.6   Lot Identification

           Each container shall be embossed or otherwise permanently marked in
code or in clear to identify the producing factory and the lot.

4.7   Date Marking and Storage Instructions

4.7.1   If not otherwise determined in an individual Codex standard, the
following date marking shall apply:

   (i)   The "date of minimum durability" shall be declared.

   (ii)   This shall consist at least of:

           -      the day and the month for products with a minimum durability of
                  not more than three months;

           -      the month and the year for products with a minimum durability of
                  more than three months. If the month is December, it is
                  sufficient to indicate the year.

   (iii)   The date shall be declared by the words:

           -      "Best before ..." where the day is indicated;
           -      "Best before end ..." in other cases.

   (iv)   The words referred to in paragraph (iii) shall be accompanied by:

           -      either the date itself; or
           -      a reference to where the date is given.

   (v)   The day, month and year shall be declared in uncoded numerical
           sequence except that the month may be indicated by letters in those
           countries where such use will not confuse the consumer.

   (vi)   Notwithstanding 4.7.1 (i) an indication of the date of minimum
           durability shall not be required for:

           -      fresh fruits and vegetables, including potatoes which have not
                  been peeled, cut or similarly treated;

           -      wines, liqueur wines, sparkling wines, aromatized wines, fruit
                  wines and sparkling fruit wines;

           -      beverages containing 10% or more by volume of alcohol;

           -      bakers' or pastry-cooks' wares which, given the nature of their
                  content, are normally consumed within 24 hours of their
                  manufacture;

           -      vinegar;

           -      food grade salt;

- solid sugars;

- confectionery products consisting of flavoured and/or coloured
  sugars;

- chewing gum.

4.7.2   In addition to the date of minimum durability, any special conditions
for the storage of the food shall be declared on the label if the validity of the
date depends thereon.

4.8   Instructions for Use

Instructions for use, including reconstitution, where applicable, shall
be included on the label, as necessary, to ensure correct utilization of the food.

5.   ADDITIONAL MANDATORY REQUIREMENTS

5.1   Quantitative Labelling of Ingredients

5.1.1   Where the labelling of a food places special emphasis on the presence
of one or more valuable and/or characterizing ingredients, or where the description
of the food has the same effect, the ingoing percentage of the ingredient (m/m) at
the time of manufacture shall be declared.

5.1.2   Similarly, where the labelling of a food places special emphasis on the
low content of one or more ingredients, the percentage of the ingredient (m/m) in
the final product shall be declared.

5.1.3   A reference in the name of a food to a particular ingredient shall not
of itself constitute the placing of special emphasis. A reference in the labelling
of a food to an ingredient used in a small quantity and only as a flavouring shall
not of itself constitute the placing of special emphasis.

5.2   Irradiated Foods

5.2.1   The label of a food which has been treated with ionizing radiation
shall carry a written statement indicating that treatment in close proximity to the
name of the food. The use of the international food irradiation symbol, as shown
below, is optional, but when it is used, it shall be in close proximity to the name
of the food.

5.2.2   When an irradiated product is used as an ingredient in another food, this shall be so declared in the list of ingredients.

5.2.3   When a single ingredient product is prepared from a raw material which has been irradiated, the label of the product shall contain a statement indicating the treatment.

6.   **EXEMPTIONS FROM MANDATORY LABELLING REQUIREMENTS**

With the exception of spices and herbs, small units, where the largest surface area is less than 10 cm^2, may be exempted from the requirements of paragraphs 4.2 and 4.6 to 4.8.

7.   **OPTIONAL LABELLING**

7.1   Any information or pictorial device written, printed, or graphic matter may be displayed in labelling provided that it is not in conflict with the mandatory requirements of this standard and those relating to claims and deception given in Section 3 - General Principles.

7.2   Grade Designations

If grade designations are used, they shall be readily understandable and not be misleading or deceptive in any way.

8.   **PRESENTATION OF MANDATORY INFORMATION**

8.1   General

8.1.1   Labels in prepackaged foods shall be applied in such a manner that they will not become separated from the container.

8.1.2   Statements required to appear on the label by virtue of this standard or any other Codex standards shall be clear, prominent, indelible and readily legible by the consumer under normal conditions of purchase and use.

8.1.3   Where the container is covered by a wrapper, the wrapper shall carry the necessary information or the label on the container shall be readily legible through the outer wrapper or not obscured by it.

8.1.4   The name and net contents of the food shall appear in a prominent position and in the same field of vision.

8.2   Language

8.2.1   If the language on the original label is not acceptable, to the consumer for whom it is intended, a supplementary label containing the mandatory information in the required language may be used instead of relabelling.

8.2.2   In the case of either relabelling or a supplementary label, the mandatory information provided shall be fully and accurately reflect that in the original label.

SECTION 4.1

CODEX GENERAL GUIDELINES ON CLAIMS

CAC/GL 1-1979 (Rev. 1-1991)

INTRODUCTION

The Codex General Guidelines on Claims was adopted by the Codex Alimentarius Commission at its 13th Session, 1979. A revised version of the Codex General Guidelines on Claims was adopted by the 19th Session of the Commission in 1991. It has been sent to all Member Nations and Associate Members of FAO and WHO as an advisory text, and it is for individual governments to decide what use they wish to make of the Guidelines.

CODEX GENERAL GUIDELINES ON CLAIMS
CAC/GL 1-1979 (Rev. 1-1991)

1.   SCOPE AND GENERAL PRINCIPLES

1.1   These guidelines relate to claims made for a food irrespective of whether or not the food is covered by an individual Codex Standard.

1.2   The principle on which the guidelines are based is that no food should be described or presented in a manner that is false, misleading or deceptive or is likely to create an erroneous impression regarding its character in any respect.

1.3   The person marketing the food should be able to justify the claims made.

2.   DEFINITION

            For the purpose of these guidelines, a claim is any representation which states, suggests or implies that a food has particular characteristics relating to its origin, nutritional properties, nature, production, processing, composition or any other quality.

3.   PROHIBITED CLAIMS

            The following claims should be prohibited:

3.1   Claims stating that any given food will provide an adequate source of all essential nutrients, except in the case of well defined products for which a Codex standard regulates such claims as admissible claims or where appropriate authorities have accepted the product to be an adequate source of all essential nutrients.

3.2   Claims implying that a balanced diet of ordinary foods cannot supply adequate amounts of all nutrients.

3.3   Claims which cannot be substantiated.

3.4   Claims as to the suitability of a food for use in the prevention, alleviation, treatment or cure of a disease, disorder, or particular physiological condition unless they are:

        (a)   in accordance with the provisions of Codex standards or guidelines for foods under jurisdiction of the Committee on Foods for Special Dietary Uses and follow the principles set forth in these guidelines.

    or,

        (b)   in the absence of an applicable Codex standard or guideline, permitted under the laws of the country in which the food is distributed.

3.5   Claims which could give rise to doubt about the safety of similar food or which could arouse or exploit fear in the consumer.

4.   **POTENTIALLY MISLEADING CLAIMS**

          The following are examples of claims which may be misleading:

4.1   Meaningless claims including incomplete comparatives and superlatives.

4.2   Claims as to good hygienic practice, such as "wholesome", "healthful", "sound".

5.   **CONDITIONAL CLAIMS**

5.1   The following claims should be permitted subject to the particular condition attached to each:

   (i)   An indication that a food has obtained an increased or special nutritive value by means of the addition of nutrients, such as vitamins, minerals and amino acids may be given only if such an addition has been made on the basis of nutritional considerations according to the Codex General Principles for the Addition of Essential Nutrients to Foods.   This kind of indication should be subject to legislation by the appropriate authorities.

   (ii)   An indication that the food has special nutritional qualities by the reduction or omission of a nutrient should be on the basis of nutritional considerations and subject to legislation by the appropriate authorities.

   (iii) Terms such as "natural", "pure", "fresh", "home made", "organically grown" and "biologically grown" when they are used, should be in accordance with the national practices in the country where the food is sold.   The use of these terms should be consistent with the prohibitions set out in Section 3.

   (iv)   Religious or Ritual Preparation (e.g. Halal, Kosher) of a food may be claimed provided that the food conforms to the requirements of the appropriate religious or ritual authorities.

   (v)   Claims that a food has special characteristics when all such foods have the same characteristics, if this fact is apparent in the claim.

   (vi)   Claims which highlight the absence or non-addition of particular substances to food may be used provided that they are not misleading and provided that the substance:

        (a) is not subject to specific requirements in any Codex Standard or Guideline;

(b) is one which consumers would normally expect to find in the
food;

(c) has not been substituted by another giving the food equivalent
characteristics unless the nature of the substitution is clearly
stated with equal prominence; and

(d) is one whose presence or addition is permitted in the food.

(vii) Claims which highlight the absence or non-addition of one or more
nutrients should be regarded as nutrition claims and therefore should
invoke mandatory nutrient declaration in accordance with the Codex
Guidelines on Nutrition Labelling.

SECTION 4.2

CODEX GUIDELINES ON NUTRITION LABELLING

CAC/GL 2-1985

INTRODUCTION

The Codex Guidelines on Nutrition Labelling was adopted by the Codex Alimentarius Commission at its 16th Session, 1985. It has been sent to all Member Nations and Associate Members of FAO and WHO as an advisory text, and it is for individual governments to decide what use they wish to make of the Guidelines.

CODEX GUIDELINES ON NUTRITION LABELLING

CAC/GL 2-1985

PURPOSE OF THE GUIDELINES

- To ensure that nutrition labelling is effective:

    (i)   In providing the consumer with information about a food so that a wise choice of food can be made;

    (ii) in providing a means for conveying information of the nutrient content of a food on the label;

    (iii) in encouraging the use of sound nutrition principles in the formulation of foods which would benefit public health;

    (iv) in providing the opportunity to include supplementary nutrition information on the label.

- To ensure that nutrition labelling does not describe a product or present information about it which is in any way false, misleading, deceptive or insignificant in any manner.

- To ensure that no nutritional claims are made without nutrition labelling.

PRINCIPLES FOR NUTRITION LABELLING

A.   Nutrient Declaration

-   Information supplied should be for the purpose of providing consumers with a suitable profile of nutrients contained in the food and considered to be of nutritional importance. The information should not lead consumers to believe that there is exact quantitative knowledge of what individuals should eat in order to maintain health, but rather to convey an understanding of the quantity of nutrients contained in the product. A more exact quantitative delineation for individuals is not valid because there is no meaningful way in which knowledge about individual requirements can be used in labelling.

B.   Supplementary Nutrition Information

-   The content of supplementary nutrition information will vary from one country to another and within any country from one target population group to another according to the educational policy of the country and the needs of the target groups.

C.   <u>Nutrition Labelling</u>

-     Nutrition labelling should not deliberately imply that a food which carries
such labelling has necessarily any nutritional advantage over a food which
is not so labelled.

1.   <u>SCOPE</u>

1.1   These guidelines recommend procedures for the nutrition labelling of
foods.

1.2   These guidelines apply to the nutrition labelling of all foods. For
foods for special dietary uses, more detailed provisions may be developed.

2.   <u>DEFINITIONS</u>

            <u>For the purpose of these guidelines</u>:

2.1   <u>Nutrition labelling</u> is a description intended to inform the consumer
of nutritional properties of a food.

2.2   <u>Nutrition labelling</u> consists of two components:

    (a)   nutrient declaration;

    (b)   supplementary nutrition information.

2.3   <u>Nutrition declaration</u> means a standardized statement or listing of the
nutrient content of a food.

2.4   <u>Nutrition claim</u> means any representation which states, suggests or
implies that a food has particular nutritional properties including but not limited
to the energy value and to the content of protein, fat and carbohydrates, as well
as the content of vitamins and minerals. The following do not constitute nutrition
claims:

    (a)   the mention of substances in the list of ingredients;

    (b)   the mention of nutrients as a mandatory part of nutrition labelling;

    (c)   quantitative or qualitative declaration of certain nutrients or
            ingredients on the label if required by national legislation.

2.5   <u>Nutrient</u> means any substance normally consumed as a constituent of
food:

    (a)   which provides energy; or

    (b)   which is needed for growth, development and maintenance of life; or

    (c)   a deficit of which will cause characteristic bio-chemical or
            physiological changes to occur.

2.6   <u>Sugars</u> means all mono-saccharides and di-saccharides present in food.

2.7   Dietary fibre means edible plant and animal material not hydrolysed by
the endogenous enzymes of the human digestive tract as determined by the agreed
upon method.

2.8   Polyunsaturated fatty acids means fatty acids with cis-cis methylene
interrupted double bonds.

3.   **NUTRIENT DECLARATION**

3.1   Application of Nutrient Declaration

3.1.1   Nutrient declaration should be mandatory for foods for which nutrition
claims, as defined in Section 2.4, are made.

3.1.2   Nutrient declaration should be voluntary for all other foods.

3.2   Listing of Nutrients

3.2.1   Where nutrient declaration is applied, the declaration of the following
should be mandatory:

3.2.1.1   Energy value;   and

3.2.1.2   The amounts of protein, available carbohydrate (i.e., carbohydrate
excluding dietary fibre) and fat;   and

3.2.1.3   The amount of any other nutrient for which a nutrition claim is made;
and

3.2.1.4   The amount of any other nutrient considered to be relevant for
maintaining a good nutritional status, as required by national legislation.

3.2.2   Where a claim is made regarding the amount and/or the type of
carbohydrate, the amount of total sugars should be listed in addition to the
requirements in Section 3.2.1.   The amounts of starch and/or other carbohydrate
constituent(s) may also be listed.   Where a claim is made regarding the dietary
fibre content, the amount of dietary fibre should be declared.

3.2.3   Where a claim is made regarding the amount and/or type of fatty acids,
the amounts of saturated fatty acids and of polyunsaturated fatty acids should be
declared in accordance with Section 3.3.7.

3.2.4   In addition to the mandatory declaration under 3.2.1, 3.2.2 and 3.2.3,
vitamins and minerals may be listed in accordance with the following criteria:

3.2.4.1   Only vitamins and minerals for which recommended intakes have been
established and/or which are of nutritional importance in the country concerned
should also be declared.

3.2.5   When nutrient declaration is applied, only those vitamins and minerals
which are present in significant amounts should be listed.[1]

---

[1]   As a rule, 5% of the recommended intake (of the population concerned)
supplied by a serving as quantified on the label should be taken into consideration
in deciding what constitutes a significant amount.

3.2.6   In the case where a product is subject to labelling requirements of a
Codex standard, the provisions for nutrient declaration set out in that standard
should take precedence over but not conflict with the provisions of Sections 3.2.1
to 3.2.5 of these guidelines.

3.2.7   Calculation of Nutrients

3.2.7.1   Calculation of Energy

        The amount of energy to be listed should be calculated by using the
following conversion factors:

        Carbohydrates   4 kcal/g - 17 kJ
        Protein   4 kcal/g - 17 kJ
        Fat   9 kcal/g - 37 kJ
        Alcohol (Ethanol)   7 kcal/g - 29 kJ
        Organic acid   3 kcal/g - 13 kJ

3.2.7.2   Calculation of Protein

        The amount of protein to be listed should be calculated using the
formula:

        Protein = Total Kjeldahl Nitrogen x 6.25

unless a different factor is given in a Codex standard or in the Codex method of
analysis for that food.

3.3   Presentation of Nutrient Content

3.3.1   The declaration of nutrient content should be numerical. However, the
use of additional means of presentation should not be excluded.

3.3.2   Information on energy value should be expressed in kJ and kcal per 100
g or per 100 ml or per package if the package contains only a single portion. In
addition, this information may be given per serving as quantified on the label or
per portion provided that the number of portions contained in the package is
stated.

3.3.3   Information on the amounts of protein, carbohydrate and fat in the food
should be expressed in g per 100 g or per 100 ml or per package if the package
contains only a single portion. In addition, this information may be given per
serving as quantified on the label or per portion provided that the number of
portions contained in the package is stated.

3.3.4   Numerical information on vitamins and minerals should be expressed in
metric units and/or as a percentage of the Reference RDA per 100 g or per 100 ml
or per package if the package contains only a single portion. In addition, this
information may be given per serving as quantified on the label or per portion
provided that the number of portions contained in the package is stated.

        In addition, information on energy value and protein may also be
expressed as percentages of Reference RDA.

        When Reference RDAs are used they should be based as far as possible
on nutrient intakes recommended by FAO/WHO. Until these have been reviewed, the

following values should be used as the Reference RDA for labelling purposes in the interests of international standardization and harmonization:

Energy MJ (kcal)	9.5 (2300)
Protein, g	50
Vitamin A, μg	1000
Vitamin D, μg	5
Vitamin E, mg	10
Vitamin C, mg	60
Thiamin, mg	1.4
Riboflavin, mg	1.6
Niacin, mg	18
Vitamin B6, mg	2
Folacin, μg	400
Vitamin B12, μg	3
Calcium, mg	800
Phosphorus, mg	800
Iron, mg	14
Magnesium, mg	300
Zinc, mg	15
Iodine, μg	150

3.3.5   In countries where serving sizes are normally used, the information required by Sections 3.3.2, 3.3.3 and 3.3.4 may be given per serving only as quantified on the label or per portion provided that the number of portions contained in the package is stated.

3.3.6   The presence of available carbohydrates should be declared on the label as "carbohydrates". Where the type of carbohydrate is declared, this declaration should follow immediately the declaration of the total carbohydrate content in the following format:

"Carbohydrate ... g, of which sugars ... g".

This may be followed by the following:

"x" ... g

where "x" represents the specific name of any other carbohydrate constituent.

3.3.7   Where the amount and/or type of fatty acids is declared, this declaration should follow immediately the declaration of the total fat in accordance with Section 3.3.3.

The following format should be used:

Fat	... g
of which polyunsaturated	... g
and saturated	... g

3.4   <u>Tolerances and Compliance</u>

3.4.1   Tolerance limits should be set in relation to public health concerns, shelf-life, accuracy of analysis, processing variability and inherent lability and variability of the nutrient in the product, and, according to whether the nutrient has been added or is naturally occurring in the product.

3.4.2   The values used in nutrient declaration should be weighted average values derived from data specifically obtained from analyses of products which are representative of the product being labelled.

3.4.3   In those cases where a product is subject to a Codex standard, requirements for tolerances for nutrient declaration established by the standard should take precedence over these guidelines.

4.   SUPPLEMENTARY NUTRITION INFORMATION

4.1   Supplementary nutrition information is intended to increase the consumer's understanding of the nutritional value of their food and to assist in interpreting the nutrient declaration. There are a number of ways of presenting such information that may be suitable for use on food labels.

4.2   The use of supplementary nutrition information on food labels should be optional and should only be given in addition to, and not in place of, the nutrient declaration, except for target populations who have a high illiteracy rate and/or comparatively little knowledge of nutrition. For these, food group symbols or other pictorial or colour presentations may be used without the nutrient declaration.

4.3   Supplementary nutrition information on labels should be accompanied by consumer education programmes to increase consumer understanding and use of the information.

5.   PERIODIC REVIEW OF NUTRITION LABELLING

5.1   Nutrient labelling should be reviewed periodically in order to maintain the list of nutrients, to be included in composition information, up-to-date and in accord with public health facts about nutrition.

5.2   A review of optional information for nutrition education including food groups will be needed as target groups increase in literacy and nutrition knowledge.

5.3   The present definition of sugars as in Section 2.6 and that of dietary fibre as in Section 2.7 and the declaration of energy as in Section 3.3.2 should be reviewed in the light of newer developments.

SECTION 5

GENERAL PRINCIPLES FOR THE USE OF FOOD ADDITIVES

INTRODUCTION

The General Principles for the Use of Food Additives were adopted by the Ninth Session of the Codex Alimentarius Commission as an advisory text (para 295, ALINORM 72/35).

GENERAL PRINCIPLES FOR THE USE OF FOOD ADDITIVES

1.   All food additives, whether actually in use or being proposed for use, should have been or should be subjected to appropriate toxicological testing and evaluation.   This evaluation should take into account, among other things,   any cumulative, synergistic or potentiating effects of their use.

2.   Only those food additives should be endorsed, which so far as can be judged on the evidence presently available, present no hazard to the health of the consumer at the levels of use proposed.

3.   All food additives should be kept under continuous observation and should be re-evaluated, whenever necessary, in the light of changing conditions of use and new scientific information.

4.   Food additives should at all times conform with an approved specification, e.g. the Specifications of Identity and Purity recommended by the Codex Alimentarius Commission.

5.   The use of food additives is justified only where they serve one or more of the purposes set out from (a) to (d) and only where these purposes cannot be achieved by other means which are economically and technologically practicable and do not present a hazard to the health of the consumer:

     (a)   to preserve the nutritional quality of the food; an intentional reduction in the nutritional quality of a food would be justified in the circumstances dealt with in sub-paragraph (b) and also in other circumstances where the food does not constitute a significant item in a normal diet;

     (b)   to provide necessary ingredients or constituents for foods manufactured for groups of consumers having special dietary needs;

     (c)   to enhance the keeping quality or stability of a food or to improve its organoleptic properties, provided that this does not so change the nature, substance or quality of the food as to deceive the consumer;

     (d)   to provide aids in the manufacture, processing, preparation, treatment, packing, transport or storage of food, provided that the additive is not used to disguise the effects of the use of faulty raw materials or of undesirable (including unhygienic) practices or techniques during the course of any of these activities.

6.   Approval or temporary approval for the inclusion of a food additive in a advisory list or in a food standard should;

     (a)   as far as possible be limited to specific foods for specific purposes and under specific conditions;

     (b)   be at the lowest level of use necessary to achieve the desired effect;

     (c)   as far as possible take into account any Acceptable Daily Intake, or equivalent assessment, established for the food additive and the probable daily intake of it from all sources.   Where the food additive is to be used in foods eaten by special groups of consumers, account should be taken of the probable daily intake of the food additive by consumers in those groups.

SECTION 5.1

INTERNATIONAL NUMBERING SYSTEM FOR FOOD ADDITIVES

INTRODUCTION

The 18th Session (July 1989) of the Codex Alimentarius Commission adopted the INS as a Codex Advisory Text on the basis that the list would be an open one and that proposals for inclusion of further additives would be considered (ALINORM 89/40, para 297).

CLASS NAMES AND THE INTERNATIONAL NUMBERING SYSTEM FOR
FOOD ADDITIVES

SECTION 1

Foreword

Background

The International Numbering System for Food Additives (INS) has been prepared by the Codex Committee on Food Additives and Contaminants (CCFAC) for the purpose of providing an agreed international numerical system for identifying food additives in ingredient lists as an alternative to the declaration of the specific name which is often lengthy and a complex chemical structure. It has been based on the restricted system already introduced successfully within the EEC.

The need for the identification of food additives on food labels arises from the provisions of the Codex General Standard for the Labelling of Prepackaged Foods (CODEX STAN 1 - 1985). This contains the following specific provisions relating to the declaration and identification of food additives in the list of ingredients.

"4.2.2.3. For food additives falling in the respective classes and appearing in lists of food additives permitted for use in foods generally, the following class titles should be used together with the specific name or recognised numerical identification as required by natural legislation."

As required by this provision, the identification numbers are for use only in conjunction with class titles which are meaningful to consumers as descriptions of the actual functions of food additives. As an example, tartrazine when used as a colour in food could be declared as either "colour (tartrazine)" or "colour 102". The advantages of the system are perhaps more apparent in the following example - "thickener (sodium carboxymethyl cellulose)" or "thickener 466".

The 18th Session (July 1989) of the Codex Alimentarius Commission adopted the INS as a Codex Advisory Text on the basis that the list would be an open one and that proposals for inclusion of further additives would be considered (ALINORM 89/40, para 297).

Composition of the INS

The INS is intended as an identification system for food additives approved for use in one or more member countries. It does not imply toxicological approval by Codex but is a means of identifying food additives on a world-wide basis. The list extends well beyond those additives currently cleared by the Joint FAO / WHO Expert Committee on Food Additives (JECFA).

The INS does not include flavours since the Codex General Standard for Labelling does not require these to be specifically identified in the list of ingredients. Further, it does not include chewing gum bases, and dietetic and nutritive additives.

Enzymes which function as food additives are included in the INS along with the technological functions they perform. It was not possible to insert these enzymes in the INS in close proximity to other food additives with similar functions (eg flour treatment agents). They have therefore been included together in an 1100 series.

Explanatory notes on the lay-out of the INS

The INS in numerical order (Section 3) is set out in three columns giving the identification number, the name of the food additive and the technological functions. The identification number for labelling purposes usually consists of three or four digits such as 100 for Curcumins and 1001 for Chlorine salts and esters. However, in some instances the number is followed by an alphabetical subscript, for example 150a identifies Caramel I-plain, 150b identifies Caramel II-caustic sulphite process, and so on. Therefore, the numbers including any alphabetical subscripts are for use on labels.

Under the column listing the name of the food additive, some additives are further subdivided by numerical subscripts, such as (i), (ii), etc. For example, Curcumins are subdivided into (i) Curcumin and (ii) Turmeric. These identifications are not for labelling purposes but simply to identify sub-classes (in this case of Curcumins) which are covered by separate specifications.

The various technological functions performed by the food additives are included in the INS in a third column. The functions listed are indicative rather that exhaustive and are not intended for labelling purposes.

For labelling purposes, the technological functions are grouped under more descriptive functional class titles which are intended to be meaningful to consumers. These are listed in Section 2 along with simple definitions of the function performed.

The twenty-three class titles given in Section 2 have been endorsed by the Codex Committee on Food Labelling and were adopted by the 19th Session (July 1991) of the Codex Alimentarius Commission (ALINORM 91/40, para 181).

A single food additive can often be used for a range of technological functions in a food and it remains the responsibility of the manufacturer to declare the most descriptive functional class in the list of ingredients. For example, sulphur dioxide may function as either a preservative or an antioxidant in foods and may therefore be declared in the list of ingredients as "preservative 220" or "antioxidant 220", as appropriate.

In preparing the INS in numerical order an effort has been made to group food additives with similar functions together in line with the previous procedure used with EEC numbers. However, because of the extension of the list and its open nature most of the three digit numbers have already been allocated. Consequently, the positioning of a food additive in the list can no longer be taken as an indication of the function, although this will often be the case.

It should be noted that a few of the numbers previously allocated within the EEC have been changed to facilitate grouping of similar additives in a more effective layout. This applies particularly to the diphosphates and polyphosphates which have now been grouped under numbers 450 to 452 and to the mineral hydrocarbons now grouped under number 905. Further changes of this nature are not expected and would be made only under exceptional and justified circumstances such as in order to prevent the confusion of consumers or avoid undue difficulties for industry.

The open nature of the list

Because of its primary purpose of identification, the INS is an open list subject to the inclusion of additional additives or removal of existing ones on an ongoing basis. Similarly, the CCFAC will maintain an ongoing review, in conjunction with the Codex Committee on Food Labelling, of the functional class titles specified for use in food labelling.

In line with the above purpose of the INS, member governments and international organizations are invited to make proposals to the CCFAC on an ongoing basis regarding

- additional food additives for which an international identification number can be justified

- additional functional class titles for use in food labelling in conjunction with the INS

- the deletion of food additives or class titles

Proposals should be directed in the first instance to the Chief, Joint FAO/WHO Food Standards Programme, FAO, 00100, Rome, ITALY.

SECTION 2

**TABLE OF FUNCTIONAL CLASSES, DEFINITIONS AND
TECHNOLOGICAL FUNCTIONS**

FUNCTIONAL CLASSES (for labelling purposes)	DEFINITION	SUB-CLASSES (technological functions)
1. Acid	Increases the acidity and/or imparts a sour taste to a food	acidifier
2. Acidity regulator	Alters or controls the acidity or alkalinity of a food	acid, alkali, base, buffer, buffering agent, pH adjusting agent
3. Anticaking agent	Reduces the tendency of particles of food to adhere to one another	anticaking agent, anti-stick agent, drying agent, dusting powder, release agent
4. Antifoaming agent	Prevents or reduces foaming	antifoaming agent
5. Antioxidant	Prolongs the shelf-life of foods by protecting against deterioration caused by oxidation, such as fat rancidity and colour changes	antioxidant, antioxidant synergist, sequestrant
6. Bulking agents	A substance, other than air or water, which contributes to the bulk of a food without contributing significantly to its available energy value	bulking agent, filler
7. Colour	Adds or restores colour in a food	colour
8. Colour retention agent	Stabilizes, retains or intensifies the colour of a food	colour fixative, colour stabilizer
9. Emulsifier	Forms or maintains a uniform mixture of two or more immiscible phases such surface as oil and water in a food	emulsifier, plasticizer, dispersing agent, surface active agent, surfactant, wetting agent
10. Emulsifying salt	Rearranges cheese proteins in the manufacture of processed cheese, in order to prevent fat separation	melding salt, sequestrant
11. Firming agent	Makes or keeps tissues of fruit or vegetables firm and crisp, or interacts with gelling agents to produce or strengthen a gel	firming agent

12. Flavour enhancer	Enhances the existing taste and/or odour of a food	flavour enhancer, flavour modifier, tenderizer
13. Flour treatment agent	A substance added to flour to improve its baking quality or colour	bleaching agent, dough improver, flour improver
14. Foaming agent	Makes it possible to form or maintain a uniform dispersion of a gaseous phase in a liquid or solid food	whipping agent, aerating agent
15. Gelling agent	Gives a food texture through formation of a gel	gelling agent
16. Glazing agent	A substance which, when applied to the external surface of a food, imparts a shiny appearance or provides a protective coating	coating, sealing agent, polish
17. Humectant	Prevents foods from drying out by counteracting the effect of an wetting agent atmosphere having a low degree of humidity	moisture/water retention agent, wetting agent
18. Preservative	Prolongs the shelf-life of a food by protecting against deterioration caused by microorganisms	antimicrobial preservative, antimycotic agent, bacteriophage control agent, chemosterilant/ wine maturing agent, disinfection agent
19. Propellant	A gas, other than air, which expels a food from a container	propellant
20. Raising agent	A substance or combination of substances which liberate gas and thereby increase the volume of a dough	leavening agent, raising agent
21. Stabilizer	Makes it possible to maintain a uniform dispersion of two or more immiscible substances in a food	binder, firming agent, moisture/water retention agent, foam stabilizer
22. Sweetener	A non-sugar substance which imparts a sweet taste to a food	sweetener, artificial sweetener, nutritive sweetener
23. Thickener	Increases the viscosity of a food	thickening agent, texturizer, bodying agent

SECTION 3

INTERNATIONAL NUMBERING SYSTEM FOR FOOD ADDITIVES

LIST IN NUMERICAL ORDER

NO.	NAME OF FOOD ADDITIVE	TECHNOLOGICAL FUNCTION(S)
100	CURCUMINS	Colour
	(i) Curcumin	
	(ii) Turmeric	
101	RIBOFLAVINS	Colour
	(i) Riboflavin	
	(ii) Riboflavin 5' - phosphate sodium	
102	TARTRAZINE	Colour
103	ALKANET	Colour
104	QUINOLINE YELLOW	Colour
107	YELLOW 2G	Colour
110	SUNSET YELLOW FCF	Colour
120	CARMINES	Colour
121	CITRUS RED 2	Colour
122	AZORUBINE	Colour
123	AMARANTH	Colour
124	PONCEAU 4R	Colour
125	PONCEAU SX	Colour
127	ERYTHROSINE	Colour
128	RED 2G	Colour
129	ALLURA RED AC	Colour
131	PATENT BLUE V	Colour
132	INDIGOTINE	Colour
133	BRILLIANT BLUE FCF	Colour
140	CHLOROPHYLL	Colour
141	COPPER CHLOROPHYLLS	Colour
	(i) Chlorophyll copper complex	
	(ii) Chlorophyllin copper complex, sodium and potassium salts	
142	GREEN S	Colour
143	FAST GREEN FCF	Colour
150a	CARAMEL I - Plain	Colour
150b	CARAMEL II - Caustic sulphite process	Colour
150c	CARAMEL III - Ammonia process	Colour
150d	CARAMEL IV - Ammonia-sulphite process	Colour
151	BRILLIANT BLACK PN	Colour
152	CARBON BLACK (hydrocarbon)	Colour
153	VEGETABLE CARBON	Colour
154	BROWN FK	Colour
155	BROWN HT	Colour
160a	CAROTENES	Colour
	(i) Beta-carotene (synthetic)	
	(ii) natural extracts	
160b	ANNATTO EXTRACTS	Colour
160c	PAPRIKA OLEORESINS	Colour

160d	LYCOPENE	Colour
160e	BETA-APO-CAROTENAL	Colour
160f	BETA-APO-8'-CAROTENOIC ACID, METHYL OR ETHYL ESTER	Colour
161a	FLAVOXANTHIN	Colour
161b	LUTEIN	Colour
161c	KRYPTOXANTHIN	Colour
161d	RUBIXANTHIN	Colour
161e	VIOLOXANTHIN	Colour
161f	RHODOXANTHIN	Colour
161g	CANTHAXANTHIN	Colour
162	BEET RED	Colour
163	ANTHOCYANINS	Colour
	(i) Anthocyanins	
	(ii) Grape skin extract	
	(iii) Blackcurrant extract	
164	SAFFRON	Colour
166	SANDALWOOD	Colour
170	CALCIUM CARBONATES	Surface colourant, anticaking agent, stabilizer
	(i) Calcium carbonate	
	(ii) Calcium hydrogen carbonate	
171	TITANIUM DIOXIDE	Colour
172	IRON OXIDES	Colour
	(i) Iron oxide, black	
	(ii) Iron oxide, red	
	(iii) Iron oxide, yellow	
173	ALUMINIUM	Colour
174	SILVER	Colour
175	GOLD	Colour
180	LITHOL RUBINE BK	Colour
181	TANNINS, FOOD GRADE	Colour, emulsifier, stabilizer, thickener
182	ORCHIL	Colour
200	SORBIC ACID	Preservative
201	SODIUM SORBATE	Preservative
202	POTASSIUM SORBATE	Preservative
203	CALCIUM SORBATE	Preservative
209	HEPTYL p-HYDROXYBENZOATE	Preservative
210	BENZOIC ACID	Preservative
211	SODIUM BENZOATE	Preservative
212	POTASSIUM BENZOATE	Preservative
213	CALCIUM BENZOATE	Preservative
214	ETHYL p-HYDROXYBENZOATE	Preservative
215	SODIUM ETHYL P-HYDROXYBENZOATE	Preservative
216	PROPYL p-HYDROXYBENZOATE	Preservative
217	SODIUM PROPYL p-HYDROXYBENZOATE	Preservative
218	METHYL p-HYDROXYBENZOATE	Preservative
219	SODIUM METHYL p-HYDROXYBENZOATE	Preservative
220	SULPHUR DIOXIDE	Preservative, antioxidant
221	SODIUM SULPHITE	Preservative, antioxidant
222	SODIUM HYDROGEN SULPHITE	Preservative, antioxidant
223	SODIUM METABISULPHITE	Preservative, bleaching agent, antioxidant
224	POTASSIUM METABISULPHITE	Preservative, antioxidant
225	POTASSIUM SULPHITE	Preservative, antioxidant
226	CALCIUM SULPHITE	Preservative, antioxidant
227	CALCIUM HYDROGEN SULPHITE	Preservative, antioxidant

228	POTASSIUM BISULPHITE	Preservative, antioxidant
230	DIPHENYL	Preservative
231	ORTHO-PHENYLPHENOL	Preservative
232	SODIUM O-PHENYLPHENOL	Preservative
233	THIABENDAZOLE	Preservative
234	NISIN	Preservative
235	PIMARICIN (NATAMYCIN)	Preservative
236	FORMIC ACID	Preservative
237	SODIUM FORMATE	Preservative
238	CALCIUM FORMATE	Preservative
239	HEXAMETHYLENE TETRAMINE	Preservative
240	FORMALDEHYDE	Preservative
241	GUM GUAICUM	Preservative
242	DIMETHYL DICARBONATE	Preservative
249	POTASSIUM NITRITE	Preservative, colour fixative
250	SODIUM NITRITE	Preservative, colour fixative
251	SODIUM NITRATE	Preservative, colour fixative
252	POTASSIUM NITRATE	Preservative, colour fixative
260	ACETIC ACID GLACIAL	Preservative, acidity regulator
261	POTASSIUM ACETATES (i) Potassium acetate (ii) Potassium diacetate	Preservative, acidity regulator
262	SODIUM ACETATES (i) Sodium acetate (ii) Sodium diacetate	Preservative, acidity regulator, sequestrant
263	CALCIUM ACETATE	Preservative, stabilizer, acidity regulator
264	AMMONIUM ACETATE	Acidity regulator
265	DEHYDROACETIC ACID	Preservative
266	SODIUM DEHYDROACETATE	Preservative
270	LACTIC ACID (L-, D- and DL-)	Acidity regulator
280	PROPIONIC ACID	Preservative
281	SODIUM PROPIONATE	Preservative
282	CALCIUM PROPIONATE	Preservative
283	POTASSIUM PROPIONATE	Preservative
290	CARBON DIOXIDE	Carbonating agent, packing gas
296	MALIC ACID (DL-)	Acidity regulator
297	FUMARIC ACID	Acidity regulator
300	ASCORBIC ACID (L-)	Antioxidant
301	SODIUM ASCORBATE	Antioxidant
302	CALCIUM ASCORBATE	Antioxidant
303	POTASSIUM ASCORBATE	Antioxidant
304	ASCORBYL PALMITATE	Antioxidant
305	ASCORBYL STEARATE	Antioxidant
306	MIXED TOCOPHEROLS CONCENTRATE	Antioxidant
307	ALPHA-TOCOPHEROL	Antioxidant
308	SYNTHETIC GAMMA-TOCOPHEROL	Antioxidant
309	SYNTHETIC DELTA-TOCOPHEROL	Antioxidant
310	PROPYL GALLATE	Antioxidant
311	OCTYL GALLATE	Antioxidant
312	DODECYL GALLATE	Antioxidant
313	ETHYL GALLATE	Antioxidant
314	GUAIAC RESIN	Antioxidant
315	ISOASCORBIC ACID (ERYTHORBIC ACID)	Antioxidant
316	SODIUM ISOASCORBATE	Antioxidant
317	POTASSIUM ISOASCORBATE	Antioxidant
318	CALCIUM ISOASCORBATE	Antioxidant

319	TERTIARY BUTYLHYDROQUINONE	Antioxidant
320	BUTYLATED HYDROXYANISOLE	Antioxidant
321	BUTYLATED HYDROXYTOLUENE	Antioxidant
322	LECITHINS	Antioxidant, emulsifier
323	ANOXOMER	Antioxidant
324	ETHOXYQUIN	Antioxidant
325	SODIUM LACTATE	Antioxidant synergist, humectant, bulking agent
326	POTASSIUM LACTATE	Antioxidant synergist, acidity regulator
327	CALCIUM LACTATE	Acidity regulator, flour treatment agent
328	AMMONIUM LACTATE	Acidity regulator, flour treatment agent
329	MAGNESIUM LACTATE (DL-)	Acidity regulator, flour treatment agent
330	CITRIC ACID	Acidity regulator, antioxidant, sequestrant
331	SODIUM CITRATES (i) Sodium dihydrogen citrate (ii) Disodium monohydrogen citrate (iii) Trisodium citrate	Acidity regulator, sequestrant, emulsifier, stabilizer
332	POTASSIUM CITRATES (i) Potassium dihydrogen citrate (ii) Tripotassium citrate	Acidity regulator, sequestrant, stabilizer
333	CALCIUM CITRATES	Acidity regulator, firming agent, sequestrant
334	TARTARIC ACID (L(+)-)	Acidity regulator, sequestrant, antioxidant synergist
335	SODIUM TARTRATES (i) Monosodium tartrate (ii) Disodium tartrate	Stabilizer, sequestrant
336	POTASSIUM TARTRATES (i) Monopotassium tartrate (ii) Dipotassium tartrate	Stabilizer, sequestrant
337	POTASSIUM SODIUM TARTRATE	Stabilizer, sequestrant
338	ORTHOPHOSPHORIC ACID	Acidity regulator, antioxidant synergist
339	SODIUM PHOSPHATES (i) Monosodium orthophosphate (ii) Disodium orthophosphate (iii) Trisodium orthophosphate	Acidity regulator, sequestrant, emulsifier, texturizer, stabilizer, water retention agent
340	POTASSIUM PHOSPHATES (i) Monopotassium orthophosphate (ii) Dipotassium orthophosphate (iii) Tripotassium orthophosphate	Acidity regulator, sequestrant, stabilizer, emulsifier, water retention agent
341	CALCIUM PHOSPHATES (i) Monocalcium orthophosphate (ii) Dicalcium orthophosphate (iii) Tricalcium orthophosphate	Acidity regulator, flour treatment agent, firming agent, texturizer, raising agent, anticaking agent, water retention agent
342	AMMONIUM PHOSPHATES (i) Monoammonium orthophosphate (ii) Diammonium orthophosphate	Acidity regulator, flour treatment agent
343	MAGNESIUM PHOSPHATES (i) Monomagnesium orthophosphate	Acidity regulator, anticaking agent

	(ii) Dimagnesium orthophosphate	
	(iii) Trimagnesium orthophosphate	
344	LECITHIN CITRATE	Preservative
345	MAGNESIUM CITRATE	Acidity regulator
349	AMMONIUM MALATE	Acidity regulator
350	SODIUM MALATES	Acidity regulator, humectant
	(i) Sodium hydrogen malate	
	(ii) Sodium malate	
351	POTASSIUM MALATES	Acidity regulator
	(i) Potassium hydrogen malate	
	(ii) Potassium malate	
352	CALCIUM MALATES	Acidity regulator
	(i) Calcium hydrogen malate	
	(ii) Calcium malate	
353	METATARTARIC ACID	Acidity regulator
354	CALCIUM TARTRATE	Acidity regulator
355	ADIPIC ACID	Acidity regulator
356	SODIUM ADIPATES	Acidity regulator
357	POTASSIUM ADIPATES	Acidity regulator
359	AMMONIUM ADIPATES	Acidity regulator
363	SUCCINIC ACID	Acidity regulator
365	SODIUM FUMARATES	Acidity regulator
366	POTASSIUM FUMARATES	Acidity regulator
367	CALCIUM FUMARATES	Acidity regulator
368	AMMONIUM FUMARATE	Acidity regulator
370	1, 4 - HEPTONOLACTONE	Acidity regulator, sequestrant
375	NICOTINIC ACID	Colour retention agent
380	AMMONIUM CITRATES	Acidity regulator
381	FERRIC AMMONIUM CITRATE	Anticaking agent
383	CALCIUM GLYCEROPHOSPHATE	Thickener, gelling agent, stabilizer
384	ISOPROPYL CITRATES	Antioxidant, preservative, sequestrant
385	CALCIUM DISODIUM ETHYLENE-DIAMINE-TETRA-ACETATE	Antioxidant, preservative, sequestrant
386	DISODIUM ETHYLENE-DIAMINE-TETRA-ACETATE	Antioxidant, preservative, synergist, sequestrant
387	OXYSTEARIN	Antioxidant, sequestrant
388	THIODIPROPIONIC ACID	Antioxidant
389	DILAURYL THIODIPROPIONATE	Antioxidant
390	DISTEARYL THIODIPROPIONATE	Antioxidant
391	PHYTIC ACID	Antioxidant
399	CALCIUM LACTOBIONATE	Stabilizer
400	ALGINIC ACID	Thickener, stabilizer
401	SODIUM ALGINATE	Thickener, stabilizer, gelling agent
402	POTASSIUM ALGINATE	Thickener, stabilizer
403	AMMONIUM ALGINATE	Thickener, stabilizer
404	CALCIUM ALGINATE	Thickener, stabilizer, gelling agent, antifoaming agent
405	PROPYLENE GLYCOL ALGINATE	Thickener, emulsifier
406	AGAR	Thickener, gelling agent, stabilizer
407	CARRAGEENAN AND ITS Na, K, NH₄ SALTS (INCLUDES FURCELLARAN)	Thickener, gelling agent, stabilizer
408	BAKERS YEAST GLYCAN	Thickener, gelling agent, stabilizer
409	ARABINOGALACTAN	Thickener, gelling agent, stabilizer
410	CAROB BEAN GUM	Thickener, stabilizer
411	OAT GUM	Thickener, stabilizer
412	GUAR GUM	Thickener, stabilizer

413	TRAGACANTH GUM	Thickener, stabilizer, emulsifier
414	GUM ARABIC (ACACIA GUM)	Thickener, stabilizer
415	XANTHAN GUM	Thickener, stabilizer
416	KARAYA GUM	Thickener, stabilizer
417	TARA GUM	Thickener, stabilizer
418	GELLAN GUM	Thickener, stabilizer, gelling agent
419	GUM GHATTI	Thickener, stabilizer, emulsifier
420	SORBITOL AND SORBITOL SYRUP	Sweetener, humectant, sequestrant, texturizer, emulsifier
421	MANNITOL	Sweetener, anticaking agent
422	GLYCEROL	Humectant, bodying agent
429	PEPTONES	Emulsifier
430	POLYOXYETHYLENE (8) STEARATE	Emulsifier
431	POLYOXYETHYLENE (40) STEARATE	Emulsifier
432	POLYOXYETHYLENE (20) SORBITAN MONOLAURATE	Emulsifier, dispersing agent
433	POLYOXYETHYLENE (20) SORBITAN MONOOLEATE	Emulsifier, dispersing agent
434	POLYOXYETHYLENE (20) SORBITAN MONOPALMITATE	Emulsifier, dispersing agent
435	POLYOXYETHYLENE (20) SORBITAN MONOSTEARATE	Emulsifier, dispersing agent
436	POLYOXYETHYLENE (20) SORBITAN TRISTEARATE	Emulsifier, dispersing agent
440	PECTINS	Thickener, stabilizer, gelling agent
441	SUPERGLYCERINATED HYDROGENATED RAPESEED OIL	Emulsifier
442	AMMONIUM SALTS OF PHOSPHATIDIC ACID	Emulsifier
443	BROMINATED VEGETABLE OIL	Emulsifier, stabilizer
444	SUCROSE ACETATE ISOBUTYRATE	Emulsifier, stabilizer
445	GLYCEROL ESTERS OF WOOD ROSIN	Emulsifier, stabilizer
446	SUCCISTEARIN	Emulsifier
450	DIPHOSPHATES (i) Disodium diphosphate (ii) Trisodium diphosphate (iii) Tetrasodium diphosphate (iv) Dipotassium diphosphate (v) Tetrapotassium diphosphate (vi) Dicalcium diphosphate (vii) Calcium dihydrogen diphosphate (viii)Dimagnesium diphosphate	Emulsifier, stabilizer, acidity regulator, raising agent, sequestrant, water retention agent
451	TRIPHOSPHATES (i) Pentasodium triphosphate (ii) Pentapotassium triphosphate	Sequestrant, acidity regulator, texturizer
452	POLYPHOSPHATES (i) Sodium polyphosphate (ii) Potassium polyphosphate (iii) Sodium calcium polyphosphate (iv) Calcium polyphosphates (v) Ammonium polyphosphates	Emulsifier, stabilizer, sequestrant, texturizer, water retent agent
460	CELLULOSE (i) Microcrystalline cellulose (ii) Powdered cellulose	Emulsifier, anticaking agent, texturizer, dispersing agent
461	METHYL CELLULOSE	Thickener, emulsifier, stabilizer
462	ETHYL CELLULOSE	Binder, filler

463	HYDROXYPROPYL CELLULOSE	Thickener, emulsifier, stabilizer
464	HYDROXYPROPYL METHYL CELLULOSE	Thickener, emulsifier, stabilizer
465	METHYL ETHYL CELLULOSE	Thickener, emulsifier, stabilizer, foaming agent
466	SODIUM CARBOXYMETHYL CELLULOSE	Thickener, stabilizer
467	ETHYL HYDROXYETHYL CELLULOSE	Emulsifier, stabilizer, thickener
470	SALTS OF FATTY ACIDS (with base Al, Ca, Na, Mg, K and NH$_4$)	Emulsifier, stabilizer, anticaking agent
471	MONO- AND DI-GLYCERIDES OF FATTY ACIDS	Emulsifier, stabilizer
472a	ACETIC AND FATTY ACID ESTERS OF GLYCEROL	Emulsifier, stabilizer, sequestrant
472b	LACTIC AND FATTY ACID ESTERS OF GLYCEROL	Emulsifier, stabilizer, sequestrant
472c	CITRIC AND FATTY ACID ESTERS OF GLYCEROL	Emulsifier, stabilizer, sequestrant
472d	TARTARIC ACID ESTERS OF MONO-AND DI-GLYCERIDES OF FATTY ACIDS	Emulsifier, stabilizer, sequestrant
472e	DIACETYLTARTARIC AND FATTY ACID ESTERS OF GLYCEROL	Emulsifier, stabilizer, sequestrant
472f	MIXED TARTARIC, ACETIC AND FATTY ACID ESTERS OF GLYCEROL	Emulsifier, stabilizer, sequestrant
472g	SUCCINYLATED MONOGLYCERIDES	Emulsifier, stabilizer, sequestrant
473	SUCROSE ESTERS OF FATTY ACIDS	Emulsifier
474	SUCROGLYCERIDES	Emulsifier
475	POLYGLYCEROL ESTERS OF FATTY ACIDS	Emulsifier
476	POLYGLYCEROL ESTERS OF INTERESTERIFIED RICINOLEIC ACID	Emulsifier
477	PROPYLENE GLYCOL ESTERS OF FATTY ACIDS	Emulsifier
478	LACTYLATED FATTY ACID ESTERS OF GLYCEROL AND PROPYLENE GLYCOL	Emulsifier
479	THERMALLY OXIDIZED SOYA BEAN OIL WITH MONO-AND DI-GLYCERIDES OF FATTY ACIDS	Emulsifier
480	DIOCTYL SODIUM SULPHOSUCCINATE	Emulsifier, wetting agent
481	SODIUM LACTYLATES (i) SODIUM STEAROYL LACTYLATE (ii) SODIUM OLEYL LACTYLATE	Emulsifier, stabilizer
482	CALCIUM LACTYLATES (i) CALCIUM STEAROYL LACTYLATE (ii) CALCIUM OLEYL LACTYLATE	Emulsifier, stabilizer
483	STEARYL TARTRATE	Flour treatment agent
484	STEARYL CITRATE	Emulsifier, sequestrant
485	SODIUM STEAROYL FUMARATE	Emulsifier
486	CALCIUM STEAROYL FUMARATE	Emulsifier
487	SODIUM LAURYLSULPHATE	Emulsifier
488	ETHOXYLATED MONO - AND DI- GLYCERIDES	Emulsifier
489	METHYL GLUCOSIDE - COCONUT OIL ESTER	Emulsifier
491	SORBITAN MONOSTEARATE	Emulsifier
492	SORBITAN TRISTEARATE	Emulsifier

493	SORBITAN MONOLAURATE	Emulsifier
494	SORBITAN MONOOLEATE	Emulsifier
495	SORBITAN MONOPALMITATE	Emulsifier
496	SORBITAN TRIOLEATE	Stabilizer, emulsifier
500	SODIUM CARBONATES (i) Sodium carbonate (ii) Sodium hydrogen carbonate (iii) Sodium sesquicarbonate	Acidity regulator, raising agent, anticaking agent
501	POTASSIUM CARBONATES (i) Potassium carbonate (ii) Potassium hydrogen carbonate	Acidity regulator, stabilizer
503	AMMONIUM CARBONATES (i) Ammonium carbonate (ii) Ammonium hydrogen carbonate	Acidity regulator, raising agent
504	MAGNESIUM CARBONATES (i) Magnesium carbonate (ii) Magnesium hydrogen carbonate	Acidity regulator, anticaking agent, colour retention agent
505	FERROUS CARBONATE	Acidity regulator
507	HYDROCHLORIC ACID	Acidity regulator
508	POTASSIUM CHLORIDE	Gelling agent
509	CALCIUM CHLORIDE	Firming agent
510	AMMONIUM CHLORIDE	Flour treatment agent
511	MAGNESIUM CHLORIDE	Firming agent
512	STANNOUS CHLORIDE	Antioxidant, colour retention agent
513	SULPHURIC ACID	Acidity regulator
514	SODIUM SULPHATES	Acidity regulator
515	POTASSIUM SULPHATES	Acidity regulator
516	CALCIUM SULPHATE	Flour treatment agent, sequestrant, firming agent
517	AMMONIUM SULPHATE	Flour treatment agent, stabilizer
518	MAGNESIUM SULPHATE	Firming agent
519	CUPRIC SULPHATE	Colour fixative, preservative
520	ALUMINIUM SULPHATE	Firming agent
521	ALUMINIUM SODIUM SULPHATE	Firming agent
522	ALUMINIUM POTASSIUM SULPHATE	Acidity regulator, stabilizer
523	ALUMINIUM AMMONIUM SULPHATE	Stabilizer, firming agent
524	SODIUM HYDROXIDE	Acidity regulator
525	POTASSIUM HYDROXIDE	Acidity regulator
526	CALCIUM HYDROXIDE	Acidity regulator, firming agent
527	AMMONIUM HYDROXIDE	Acidity regulator
528	MAGNESIUM HYDROXIDE	Acidity regulator, colour retention agent
529	CALCIUM OXIDE	Acidity regulator, flour treatment agent
530	MAGNESIUM OXIDE	Anticaking agent
535	SODIUM FERROCYANIDE	Anticaking agent
536	POTASSIUM FERROCYANIDE	Anticaking agent
537	FERROUS HEXACYANOMANGANATE	Anticaking agent
538	CALCIUM FERROCYANIDE	Anticaking agent
539	SODIUM THIOSULPHATE	Antioxidant, sequestrant
541	SODIUM ALUMINIUM PHOSPHATE (i) Acidic (ii) Basic	Acidity regulator, emulsifier
542	BONE PHOSPHATE (essentially Calcium phosphate, tribasic)	Emulsifier, anticaking agent, water retention agent
550	SODIUM SILICATES (i) Sodium silicate	Anticaking agent

	(ii) Sodium metasilicate	
551	SILICON DIOXIDE AMORPHOUS	Anticaking agent
552	CALCIUM SILICATE	Anticaking agent
553	MAGNESIUM SILICATES	Anticaking agent, dusting powder
	(i) Magnesium silicate	
	(ii) Magnesium trisilicate	
	(iii) Talc	
554	SODIUM ALUMINOSILICATE	Anticaking agent
555	POTASSIUM ALUMINIUM SILICATE	Anticaking agent
556	CALCIUM ALUMINIUM SILICATE	Anticaking agent
557	ZINC SILICATE	Anticaking agent
558	BENTONITE	Anticaking agent
559	ALUMINIUM SILICATE	Anticaking agent
560	POTASSIUM SILICATE	Anticaking agent
570	FATTY ACIDS	Foam stabilizer, glazing agent, antifoaming agent
574	GLUCONIC ACID (D-)	Acidity regulator, raising agent
575	GLUCONO DELTA-LACTONE	Acidity regulator, raising agent
576	SODIUM GLUCONATE	Sequestrant
577	POTASSIUM GLUCONATE	Sequestrant
578	CALCIUM GLUCONATE	Acidity regulator, firming agent
579	FERROUS GLUCONATE	Colour retention agent
580	MAGNESIUM GLUCONATE	Acidity regulator, firming agent
585	FERROUS LACTATE	Colour retention agent
620	GLUTAMIC ACID (L(+)-)	Flavour enhancer
621	MONOSODIUM GLUTAMATE	Flavour enhancer
622	MONOPOTASSIUM GLUTAMATE	Flavour enhancer
623	CALCIUM GLUTAMATE	Flavour enhancer
624	MONOAMMONIUM GLUTAMATE	Flavour enhancer
625	MAGNESIUM GLUTAMATE	Flavour enhancer
626	GUANYLIC ACID	Flavour enhancer
627	DISODIUM 5'-GUANYLATE	Flavour enhancer
628	DIPOTASSIUM 5'-GUANYLATE	Flavour enhancer
629	CALCIUM 5'-GUANYLATE	Flavour enhancer
630	INOSINIC ACID	Flavour enhancer
631	DISODIUM 5'-INOSINATE	Flavour enhancer
632	POTASSIUM INOSINATE	Flavour enhancer
633	CALCIUM 5'-INOSINATE	Flavour enhancer
634	CALCIUM 5'- RIBONUCLEOTIDES	Flavour enhancer
635	DISODIUM 5' -RIBONUCLEOTIDES	Flavour enhancer
636	MALTOL	Flavour enhancer
637	ETHYL MALTOL	Flavour enhancer
640	GLYCINE	Flavour modifier
641	L-LEUCINE	Flavour modifier
900a	POLYDIMETHYLSILOXANE	Antifoaming agent, emulsifier, anticaking agent
900b	METHYLPHENYLPOLYSILOXANE	Antifoaming agent
901	BEESWAX, WHITE AND YELLOW	Glazing agent, release agent
902	CANDELILLA WAX	Glazing agent
903	CARNAUBA WAX	Glazing agent
904	SHELLAC	Glazing agent
905a	MINERAL OIL, FOOD GRADE	Glazing agent, release agent, sealing agent
905b	PETROLATUM (PETROLEUM JELLY)	Glazing agent, release agent, sealing agent
905c	PETROLEUM WAX	Glazing agent, release agent, sealing agent

906	BENZOIN GUM	Glazing agent
908	RICE BRAN WAX	Glazing agent
909	SPERMACETI WAX	Glazing agent
910	WAX ESTERS	Glazing agent
911	METHYL ESTERS OF FATTY ACIDS	Glazing agent
913	LANOLIN	Glazing agent
915	GLYCEROL -, METHYL - OR PENTA - ERITHRYTOL ESTERS OF COLOPHANE	Glazing agent
916	CALCIUM IODATE	Flour treatment agent
917	POTASSIUM IODATE	Flour treatment agent
918	NITROGEN OXIDES	Flour treatment agent
919	NITROSYL CHLORIDE	Flour treatment agent
920	L-CYSTEINE AND ITS HYDROCHLORIDES - SODIUM AND POTASSIUM SALTS	Flour treatment agent
921	L-CYSTINE AND ITS HYDROCHLORIDES - SODIUM AND POTASSIUM SALTS	Flour treatment agent
922	POTASSIUM PERSULPHATE	Flour treatment agent
923	AMMONIUM PERSULPHATE	Flour treatment agent
924a	POTASSIUM BROMATE	Flour treatment agent
924b	CALCIUM BROMATE	Flour treatment agent
925	CHLORINE	Flour treatment agent
926	CHLORINE DIOXIDE	Flour treatment agent
927a	AZODICARBONAMIDE	Flour treatment agent
927b	CARBAMIDE (UREA)	Flour treatment agent
928	BENZOYL PEROXIDE	Flour treatment agent, preservative
929	ACETONE PEROXIDE	Flour treatment agent
930	CALCIUM PEROXIDE	Flour treatment agent
940	DICHLORODIFLUOROMETHANE	Propellant, liquid freezant
941	NITROGEN	Packing gas, freezant
942	NITROUS OXIDE	Propellant
943a	BUTANE	Propellant
943b	ISOBUTANE	Propellant
944	PROPANE	Propellant
945	CHLOROPENTAFLUOROETHANE	Propellant
946	OCTAFLUOROCYCLOBUTANE	Propellant
950	ACESULFAME POTASSIUM	Sweetener
951	ASPARTAME	Sweetener, flavour enhancer
952	CYCLAMIC ACID (and Na, K, Ca salts)	Sweetener
953	ISOMALT (ISOMALTITOL)	Sweetener, anticaking agent, bulking agent, glazing agent
954	SACCHARIN (and Na, K, Ca salts)	Sweetener
957	THAUMATIN	Sweetener, flavour enhancer
958	GLYCYRRHIZIN	Sweetener, flavour enhancer
959	NEOHESPERIDINE DIHYDROCHALCONE	Sweetener
965	MALTITOL AND MALTITOL SYRUP	Sweetener, stabilizer, emulsifier
966	LACTITOL	Sweetener, texturizer
967	XYLITOL	Sweetener, humectant, stabilizer, emulsifier, thickener
999	QUILLAIA EXTRACTS	Foaming agent
1000	CHOLIC ACID	Emulsifier
1001	CHOLINE SALTS AND ESTERS (i) Choline acetate	Emulsifier

	(ii)	Choline carbonate	
	(iii)	Choline chloride	
	(iv)	Choline citrate	
	(v)	Choline tartrate	
	(vi)	Choline lactate	
1100	AMYLASES		Flour treatment agent
1101	PROTEASES		Flour treatment agent,
	(i)	Protease	stabilizer, tenderizer,
	(ii)	Papain	flavour enhancer
	(iii)	Bromelain	
	(iv)	Ficin	
1102	GLUCOSE OXIDASE		Antioxidant
1103	INVERTASES		Stabilizer
1104	LIPASES		Flavour enhancer
1105	LYSOZYME		Preservative
1200	POLYDEXTROSES A AND N		Bulking agent, stabilizer, thickener, humectant, texturizer
1201	POLYVINYLPYRROLIDONE		Bodying agent, stabilizer, clarifying agent, dispersing agent
1202	POLYVINYLPOLYPYRROLIDONE		Colour stabilizer, colloidal stabilizer
1503	CASTOR OIL		Release agent
1505	TRIETHYL CITRATE		Foam stabilizer
1518	TRIACETIN		Humectant
1520	PROPYLENE GLYCOL		Humectant, wetting agent, dispersing agent
1521	POLYETHYLENE GLYCOL		Antifoaming agent

SUPPLEMENTARY LIST - MODIFIED STARCHES

EXPLANATORY NOTE

The Codex General Standard for the Labelling of Prepackaged Foods (CODEX STAN 1 - 1985) specifies that modified starches may be declared as such in the list of ingredients. However, as some countries presently require the specific identification of modified starches the following numbers are provided as a guide and as a means of facilitating uniformity. Where these starches are specifically identified in the list of ingredients then it would be appropriate to include them under the relevant class name eg Thickener.

1400	DEXTRINS, ROASTED STARCH WHITE AND YELLOW	Stabilizer, thickener, binder
1401	ACID-TREATED STARCH	Stabilizer, thickener, binder
1402	ALKALINE TREATED STARCH	Stabilizer, thickener, binder
1403	BLEACHED STARCH	Stabilizer, thickener, binder
1404	OXIDIZED STARCH	Emulsifier, thickener, binder
1405	STARCHES, ENZYME-TREATED	Thickener
1410	MONOSTARCH PHOSPHATE	Stabilizer, thickener, binder
1411	DISTARCH GLYCEROL	Stabilizer, thickener
1412	DISTARCH PHOSPHATE ESTERIFIED WITH SODIUM TRIMETASPHOSPHATE; ESTERIFIED WITH PHOSPHORUS-OXYCHLORIDE	Stabilizer, thickener, binder
1413	PHOSPHATED DISTARCH PHOSPHATE	Stabilizer, thickener, binder
1414	ACETYLATED DISTARCH PHOSPHATE	Emulsifier, thickener
1420	STARCH ACETATE ESTERIFIED WITH ACETIC ANHYDRIDE	Stabilizer, thickener
1421	STARCH ACETATE ESTERIFIED WITH VINYL ACETATE	Stabilizer, thickener
1422	ACETYLATED DISTARCH ADIPATE	Stabilizer, thickener, binder
1423	ACETYLATED DISTARCH GLYCEROL	Stabilizer, thickener
1440	HYDROXYPROPYL STARCH	Emulsifier, thickener, binder
1442	HYDROXYPROPYL DISTARCH PHOSPHATE	Stabilizer, thickener
1443	HYDROXYPROPYL DISTARCH GLYCEROL	Stabilizer, thickener
1450	STARCH SODIUM OCTENYL SUCCINATE	Stabilizer, thickener, binder, emulsifier

SECTION 4

INTERNATIONAL NUMBERING SYSTEM FOR FOOD ADDITIVES

LIST IN ALPHABETICAL ORDER

NAME OF FOOD ADDITIVE	No.	TECHNOLOGICAL FUNCTION(S)
ACESULFAME POTASSIUM	950	Sweetener
ACETIC ACID GLACIAL	260	Preservative, acidity regulator
ACETIC AND FATTY ACID ESTERS OF GLYCEROL	472a	Emulsifier, stabilizer, sequestrant
ACETONE PEROXIDE	929	Flour treatment agent
ADIPIC ACID	355	Acidity regulator
AGAR	406	Thickener, stabilizer, gelling agent
ALGINIC ACID	400	Thickener, stabilizer
ALKANET	103	Colour
ALLURA RED AC	129	Colour
ALPHA-TOCOPHEROL	307	Antioxidant
ALUMINIUM	173	Colour
ALUMINIUM AMMONIUM SULPHATE	523	Stabilizer, firming agent
ALUMINIUM POTASSIUM SULPHATE	522	Acidity regulator, stabilizer
ALUMINIUM SILICATE	559	Anticaking agent
ALUMINIUM SODIUM SULPHATE	521	Firming agent
ALUMINIUM SULPHATE	520	Firming agent
AMARANTH	123	Colour
AMMONIUM ACETATE	264	Acidity regulator
AMMONIUM ADIPATES	359	Acidity regulator
AMMONIUM ALGINATE	403	Thickener, stabilizer
AMMONIUM CARBONATE	503	Acidity regulator, raising agent
AMMONIUM CHLORIDE	510	Flour treatment agent
AMMONIUM CITRATES	380	Acidity regulator
AMMONIUM FURMATE	368	Acidity regulator
AMMONIUM HYDROGEN CARBONATE	503	Acidity regulator, raising agent
AMMONIUM HYDROXIDE	527	Acidity regulator
AMMONIUM LACTATE	328	Acidity regulator, flour treatment agent
AMMONIUM MALATE	349	Acidity regulator
AMMONIUM PERSULPHATE	923	Flour treatment agent
AMMONIUM PHOSPHATES	342	Acidity regulator, flour treatment agent
AMMONIUM POLYPHOSPHATES	452	Emulsifier, stabilizer, sequestrant, texturizer, water retention agent
AMMONIUM SALTS OF PHOSPHATIDIC ACID	442	Emulsifier
AMMONIUM SULPHATE	517	Flour treatment agent, stabilizer
AMYLASES	1100	Flour treatment agent
ANNATTO EXTRACTS	160b	Colour
ANOXOMER	323	Antioxidant
ANTHOCYANINS	163	Colour
ARABINOGALACTAN	409	Thickener, gelling agent, stabilizer
ASCORBYL PALMITATE	304	Antioxidant
ASCORBYL STEARATE	305	Antioxidant
ASORBIC ACID (L-)	300	Antioxidant
ASPARTAME	951	Sweetener, flavour enhancer
AZODICARBONAMIDE	927a	Flour treatment agent

AZORUBINE	122	Colour
BAKERS YEAST GLYCAN	408	Thickener, gelling agent, stabilizer
BEESWAX, WHITE AND YELLOW	901	Glazing agent, release agent
BEET RED	162	Colour
BENTONITE	558	Anticaking agent
BENZOIC ACID	210	Preservative
BENZOIN GUM	906	Glazing agent
BENZOYL PEROXIDE	928	Flour treatment agent, preservative
BETA-APO-CAROTENAL	160e	Colour
BETA-APO-8'-CAROTENOIC ACID, METHYL OR ETHYL ESTER	160f	Colour
BETA-CAROTENE (NATURAL EXTRACTS)	160a	Colour
BETA-CAROTENE (SYNTHETIC)	160a	Colour
BLACKCURRANT EXTRACT	163	Colour
BONE PHOSPHATE (essentially Calcium phosphate, tribasic)	542	Emulsifier, anticaking agent, water retention agent
BRILLIANT BLACK PN	151	Colour
BRILLIANT BLUE FCF	133	Colour
BROMELAIN	1101	Flour treatment agent, stabilizer tenderizer, flavour enhancer
BROMINATED VEGETABLE OIL	443	Emulsifier, stabilizer
BROWN FK	154	Colour
BROWN HT	155	Colour
BUTANE	943a	Propellant
BUTYLATED HYDROXYANISOLE	320	Antioxidant
BUTYLATED HYDROXYTOLUENE	321	Antioxidant
CALCIUM ACETATE	263	Preservative, stabilizer, acidity regulator
CALCIUM ALGINATE	404	Thickener, stabilizer, gelling agent, antifoaming agent
CALCIUM ALUMINIUM SILICATE	556	Anticaking agent
CALCIUM ASCORBATE	302	Antioxidant
CALCIUM BENZOATE	213	Preservative
CALCIUM BROMATE	924b	Flour treatment agent
CALCIUM CARBONATE	170	Surface colourant, anticaking agent, stabilizer
CALCIUM CHLORIDE	509	Firming agent
CALCIUM CITRATES	333	Acidity regulator, firming agent, sequestrant
CALCIUM DIHYDROGEN DIPHOSPHATE	450	Emulsifier, stabilizer, acidity regulator, raising agent, sequestrant, water retention agent
CALCIUM DISODIUM ETHYLENE-DIAMINE-TETRA-ACETATE	385	Antioxidant, preservative, sequestrant
CALCIUM FERROCYANIDE	538	Anticaking agent
CALCIUM FORMATE	238	Preservative
CALCIUM FUMARATE	367	Acidity regulator
CALCIUM GLUCONATE	578	Acidity regulator, firming agent
CALCIUM GLUTAMATE	623	Flavour enhancer
CALCIUM GLYCEROPHOSPHATE	383	Thickener, gelling agent, stabilizer
CALCIUM 5' - GUANYLATE	629	Flavour enhancer
CALCIUM HYDROGEN CARBONATE	170	Surface colourant, anticaking agent, stabilizer
CALCIUM HYDROGEN MALATE	352	Acidity regulator
CALCIUM HYDROGEN SULPHITE	227	Preservative, antioxidant
CALCIUM HYDROXIDE	526	Acidity regulator, firming agent
CALCIUM 5' -INOSINATE	633	Flavour enhancer

CALCIUM IODATE	916	Flour treatment agent
CALCIUM ISOASCORBATE	318	Antioxidant
CALCIUM LACTATE	327	Acidity regulator, flour treatment agent,
CALCIUM LACTOBIONATE	399	Stabilizer
CALCIUM MALATE	352	Acidity regulator
CALCIUM 5'-RIBONUCLEOTIDES	634	Flavour enhancer
CALCIUM OLEYL LACTYLATE	482	Emulsifier, stabilizer
CALCIUM OXIDE	529	Acidity regulator, flour treatment agent
CALCIUM PEROXIDE	930	Flour treatment agent
CALCIUM POLYPHOSPHATES	452	Texturizer, water retention agent sequestrant, emulsifier, stabilizer
CALCIUM PROPIONATE	282	Preservative
CALCIUM SILICATE	552	Anticaking agent
CALCIUM SORBATE	203	Preservative
CALCIUM STEAROYL FUMARATE	486	Emulsifier
CALCIUM STEAROYL LACTYLATE	482	Emulsifier, stabilizer
CALCIUM SULPHATE	516	Flour treatment agent, sequestrant, firming agent
CALCIUM SULPHITE	226	Preservative, antioxidant
CALCIUM TARTRATE	354	Acidity regulator
CANDELILLA WAX	902	Glazing agent
CANTHAXANTHIN	161g	Colour
CARAMEL I (PLAIN)	150a	Colour
CARAMEL II (CAUSTIC SULPHITE PROCESS)	150b	Colour
CARAMEL III (AMMONIA PROCESS)	150c	Colour
CARAMEL IV (AMMONIA- SULPHITE PROCESS)	150d	Colour
CARBAMIDE (UREA)	927b	Flour treatment agent
CARBON BLACK (hydrocarbon)	152	Colour
CARBON DIOXIDE	290	Carbonating agent, packing gas
CARMINES	120	Colour
CARNAUBA WAX	903	Glazing agent
CAROB BEAN GUM	410	Thickener, stabilizer
CAROTENES	160a	Colour
CARRAGEENAN AND ITS Na, K, NH₄ SALTS (INCLUDES FURCELLARAN)	407	Thickener, gelling agent, stabilizer
CASTOR OIL	1503	Release agent
CHLORINE	925	Flour treatment agent
CHLORINE DIOXIDE	926	Flour treatment agent
CHLOROPENTAFLUOROETHANE	945	Propellant
CHLOROPHYLL	140	Colour
CHLOROPHYLL COPPER COMPLEX	141	Colour
CHLOROPHYLLIN COPPER COMPLEX, SODIUM AND POTASSIUM SALTS	141	Colour
CHOLIC ACID	1000	Emulsifier
CHOLINE ACETATE	1001	Emulsifier
CHOLINE CARBONATE	1001	Emulsifier
CHOLINE CHLORIDE	1001	Emulsifier
CHOLINE CITRATE	1001	Emulsifier
CHOLINE LACTATE	1001	Emulsifier
CHOLINE TARTRATE	1001	Emulsifier
CITRIC ACID	330	Acidity regulator, antioxidant, sequestrant
CITRIC AND FATTY ACID ESTERS	472c	Emulsifier, sequestrant,

OF GLYCEROL		stabilizer
CITRUS RED 2	121	Colour
CUPRIC SULPHATE	519	Colour fixative, preservative
CURCUMIN	100	Colour
CYCLAMIC ACID (and Na, K, Ca salts)	952	Sweetener
DEHYDROACETIC ACID	265	Preservative
DIACETYLTARTARIC AND FATTY ACID ESTERS OF GLYCEROL	472e	Emulsifier, stabilizer, sequestrant
DIAMMONIUM ORTHOPHOSPHATE	342	Acidity regulator, flour treatment agent
DICALCIUM DIPHOSPHATE	450	Acidity regulator, emulsifier, stabilizer, raising agent, sequestrant, water retention agent
DICALCIUM ORTHOPHOSPHATE	341	Acidity regulator, flour treatment agent, firming agent, texturizer, raising agent, anticaking agent, water retention agent
DICHLORODIFLUOROMETHANE	940	Propellant, liquid freezant
DILAURYL THIODIPROPIONATE	389	Antioxidant
DIMAGNESIUM DIPHOSPHATE	450	Emulsifier, stabilizer, acidity regulator, raising agent, sequestrant, water retention agent
DIMAGNESIUM ORTHOPHOSPHATE	343	Acidity regulator, anticaking agent
DIMETHYL DICARBONATE	242	Preservative
DIOCTYL SODIUM SULPHOSUCCINATE	480	Emulsifier, wetting agent
DIPHENYL	230	Preservative
DIPOTASSIUM DIPHOSPHATE	450	Emulsifier, stabilizer, acidity regulator, raising agent, sequestrant, water retention agent
DIPOTASSIUM 5'-GUANYLATE	628	Flavour enhancer
DIPOTASSIUM ORTHOPHOSPHATE	340	Acidity regulator, sequestrant, stabilizer, emulsifier, water retention agent
DIPOTASSIUM TARTRATE	336	Stabilizer, sequestrant
DISODIUM DIPHOSPHATE	450	Emulsifier, stabilizer, acidity regulator, raising agent, sequestrant, water retention agent
DISODIUM ETHYLENE-DIAMINE-TETRA-ACETATE	386	Antioxidant, preservative, synergist, sequestrant
DISODIUM 5'-GUANYLATE	627	Flavour enhancer
DISODIUM 5'-INOSINATE	631	Flavour enhancer
DISODIUM MONOHYDROGEN CITRATE	331	Acidity regulator, sequestrant, emulsifier, stabilizer
DISODIUM ORTHOPHOSPHATE	339	Acidity regulator, sequestrant, emulsifier, texturizer, stabilizer, water retention agent
DISODIUM 5'-RIBONUCLEOTIDES	635	Flavour enhancer
DISODIUM TARTRATE	335	Stabilizer, seqestrant
DISTEARYL THIODIPROPIONATE	390	Antioxidant
DODECYL GALLATE	312	Antioxidant
ERYTHROSINE	127	Colour
ETHOXYLATED MONO - AND DI-GLYCIDERIDES	488	Emulsifier
ETHOXYQUIN	324	Antioxidant
ETHYL CELLULOSE	462	Binder, filler
ETHYL GALLATE	313	Antioxidant

ETHYL HYDROXYETHYL CELLULOSE	467	Emulsifier, stabilizer, thickener
ETHYL MALTOL	637	Flavour enhancer
ETHYL p-HYDROXYBENZOATE	214	Preservative
FAST GREEN FCF	143	Colour
FATTY ACIDS	570	Foam stabilizer, glazing agent, antifoaming agent
FERRIC AMMONIUM CITRATE	381	Anticaking agent
FERROUS CARBONATE	505	Acidity regulator
FERROUS GLUCONATE	579	Colour retention agent
FERROUS HEXACYANOMANGANATE	537	Anticaking agent
FERROUS LACTATE	585	Colour retention agent
FICIN	1101	Flour treatment agent, stabilizer, tenderizer, flavour enhancer
FLAVOXANTHIN	161a	Colour
FORMIC ACID	236	Preservative
FORMALDEHYDE	240	Preservative
FUMARIC ACID	297	Acidity regulator
FURCELLARAN	407	Thickener, gelling agent, stabilizer
GELLAN GUM	418	Thickener, stabilizer, gelling agent
GLUCONIC ACID (D-)	574	Acidity regulator, raising agent
GLUCONO DELTA-LACTONE	575	Acidity regulator, raising agent
GLUCOSE OXIDASE	1102	Antioxidant
GLUTAMIC ACID (L(+)-)	620	Flavour enhancer,
GLYCEROL	422	Humectant, bodying agent
GLYCEROL ESTERS OF WOOD ROSIN	445	Stabilizer, emulsifier
GLYCEROL -, METHYL - OR PENTA - ERITHRYTOL ESTERS OF COLOPHANE	915	Glazing agent
GLYCINE	640	Flavour modifier
GLYCYRRHIZIN	958	Sweetener, flavour enhancer
GOLD	175	Colour
GRAPE SKIN EXTRACT	163	Colour
GREEN S	142	Colour
GUAIAC RESIN	314	Antioxidant
GUANYLIC ACID	626	Flavour enhancer
GUAR GUM	412	Thickener, stabilizer
GUM ARABIC (ACACIA GUM)	414	Thickener, stabilizer
1, 4 - HEPTONOLACTONE	370	Acidity regulator, sequestrant
GUM GHATTI	419	Thickener, stabilizer, emulsifier
GUM GUAICUM	241	Preservative
HEPTYL p-HYDROXYBENZOATE	209	Preservative
HEXAMETHYLENE TETRAMINE	239	Preservative
HYDROCHLORIC ACID	507	Acidity regulator
HYDROXYPROPYL CELLULOSE	463	Thickener, emulsifier, stabilizer
HYDROXYPROPYL METHYL CELLULOSE	464	Thickener, emulsifier, stabilizer
INDIGOTINE	132	Colour
INVERTASES	1103	Stabilizer
INOSINIC ACID	630	Flavour enhancer
IRON OXIDE BLACK	172	Colour
IRON OXIDE RED	172	Colour
IRON OXIDE YELLOW	172	Colour
ISOASCORBIC ACID (ERYTHORBIC ACID)	315	Antioxidant
ISOBUTANE	943b	Propellant
ISOMALT (ISOMALTITOL)	953	Sweetener, anticaking agent, bulking agent, glazing agent
ISOPROPYL CITRATES	384	Antioxidant, preservative, sequestrant
KARAYA GUM	416	Thickener, stabilizer

KRYPTOXANTHIN	161c	Colour
LACTIC ACID (L-, D- AND DL-)	270	Acidity regulator
LACTIC AND FATTY ACID ESTERS OF GLYCEROL	472b	Emulsifier, stabilizer, sequestrant
LACTITOL	966	Sweetener, texturizer
LACTYLATED FATTY ACID ESTERS OF GLYCEROL AND PROPYLENE GLYCOL	478	Emulsifier
LANOLIN	913	Glazing agent
L-CYSTEINE AND ITS HYDROCHLORIDES - SODIUM AND POTASSIUM SALTS	920	Flour treatment agent
L-CYSTINE AND ITS HYDROCHLORIDES - SODIUM AND POTASSIUM SALTS	921	Flour treatment agent
LECITHIN CITRATE	344	Preservative
LECITHINS	322	Antioxidant, emulsifier
LIPASES	1104	Flavour enhancer
LITHOL RUBINE BK	180	Colour
L-LEUCINE	641	Flavour modifier
LUTEIN	161b	Colour
LYCOPENE	160d	Colour
LYSOZYME	1105	Preservative
MAGNESIUM CARBONATE	504	Acidity regulator, anticaking agent, colour retention agent
MAGNESIUM CHLORIDE	511	Firming agent
MAGNESIUM CITRATE	345	Acidity regulator
MAGNESIUM GLUTAMATE	625	Flavour enhancer
MAGNESIUM GLUCONATE	580	Acidity regulator, firming agent
MAGNESIUM HYDROGEN CARBONATE	504	Acidity regulator, anticaking agent, colour retention agent
MAGNESIUM HYDROXIDE	528	Acidity regulator, colour retention agent
MAGNESIUM LACTATE (DL-)	329	Acidity regulator, flour treatment agent
MAGNESIUM OXIDE	530	Anticaking agent
MAGNESIUM SILICATE	553	Anticaking agent,, dusting powder
MAGNESIUM SULPHATE	518	Firming agent
MAGNESIUM TRISILICATE	553	Anticaking agent, dusting powder
MALIC ACID (DL-)	296	Acidity regulator
MALTITOL AND MALTITOL SYRUP	965	Sweetener, stabilizer, emulsifier
MALTOL	636	Flavour enhancer
MANNITOL	421	Sweetener, anticaking agent
METATARTARIC ACID	353	Acidity regulator
METHYL CELLULOSE	461	Thickener, emulsifier, stabilizer
METHYL ESTERS OF FATTY ACIDS	911	Glazing agent
METHYL ETHYL CELLULOSE	465	Thickener, emulsifier, stabilizer, foaming agent
METHYL GLUCOSIDE - COCONUT OIL ESTER	489	Emulsifier
METHYL p-HYDROXYBENZOATE	218	Preservative
METHYLPHENYLPOLYSILOXANE	900b	Antifoaming agent
MICROCRYSTALLINE CELLULOSE	460	Emulsifier, anticaking agent, dispersing agent, texturizer
MINERAL OIL, FOOD GRADE	905a	Glazing agent, release agent, sealing agent
MIXED TARTARIC, ACETIC AND FATTY	472f	Emulsifier, stabilizer, sequestrant

ACID ESTERS OF GLYCEROL

MIXED TOCOPHEROLS CONCENTRATE	306	Antioxidant
MONO- AND DI-GLYCERIDES OF FATTY ACIDS	471	Emulsifier, stabilizer
MONOAMMONIUM GLUTAMATE	624	Flavour enhancer
MONOAMMONIUM ORTHOPHOSPHATE	342	Acidity regulator, flour treatment agent
MONOCALCIUM ORTHOPHOSPHATE	341	Acidity regulator, flour treatment agent, firming agent, texturizer, raising agent, aqnticaking agent, water retention agent
MONOMAGNESIUM ORTHOPHOSPHATE	343	Acidity regulator, anticaking agent
MONOPOTASSIUM GLUTAMATE	622	Flavour enhancer
MONOPOTASSIUM ORTHOPHOSPHATE	340	Acidity regulator, sequestrant, stabilizer, emulsifier, water retention agent
MONOPOTASSIUM TARTRATE	336	Stabilizer, sequestrant
MONOSODIUM GLUTAMATE	621	Flavour enhancer
MONOSODIUM ORTHOPHOSPHATE	339	Acidity regulator, sequestrant, emulsifier, texturiser, stabilizer, water retention agent
MONOSODIUM TARTRATE	335	Stabilizer, sequestrant
NEOHESPERIDINE DIHYDROCHALCONE	959	Sweetener
NICOTINIC ACID	375	colour retention agent
NISIN	234	Preservative
NITROGEN	941	Packing gas, freezant
NITROGEN OXIDES	918	Flour treatment agent
NITROSYL CHLORIDE	919	Flour treatment agent
NITROUS OXIDE	942	Propellant
OAT GUM	411	Thickener, stabilizer
OCTAFLUOROCYCLOBUTANE	946	Propellant
OCTYL GALLATE	311	Antioxidant
ORCHIL	182	Colour
ORTHOPHOSPHORIC ACID	338	Acidity regulator, antioxidant, syngerist,
ORTHO-PHENYLPHENOL	231	Preservative
OXYSTEARIN	387	Antioxidant, sequestrant
PAPAIN	1101	Flour treatment agent, stabilizer tenderizer, flavour enhancer
PAPRIKA OLEORESINS	160c	Colour
PATENT BLUE V	131	Colour
PECTINS	440	Thickener, stabilizer, gelling agent
PENTAPOTASSIUM TRIPHOSPHATE	451	Texturizer, sequestrant, acidity regulator
PENTASODIUM TRIPHOSPHATE	451	Texturizer, sequestrant, acidity regulator
PEPTONES	429	Emulsifier
PETROLATUM (PETROLEUM JELLY)	905b	Glazing agent, release agent, sealing agent
PETROLEUM WAX	905c	Glazing agent, release agent, sealing agent
PHYTIC ACID	391	Antioxidant
PIMARICIN (NATAMYCIN)	235	Preservative
POLYDEXTROSES A AND N	1200	Bulking agent, stabilizer thickener, humectant, texturizer
POLYDIMETHYLSILOXANE	900a	Antifoaming agent, emulsifier anticaking agent

POLYETHYLENE GLYCOL	1521	Antifoaming agent
POLYGLYCEROL ESTERS OF FATTY ACIDS	475	Emulsifier
POLYGLYCEROL ESTERS OF FATTY INTERESTERIFIED RICINOLEIC ACIDS	476	Emulsifier
POLYOXYETHYLENE (20) SORBITAN MONOLAURATE	432	Emulsifier, dispersing agent
POLYOXYETHYLENE (20) SORBITAN MONOOLEATE	433	Emulsifier, dispersing agent
POLYOXYETHYLENE (20) SORBITAN MONOPALMITATE	434	Emulsifier, dispersing agent
POLYOXYETHYLENE (20) SORBITAN MONOSTEARATE	435	Emulsifier, dispersing agent
POLYOXYETHYLENE (20) SORBITAN TRISTEARATE	436	Emulsifier, dispersing agent
POLYOXYETHYLENE (8) STEARATE	430	Emulsifier
POLYOXYETHYLENE (40) STEARATE	431	Emulsifier
POLYVINYLPOLYPYRROLIDINE	1202	Colour stabilizer, colloidal stabilizer
POLYVINYLPYRROLIDONE	1201	Bodying agent, stabilizer, clarifying agent, dispersing agent
PONCEAU 4R	124	Colour
PONCEAU SX	125	Colour
POTASSIUM ACETATE	261	Preservative, acidity regulator
POTASSIUM ADIPATES	357	Acidity regulator
POTASSIUM ALGINATE	402	Thickener, stabilizer
POTASSIUM ALUMINIUM SILICATE	555	Anticaking agent
POTASSIUM ASCORBATE	303	Antioxidant
POTASSIUM BENZOATE	212	Preservative
POTASSIUM BISULPHITE	228	Preservative, antioxidant
POTASSIUM BROMATE	924a	Flour treatment agent
POTASSIUM CARBONATE	501	Acidity regulator, stabilizer
POTASSIUM CHLORIDE	508	Gelling agent
POTASSIUM DIACETATE	261	Preservative, acidity regulator
POTASSIUM DIHYDROGEN CITRATE	332	Acidity regulator, sequestrant, stabilizer
POTASSIUM FERROCYANIDE	536	Anticaking agent
POTASSIUM FUMARATES	366	Acidity regulator
POTASSIUM GLUCONATE	577	Sequestrant
POTASSIUM HYDROGEN CARBONATE	501	Acidity regulator, stabilizer
POTASSIUM HYDROGEN MALATE	351	Acidity regulator
POTASSIUM HYDROXIDE	525	Acidity regulator
POTASSIUM INOSINATE	632	Flavour enhancer
POTASSIUM IODATE	917	Flour treatment agent
POTASSIUM ISOASCORBATE	317	Antioxidant
POTASSIUM LACTATE	326	Antioxidant synergist, acidity regulator
POTASSIUM MALATE	351	Acidity regulator
POTASSIUM METABISULPHITE	224	Preservative, antioxidant
POTASSIUM NITRATE	252	Preservative, colour fixative
POTASSIUM NITRITE	249	Preservative, colour fixative
POTASSIUM PERSULPHATE	922	Flour treatment agent
POTASSIUM POLYPHOSPHATE	452	Emulsifier, sequestrant, texturizer, water retention agent, stabilizer
POTASSIUM PROPIONATE	283	Preservative
POTASSIUM SILICATE	560	Anticaking agent

POTASSIUM SODIUM TARTRATE	337	Stabilizer, sequestrant
POTASSIUM SORBATE	202	Preservative
POTASSIUM SULPHATES	515	Acidity regulator
POTASSIUM SULPHITE	225	Preservative, antioxidant
POWDERED CELLULOSE	460	Anticaking agent, dispersing agent, texturizer, emulsifier
PROPANE	944	Propellant
PROPIONIC ACID	280	Preservative
PROPYLENE GLYCOL	1520	Humectant, wetting agent, dispersing agent
PROPYL GALLATE	310	Antioxidant
PROPYL p-HYDROXYBENZOATE	216	Preservative
PROPYLENE GLYCOL ALGINATE	405	Thickener, emulsifier,
PROPYLENE GLYCOL ESTERS OF FATTY ACIDS	477	Emulsifier
PROTEASE	1101	Flour treatment agent, stabilizer, tenderizer, flavour enhancer
QUILLAIA EXTRACTS	999	Foaming agent
QUINOLINE YELLOW	104	Colour
RED 2G	128	Colour
RHODOXANTHIN	161f	Colour
RIBOFLAVIN	101	Colour
RIBOFLAVIN 5'-PHOSPHATE SODIUM	101	Colour
RICE BRAN WAX	908	Glazing agent
RUBIXANTHIN	161d	Colour
SACCHARIN (and Na, K, Ca salts)	954	Sweetener
SAFFRON	164	Colour
SALTS OF FATTY ACIDS (with base Al, Ca, Na, Mg, K and NH$_4$)	470	Emulsifier, anticaking agent, stabilizer
SANDALWOOD	166	Colour
SHELLAC	904	Glazing agent
SILICON DIOXIDE AMORPHOUS	551	Anticaking agent
SILVER	174	Colour
SODIUM ACETATE	262	Preservative, acidity regulator, sequestrant
SODIUM ADIPATES	356	Acidity regulator
SODIUM ALGINATE	401	Thickener, stabilizer, gelling agent
SODIUM ALUMINIUM PHOSPHATE, BASIC AND ACIDIC	541	Acidity regulator, emulsifier
SODIUM ALUMINOSILICATE	554	Anticaking agent
SODIUM ASCORBATE	301	Antioxidant
SODIUM BENZOATE	211	Preservative
SODIUM CALCIUM POLYPHOSPHATE	452	Emulsifier, stabilizer, sequestrant, texturizer, water retention agent
SODIUM CARBONATE	500	Acidity regulator, raising agent, anticaking agent
SODIUM CARBOXYMETHYL CELLULOSE	466	Thickener, stabilizer
SODIUM DEHYDROACETATE	266	Preservative
SODIUM DIACETATE	262	Preservative, sequestrant, acidity regulator
SODIUM DIHYDROGEN CITRATE	331	Acidity regulator, sequestrant, emulsifier, stabilizer
SODIUM ETHYL P-HYDROXYBENZOATE	215	Preservative
SODIUM FERROCYANIDE	535	Anticaking agent
SODIUM FORMATE	237	Preservative
SODIUM FUMARATES	365	Acidity regulator

SODIUM GLUCONATE	576	Sequestrant
SODIUM HYDROGEN CARBONATE	500	Acidity regulator, raising agent, anticaking agent
SODIUM HYDROGEN MALATE	350	Acidity regulator, humectant
SODIUM HYDROGEN SULPHITE	222	Preservative, antioxidant
SODIUM HYDROXIDE	524	Acidity regulator
SODIUM ISOASCORBATE	316	Antioxidant
SODIUM LACTATE	325	Antioxidant synergist, humectant, bulking agent
SODIUM LAURYLSULPHATE	487	Emulsifier
SODIUM MALATE	350	Acidity regulator, humectant
SODIUM METABISULPHITE	223	Preservative, bleaching agent, antioxidant
SODIUM METASILICATE	550	Anticaking agent
SODIUM METHYL p-HYDROXYBENZOATE	219	Preservative
SODIUM NITRATE	251	Preservative, colour fixative
SODIUM NITRITE	250	Colour fixative, preservative
SODIUM OLEYL LACTYLATE	481	Emulsifier, stabilizer
SODIUM o-PHENYLPHENOL	232	Preservative
SODIUM POLYPHOSPHATE	452	Emulsifier, texturizer, sequestrant, stabilizer, water retention agent
SODIUM PROPIONATE	281	Preservative
SODIUM PROPYL p-HYDROXYBENZOATE	217	Preservative
SODIUM SESQUICARBONATE	500	Acidity regulator, raising agent, anticaking agent
SODIUM SILICATE	550	Anticaking agent
SODIUM SORBATE	201	Preservative
SODIUM STEAROYL FUMARATE	485	Emulsifier
SODIUM STEAROYL LACTYLATE	481	Emulsifier, stabilizer
SODIUM SULPHATES	514	Acidity regulator
SODIUM SULPHITE	221	Preservative, antioxidant
SODIUM THIOSULPHATE	539	Antioxidant, sequestrant
SORBIC ACID	200	Preservative
SORBITAN MONOLAURATE	493	Emulsifier
SORBITAN MONOOLEATE	494	Emulsifier
SORBITAN MONOPALMITATE	495	Emulsifier
SORBITAN MONOSTEARATE	491	Emulsifier
SORBITAN TRIOLEATE	496	Stabilizer, emulsifier
SORBITAN TRISTEARATE	492	Emulsifier
SORBITOL AND SORBITOL SYRUP	420	Sweetener, humectant, sequestrant, texturizer, emulsifier
SPERMACETI WAX	909	Glazing agent
STANNOUS CHLORIDE	512	Antioxidant, colour retention agent
STEARYL CITRATE	484	Emulsifier, sequestrant
STEARYL TARTRATE	483	Flour treatment agent
SUCCINIC ACID	363	Acidity regulator
SUCCINYLATED MONOGLYCERIDES	472g	Emulsifier, stabilizer, sequestrant
SUCCISTEARIN	446	Emulsifier
SUCROGLYCERIDES	474	Emulsifier
SUCROSE ACETATE ISOBUTYRATE	444	Emulsifier, stabilizer
SUCROSE ESTERS OF FATTY ACIDS	473	Emulsifier
SULPHUR DIOXIDE	220	Preservative, antioxidant
SULPHURIC ACID	513	Acidity regulator
SUNSET YELLOW FCF	110	Colour
SUPERGLYCERINATED HYDROGENATED RAPESEED OIL	441	Emulsifier
SYNTHETIC DELTA-TOCOPHEROL	309	Antioxidant

SYNTHETIC GAMMA-TOCOPHEROL	308	Antioxidant
TALC	553	Anticaking agent, dusting powder
TANNINS, FOOD GRADE	181	Colour, emulsifier, stabilizer, thickener
TARA GUM	417	Thickener, stabilizer
TARTARIC ACID ESTERS OF MONO-AND DI-GLYCERIDES OF FATTY ACIDS	472d	Emulsifier, stabilizer, sequestrant
TARTARIC ACID (L(+)-)	334	Acidity regulator, sequestrant, antioxidant synergist
TARTRAZINE	102	Colour
TERTIARY BUTYLHYDROQUINONE	319	Antioxidant
TETRAPOTASSIUM DIPHOSPHATE	450	Emulsifier, stabilizer, acidity regulator, raising agent, sequestrant, water retention agent
TETRASODIUM DIPHOSPHATE	450	Emulsifier, stabilizer, acidity regulator, raising agent, sequestrant, water retention agent
THAUMATIN	957	Sweetener, flavour enhancer
THERMALLY OXIDIZED SOYA BEAN OIL WITH MONO-AND DI-GLYCERIDES OF FATTY ACIDS	479	Emulsifier
THIABENDAZOLE	233	Preservative
THIODIPROPIONIC ACID	388	Antioxidant
TITANIUM DIOXIDE	171	Colour
TRAGACANTH GUM	413	Thickener, stabilizer, emulsifier
TRIACETIN	1518	Humectant
TRICALCIUM ORTHOPHOSPHATE	341	Acidity regulator, flour treatment agent, firming agent, texturizer, raising agent, anticaking agent, water retention agent
TRIETHYL CITRATE	1505	Foam stabilizer
TRIMAGNESIUM ORTHOPHOSPHATE	343	Acidity regulator, anticaking agent
TRIPOTASSIUM CITRATE	332	Acidity regulator, stabilizer, sequestrant
TRIPOTASSIUM ORTHOPHOSPHATE	340	Acidity regulator, sequestrant, stabilizer, emulsifier, water retention agent
TRISODIUM CITRATE	331	Acidity regulator, emulsifier stabilizer, sequestrant
TRISODIUM DIPHOSPHATE	450	Emulsifier, stabilizer, acidity regulator, raising agent, sequestrant, water retention agent
TRISODIUM ORTHOPHOSPHATE	339	Acidity regulator, sequestrant, emulsifier, texturizer, stabilizer, water retention agent
TURMERIC	100	Colour
VEGETABLE CARBON	153	Colour
VIOLOXANTHIN	161e	Colour
WAX ESTERS	910	Glazing agent
XANTHAN GUM	415	Thickener, stabilizer
XYLITOL	967	Sweetener, humectant, stabilizer, emulsifier, thickener
YELLOW 2G	107	Colour
ZINC SILICATE	557	Anticaking agent

SUPPLEMENTARY LIST - MODIFIED STARCHES

EXPLANATORY NOTE

The Codex General Standard for the Labelling of Prepackaged Foods (CODEX STAN 1 - 1985) specifies that modified starches may be declared as such in the list of ingredients.   However, as some countries presently require the specific identification of modified starches the following numbers are provided as a guide and as a means of facilitating uniformity.   Where these starches are specifically identified in the list of ingredients then it would seem appropriate to include them under the relevant class name eg Thickener.

ACETYLATED DISTARCH ADIPATE	1422	Stabilizer, thickener, binder
ACETYLATED DISTARCH GLYCEROL	1423	Emulsifier, thickener
ACETYLATED DISTARCH PHOSPHATE	1414	Emulsifier, thickener
ACID-TREATED STARCH	1401	Stabilizer, thickener, binder
ALKALINE TREATED STARCH	1402	Stabilizer, thickener, binder
BLEACHED STARCH	1403	Stabilizer, thickener, binder
DEXTRINS, ROASTED STARCH WHITE AND YELLOW	1400	Stabilizer, thickener, binder
DISTARCH GLYCEROL	1411	Stabilizer, thickener
DISTARCH PHOSPHATE ESTERIFIED WITH SODIUM TRIMETAPHOSPHATE; ESTERIFIED WITH PHOSPHORUS-OXYCHLORIDE	1412	Stabilizer, thickener, binder
HYDROXYPROPYL DISTARCH GLYCEROL	1443	Stabilizer, thickener
HYDROXYPROPYL DISTARCH PHOSPHATE	1442	Stabilizer, thickener
HYDROXYPROPYL STARCH	1440	Emulsifier, thickener, binder
MONOSTARCH PHOSPHATE	1410	Stabilizer, thickener, binder
OXIDIZED STARCH	1404	Emulsifier, thickener, binder
PHOSPHATED DISTARCH PHOSPHATE	1413	Stabilizer, thickener, binder
STARCH ACETATE ESTERIFIED WITH ACETIC ANHYDRIDE	1420	Stabilizer, thickener
STARCH ACETATE ESTERIFIED WITH VINYL ACETATE	1421	Stabilizer, thickener
STARCH SODIUM OCTENYL SUCCINATE	1450	Stabilizer, thickener, binder, emulsifier
STARCHES, ENZYME-TREATED	1405	Thickener

SECTION 5.2

THE PRINCIPLE RELATING TO THE CARRY-OVER
OF FOOD ADDITIVES INTO FOODS

INTRODUCTION

The Codex Alimentarius Commission at its 17th Session 1987 adopted the revised statement of "Principle Relating to the Carry-Over of Food Additives in Foods" as an advisory text for the use of governments but not subject to acceptance. At its 13th Session (1979) the Commission had concurred with the view of the Codex Committees on Food Additives and Labelling that food additives carried over in accordance with Section 3 of the Carry-Over Principle would not be declared on the label in the list of ingredients.

THE PRINCIPLE RELATING TO THE CARRY-OVER OF FOOD ADDITIVES INTO FOODS

SECTION 1 - SCOPE

For the purposes of the Codex Alimentarius, the Principle relating to the Carry-Over of Food Additives into Foods (the "Carry-Over Principle") applies to the presence of additives in food as a result of the use of raw materials or other ingredients in which these additives are used.

SECTION 2 - APPLICATION

The Carry-Over Principle applies to all foods covered by Codex Standards, unless otherwise specified in such standards (see Section 4).

SECTION 3 - CONDITIONS UNDER WHICH THE CARRY-OVER PRINCIPLE APPLIES

The presence of an additive in food, through the application of the Carry-Over Principle, is generally permitted if:

(a) the additive is permitted in the raw materials or other ingredients (including food additives) by an applicable Codex Standard or under any other acceptable provision which takes into account the safety aspects of food additives;

(b) the amount of the additive in the raw materials or other ingredients (including food additives) does not exceed the maximum amount so permitted;

(c) the food into which the additive is carried over does not contain the food additive in greater quantity than would be introduced by the use of the ingredients under proper technological conditions or manufacturing practice, and

(d) the food additive carried over is present at a level which is non-functional, i.e., at a level significantly less than that normally required to achieve an efficient technological function in its own right in the food.

SECTION 4 - SPECIAL CONDITIONS

4.1   An additive carried over into a particular food in a significant quantity or in an amount sufficient to perform a technological function in that food as a result of the use of raw materials or other ingredients in which this additive was used, shall be treated and regarded as an additive to that food, and shall be provided for in the Section on Food Additives of the applicable Codex Standard.

SECTION 5 - STATEMENTS IN CODEX STANDARDS REGARDING CARRIED OVER ADDITIVES

5.1   Where the Carry-Over Principle does not apply to a food, i.e., where the presence of additives carried over is not permitted in the food, this should be clearly stated in the relevant Codex standard using the following statement:

"no food additives shall be present as a result of Carry-Over from raw materials or other ingredients".

5.2   Where reference to the applicability of the Carry-Over Principle is
specifically made in a Codex Standard, the following statement should be used:

> "Section 3 of the Principle relating to the Carry-Over of
> Additives into Foods shall apply".

SECTION 5.3

CODEX GENERAL STANDARD
FOR THE LABELLING OF FOOD ADDITIVES WHEN SOLD AS SUCH
(Worldwide Standard)

CODEX STAN 107-1981

INTRODUCTION

The Codex General Standard for the Labelling of Food Additives When Sold as Such was adopted by the Codex Alimentarius at its 14th Session in 1981. This Standard has been submitted to all Member Nations and Associate Members of FAO and WHO for **acceptance** in accordance with the General Principles of the Codex Alimentarius.

CODEX GENERAL STANDARD
FOR THE LABELLING OF FOOD ADDITIVES WHEN SOLD AS SUCH
(Worldwide Standard)

CODEX STAN 107-1981

1.   SCOPE

This standard applies to the labelling of "food additives" sold as such whether by retail or other than by retail, including sales to caterers and food manufacturers for the purpose of their businesses. This standard also applies to food "processing aids"; any reference to food additives includes food processing aids.

2.   DEFINITION OF TERMS

For the purpose of this standard:

(a)   food additive means any substance not normally consumed as a food by itself and not normally used as a typical ingredient of the food, whether or not it has nutritive value, the intentional addition of which to food for a technological (including organoleptic) purpose in the manufacture, processing, preparation, treatment, packing, packaging, transport or holding of such food results, or may be reasonably expected to result, (directly or indirectly) in it or its by-products becoming a component of or otherwise affecting the characteristics of such foods. The term does not include contaminants, or substances added to food for maintaining or improving nutritional qualities, or sodium chloride;

(b)   processing aid means a substance or material not including apparatus or utensils and not consumed as a food ingredient by itself, intentionally used in the processing of raw materials, foods or its ingredients to fulfil a certain technological purpose during treatment or processing and which may result in the non-intentional but unavoidable presence of residues or derivatives in the final product;

(c)   contaminant means any substance not intentionally added to food, which is present in such food as a result of the production (including operations carried out in crop husbandry, animal husbandry and veterinary medicine), manufacture, processing, preparation, treatment, packing, packaging, transport or holding of such food or as a result of environmental contamination;

(d)   label includes any tag, brand, mark, pictorial or other descriptive matter, written, painted, stencilled, marked, embossed or impressed on, or attached to, a container;

(e)   labelling includes the label and any written, printed or graphic matter relating to and accompanying the food additives. The term does not include bills, invoices and similar material which may accompany the food additives;

(f)   container means any form of packaging of food additives for sale as a single item, whether by completely or partially enclosing the food additives, and includes wrappers;

(g) <u>ingredient</u> means any substance, excluding a food additive, used in the manufacture or preparation of a food and present in the final product;

(h) <u>sale by retail</u> means any sale to a person buying otherwise than for the purpose of resale but does not include a sale to caterers for the purposes of their catering business or a sale to manufacturers for the purposes of their manufacturing business.

3. GENERAL PRINCIPLES

3.1   Food additives[1] shall not be described or presented on any label or in any labelling in a manner than is false, misleading or deceptive or is likely to create an erroneous impression regarding their character in any respect.

3.2   Food additives[1] shall not be described or presented on any label or in any labelling by words, pictorial or other devices which refer to or are suggestive, either directly or indirectly, of any other product with which such food additives might be confused, or in such a manner as to lead the purchaser or consumer to suppose that the food additive is connected with or derived from such other product; provided that the term "x flavour" may be used to describe a flavour which is not derived from, but reproduces the flavour of "x".

4. MANDATORY LABELLING OF PREPACKAGED FOOD ADDITIVES SOLD BY RETAIL

The labels of all food additives sold by retail shall bear the information required by sub-sections 4.1 to 4.5 of this section, as applicable to the food additive[1] being labelled.

4.1   <u>Details of the Food Additive</u>

(a) The name of each food additive present shall be given. The name shall be specific and not generic and shall indicate the true nature of the food additive. Where a name has been established for a food additive in a Codex list of additives, that name shall be used. In other cases the common or usual name shall be listed or, where none exists, an appropriate descriptive name shall be used.

(b) If two or more food additives are present, their names shall be given in the form of a list. The list shall be in the order of the proportion by weight which each food additive bears to the total contents of the container, the food additive present in the greatest proportion by weight being listed first. Where one or more of the food additives is subject to a quantitative limitation in a food covered by a Codex standard, the quantity or proportion of that additive may be stated. If food ingredients are part of the preparation, they shall be declared in the list of ingredients in descending order of proportion.

(c) In the case of mixtures of flavourings, the name of each flavouring present in the mixture need not be given. The generic expression "flavour" or "flavouring" may be used, together with a true indication of the nature of the flavour. The expression "flavour" or "flavouring" may be qualified by the words "natural", "nature-identical", "artificial", or a combination of these words, as

---

[1] The term includes "processing aids" as defined (see Scope Section).

appropriate. This provision does not apply to flavour modifiers, but does apply to "herbs" and "spices", which generic expressions may be used where appropriate.

(d)   Food additives with a shelf-life not exceeding 18 months shall carry the date of minimum durability using words such as "will keep at least until ....".

(e)   The words "For Food Use" or a statement substantially similar thereto shall appear in a prominent position on the label.

4.2   Instructions on Keeping and Use

Adequate information shall be given about the manner in which the food additive is to be kept and is to be used in food.

4.3   Net Contents

The net contents shall be declared in either the metric (Système International Units) or avoirdupois or both systems of measurement as required by the country in which the food additive is sold. This declaration shall be made in the following manner:

(a)   for liquid food additives, by volume or weight;

(b)   for solid food additives, other than those sold in tablet form, by weight;

(c)   for semi-solid or viscous food additives, either by weight or volume;

(d)   for food additives sold in tablet form, by weight together with the number of tablets in the package.

4.4   Name and Address

The name and address of the manufacturer, packer, distributor, importer, exporter or vendor of the food additive shall be declared.

4.5   Country of Origin

(a)   The country of origin of a food additive shall be declared if its omission is likely to mislead or deceive the consumer.

(b)   When a food additive undergoes processing in a second country which changes its chemical or physical nature, the country in which the processing is performed shall be considered to be the country of origin for the purposes of labelling.

4.6   Lot Identification

Each container shall be marked in code or in clear to identify the producing factory and the lot.

5.   **MANDATORY LABELLING OF PREPACKAGED FOOD ADDITIVES SOLD OTHER THAN BY RETAIL**

The labels of all food additives sold other than by retail shall bear the information required by sub-sections 5.1 to 5.5 of this section, as applicable to the food additive being labelled; except that, where the food additives in non-retail containers are solely destined for further industrial processing, the required information, other than that described in sections 5.1(a) and 5.1(d), may be given on the documents relating to the sale.

5.1   Details of the Food Additive

(a)   The name of each food additive present shall be given. The name shall be specific and not generic and shall indicate the true nature of the food additive. Where a name has been established for a food additive in a Codex list of additives, that name shall be used. In other cases, the common or usual name shall be listed or, where none exists, an appropriate descriptive name shall be used.

(b)   If two or more food additives are present, their names shall be given in the form of a list. The list shall be in the order of the proportion by weight which each food additive bears to the total contents of the container, the food additive present in the greatest proportion by weight being listed first. Where one or more food additives is subject to a quantitative limitation in a food in the country in which the food additive is to be used, the quantity or proportion of that additive and/or adequate instruction to enable the compliance with the limitation shall be given. If food ingredients are part of the preparation, they shall be declared in the list of ingredients in descending order of proportion.

(c)   In the case of mixtures of flavourings, the name of each flavouring present in the mixture need not be given. The generic expression "flavour" or "flavouring" may be used together with a true indication of the nature of the flavour. The expression "flavour" or "flavouring" may be qualified by the words "natural", "nature-identical", "artificial", or a combination of these words, as appropriate. This provision does not apply to flavour modifiers, but does apply to "herbs" and "spices" which generic expressions may be used where appropriate.

(d)   Food additives with a shelf-life not exceeding 18 months shall carry the date of minimum durability using words such as "will keep at least until ...".

(e)   The words "For Food Use" or a statement substantially similar thereto shall appear in a prominent position on the label.

5.2   Instructions on Keeping and Use

Adequate information shall be given about the manner in which the food additive is to be kept and is to be used in food. This information may be given on the label or in the documents relating to the sale.

5.3   Net Contents

The net contents shall be declared in either (a) metric units or "Système International" units or (b) avoirdupois, unless both systems of measurement are specifically required by the country in which the food additive is sold. The declaration shall be made in the following manner:

(i)   for liquid food additives, by volume or weight;
(ii)   for solid food additives, by weight;
(iii) for semi-solid or viscous food additives, either by weight or volume.

5.4   Name and Address

The name and address of the manufacturer, packer, distributor, importer, exporter or vendor of the food additive shall be declared.

5.5   Country of Origin

(a)   The country of origin of a food additive shall be declared if its omission is likely to mislead or deceive the user.

(b)   When a food additive undergoes processing in a second country which changes its chemical or physical nature, the country in which the processing is performed shall be considered to be the country of origin for the purposes of labelling.

5.6   Lot Identification

Each container shall be marked, in code or in clear, to identify the producing factory and the lot.

6.   PRESENTATION OF MANDATORY INFORMATION

6.1   General

Statements required to appear on the label by virtue of this standard or any other Codex standard shall be clear, prominent and readily legible by the consumer under normal conditions of purchase and use. Such information shall not be obscured by designs or by other written, printed or graphic matter and shall be on contrasting ground to that of the background. The letters in the name of the food additive shall be in a size reasonably related to the most prominent printed matter on the label. Where the container is covered by a wrapper, the wrapper shall carry the necessary information, or the label on the container shall be readily legible through the outer wrapper or not obscured by it. In general the name and net contents of the food additive shall appear on that portion of the label normally intended to be presented to the consumer at the time of sale.

6.2   Language

The language used for the declaration of the statements referred to in paragraph 6.1 shall be a language acceptable to the country in which the food additive is intended for sale. If the language on the original label is not acceptable, a supplementary label containing the mandatory information in an acceptable language may be used instead of relabelling.

7.   <u>ADDITIONAL OR DIFFERENT REQUIREMENTS FOR SPECIFIC FOOD ADDITIVES</u>

7.1   Nothing in this standard shall preclude the adoption of additional or
different provisions in a Codex standard, in respect of labelling, where the
circumstances of a particular food additive would justify their incorporation in
that standard.

7.2   <u>Irradiated Food Additives</u>

Food additives which have been treated with ionizing radiation, shall
be so designated.

8.   <u>OPTIONAL LABELLING</u>

8.1   <u>General</u>

Any information or pictorial device may be displayed in labelling
provided that it is not in conflict with the mandatory requirement nor would
mislead or deceive the consumer in any way whatsoever in respect of the food
additive.

SECTION 5.4

LIST OF CODEX ADVISORY SPECIFICATIONS FOR FOOD ADDITIVES

INTRODUCTION

The General Principles for the Use of Food Additives specify that food additives should at all times conform with an approved specification, for example, the Specifications of Identity and Purity recommended by the Codex Alimentarius Commission. The following index lists all of the Specifications adopted by the Commission as well as their year of adoption. The Specifications are being published in the FAO Food and Nutrition Paper series. This will be a comprehensive compendium of all specifications prepared by the Joint FAO/WHO Expert Committee on Food Additives where the Specifications adopted as Codex Advisory Specifications are indicated by the reference "CXAS". Codex Advisory Specifications are not subject to acceptance by governments.

LIST OF CODEX ADVISORY SPECIFICATIONS FOR FOOD ADDITIVES

Food Additive	Year of adoption
Acetic Acid, Glacial	1979
Acetic and Fatty Acid Esters of Glycerol	1981
Activated Carbon	1991
Adipic Acid	1979
Allura Red AC	1987
Aluminium Ammonium Sulfate	1989
Aluminium Powder	1979
Aluminium Sodium Sulfate	1981
Amaranth	1987
Ammonium Carbonate	1985
Ammonium Chloride	1983
Ammonium Dihydrogen Phosphate	1987
Ammonium Hydrogen Carbonate	1989
Amyl Acetate	1983
Ascorbic Acid	1981
Aspartame	1983
Azodicarbonamide	1979
Azorubine	1987
Beet Red	1991
Benzoyl Peroxide	1979
Benzyl Acetate	1987
Benzyl Alcohol	1983
Benzyl Benzoate	1983
Beta-Apo-8'-Carotenoic Acid, Ethyl Ester	1987

Food Additive	Year of adoption
Beta-Apo-8'-Carotenal	1987
Beta Carotene (Synthetic)	1991
Bone Phosphate	1991
Brilliant Blue FCF	1987
Brown HT	1987
Butan-1-ol	1987
Butan-2-ol	1983
Butane-1,3-diol	1983
Buytl p-Hydroxybenzoate	1981
Butylated Hydroxyanisole	1991
Calcium Acetate	1981
Calcium Aluminium Silicate	1987
Calcium Ascorbate	1983
Calcium Benzoate	1987
Calcium Carbonate	1981
Calcium Chloride	1979
Calcium Citrate	1979
Calcium Cylamates	1983
Calcium Di-L-Glutamate	1991
Calcium Disodium Ethylenediaminetetracetate	1989
Calcium Gluconate	1978
Calcium 5'-Guanylate	1978
Calcium Hydrogen Sulphite	1979
Calcium Hydroxide	1979
Calcium 5'Inosinate	1978
Calcium Lactate	1978

Food Additive	Year of adoption
Calcium DL-Malate	1987
Calcium Monohydrogen Phosphate	1979
Calcium Oxide	1979
Calcium Propionate	1981
Calcium 5'-Ribonucleotides	1978
Calcium Sorbate	1981
Calcium Sulfate	1979
Canthaxanthin	1991
Caramel Colours	1991
Carbohydrase from *Bacillus licheniformis*	1989
Carrageenan	1989
Carthamus Yellow	1991
Castor Oil	1987
Catalase from *Micrococcus lisodeicticus*	1983
Chlorine	1987
Chlorophylls	1991
Chlorophylls Copper Complexes	1991
Chlorophylls Copper Complexes, Sodium and Potassium Salts	1991
Cholic Acid	1981
Cinnamaldehyde	1987
Citral	1985
Citranaxanthin	1991
Citric and Fatty Acid Esters of Glycerol	1991
Cupric Sulfate	1981
Cyclohexane	1983

Food Additive	Year of adoption
Desoxycholic Acid	1981
Diammonium Hydrogen Phosphate	1985
Dicalcium Pyrophospate	1983
Diethyl Tartrate	1989
Dilauryl Thiodipropionate	1981
Dipotassium 5'-Guanylate	1989
Dipotassium Hydrogen Phosphate	1979
Dipotassium 5'-Inosinate	1989
Disodium Ethylenediamine-tetraacetate	1981
Disodium 5'-Guanylate	1978
Disodium 5'-Inosinate	1978
Disodium 5'-Ribonucleotides	1978
Erythorbic Acid	1981
Ethyl Cellulose	1985
Ethyl Formate	1985
Ethyl Heptanoate	1985
Ethyl Lactate	1985
Ethyl Laurate	1983
Ethyl Maltol	1978
Ethyl Methyl Ketone	1987
Ethyl Methylphenylglycidate	1987
Ethyl Nonanoate	1987
Ethyl Phenylglycidate	1983
Ethyl Protocatechuate	1981
Ethyl Vanillin	1991
Eugenol	1985
Eugenyl Methyl Ether	1989

Food Additive	Year of adoption
Fast Green FCF	1989
Fast Red E	1987
Ferric Ammonium Citrate	1987
Ferrocyanides of Calcium, Potassium and Sodium	1981
Ferrous Gluconate	1987
Ferrous Lactate	1991
Ficin	1983
Fumaric Acid	1991
Furfural	1983
Geranyl Acetate	1983
Glucose Isomerase from *Actinoplanes missouriensis* (Immobilized)	1987
Glucose Isomerase from *Bacillus coagulans* (Immobilized)	1987
Glucose Isomerase from *Streptomyces olivaceous* (Immobilized)	1987
Glucose Isomerase from *Streptomyces olivochromo-genes* (Immobilized)	1987
Glucose Isomerase from *Streptomyces rubiginosus* (Immobilized)	1989
Glucose Isomerase from *Streptomyces violaceoniger*	1987
Glucose Oxidase and Catalese from *Aspergillus niger*	1983
L-Glutamic Acid	1991
Glycerol	1979
Glycerol Diacetate	1979
Green S	1987

Food Additive	Year of adoption
5' Guanylic Acid	1989
Heptane	1989
Hexamethylenetetramine	1978
Hydrogen Peroxide	1989
Indigotine	1987
5' Inosinic Acid	1989
Insoluble Polyvinylpyrrolidon	1991
Alpha-Ionone	1987
Beta-Ionone	1987
Isoamyl Butyrate	1983
Isobutanol	1987
Isomalt	1991
Isopropyl Acetate	1985
Isopropyl Citrate Mixture	1981
Isopropyl Myristate	1983
Karaya Gum	1991
Lactic Acid and Fatty Acid Esters of Glycerol	1981
Light Petroleum	1983
Linalool	1985
Linalyl Acetate	1985
Lithol Rubine BK	1987
Magnesium Chloride	1987
Magnesium Di-L-Glutamate	1991
Magnesium Gluconate	1987
Magnesium Hydrogen Carbonate	1987
Magnesium Hydrogen Phosphate	1985
Magnesium Hydroxide	1979

Food Additive	Year of adoption
Magnesium DL-Lactate	1987
Magnesium L-Lactate	1987
Magnesium Silicate (synthetic)	1985
DL-Malic Acid	1979
Maltitol	1991
Maltol	1983
Mannitol	1991
Methanol	1987
Methyl Anthranilate	1983
Methyl Cellulose	1987
Methyl N-Methylanthranilate	1983
Methyl Beta-Naphthyl Ketone	1987
Modified Starches	1991
Monoammonium L-Glutamate	1991
Monoglyceride Citrate	1981
Monopotassium L-Glutamate	1991
Monosodium L-Glutamate	1991
Nitrogen	1985
Nitrous Oxide	1989
Nonanal	1983
Octanal	1987
Paprika Oleoresins	1991
Patent Blue V	1991
Pectin	1987
Pentapotassium Triphosphate	1989
Pimaricin	1979
Polydextroses	1983
Polydimethylsiloxane	1989

Food Additive	Year of adoption
Polyoxyethylene (20) Sorbitan Monostearate	1983
Polyoxyethylene (20) Sorbitan Tristearate	1983
Potassium Acetate	1978
Potassium Benzoate	1981
Potassium Bromate	1991
Potassium Carbonate	1979
Potassium Chloride	1983
Potassium Dihydrogen Citrate	1991
Potassium Dihydrogen Phosphate	1979
Potassium Gluconate	1983
Potassium Hydrogen Carbonate	1979
Potassium Hydroxide	1979
Potassium Iodate	1991
Potassium Lactate (Solution)	1978
Potassium Metabisulfite	1981
Potassium Polyphosphates	1985
Potassium Saccharin	1987
Potassium Sorbate	1981
Potassium Sulfate	1989
Potassium Sulfite	1989
Powdered Cellulose	1979
Propan-2-ol	1987
Protease from *Streptomyces fradiae*	1985
Pullulanase from *Klebsiella aerogenes*	1983
Quinine Hydrochloride	1991

Food Additive	Year of adoption
Quinine Sulfate	1985
Quinoline Yellow	1987
Red 2G	1987
Riboflavin	1991
Riboflavin 5'-Phosphate Sodium	1991
Saccharin	1991
Saffron	1989
Salts of Fatty Acids	1991
Silicon Dioxide Amorphous	1981
Sodium Acetate	1978
Sodium Aluminium Phosphate, Acidic	1989
Sodium Aluminium Phosphate, Basic	1985
Sodium Carbonate	1979
Sodium Carboxymethyl Cellulose	1987
Sodium Cyclamate	1983
Sodium Diacetate	1981
Sodium Dihydrogen Citrate	1989
Sodium Erythorbate	1981
Sodium Fumarate	1989
Sodium Gluconate	1983
Sodium Hydrogen Carbonate	1979
Sodium Hydrogen DL-Malate	1985
Sodium Hydrogen Sulfite	1981
Sodium Hydroxide	1979
Sodium Lactate (Solution)	1978
Sodium DL-Malate	1989
Sodium Metabisulfite	1981

Food Additive	Year of adoption
Sodium Percarbonate	1991
Sodium Sesquicarbonate	1987
Sodium Sulfite	1981
Sodium Thiosulfate	1981
Sorbic Acid	1979
Sorbitan Monoleate	1991
Sorbitan Monopalmitate	1981
Sorbitan Monostearate	1981
Sorbitan Tristearate	1981
Sorbitol	1991
Sorbitol Syrup	1991
Stannous Chloride	1981
Stearyl Citrate	1981
Stearyl Monoglyceridyl Citrate	1985
Succinylated Monoglycerides	1985
Sucroglycerides	1987
Sucrose Esters of Fatty Acids	1991
Sunset Yellow FCF	1987
Tara Gum	1989
DL-Tartaric Acid	1987
L(+)Tartaric Acid	1979
Tartrazine	1987
Tertiary Butylhydroquinone	1989
Thaumatin	1987
Thiodipropionic Acid	1981
Tocopherol Concentrate (Mixed)	1989
Tocopherol, Alpha (DL-)	1989

Food Additive	Year of adoption
Toluene	1983
Tragacanth Gum	1989
Tricalcium Phosphate	1981
Trichlorotrifluorethane (1,1,2)	1985
Triethyl Citrate	1987
Trimagnesium Phosphate	1981
Tripotassium Citrate	1979
Tripotassium Phosphate	1979
Trisodium Citrate	1979
Trisodium Phosphate	1979
Turmeric	1983
Turmeric Oleoresin	1991
Xylitol	1991

SECTION 5.5

CODEX STANDARD FOR FOOD GRADE SALT
(World-wide Standard)

CODEX STAN 150-1985

INTRODUCTION

The Codex Standard for Food Grade Salt was adopted by the Codex Alimentarius Commission at its 16th Session in 1985. This Standard has been submitted to all Member Nations and Associate Members of FAO and WHO for **acceptance** in accordance with the General Principles of the Codex Alimentarius.

CODEX STANDARD FOR FOOD GRADE SALT
(World-wide Standard)

CODEX STAN 150-1985

1.   SCOPE

        This standard applies to salt used as an ingredient of food, both for
direct sale to the consumer and for food manufacture. It applies also to salt used
as a carrier of food additives and/or nutrients. Subject to the provisions of this
standard more specific requirements for special needs may be applied. It does not
apply to salt from origins other than those mentioned in Section 2, notably the
salt which is a by-product of chemical industries.

2.   DESCRIPTION

        Food grade salt is a crystalline product consisting predominantly of
sodium chloride. It is obtained from the sea, from underground rock salt deposits
or from natural brine.

3.   ESSENTIAL COMPOSITION AND QUALITY FACTORS

3.1   Minimum NaCl Content

        The content of NaCl shall not be less than 97% on a dry matter basis,
exclusive of additives.

3.2   Naturally Present Secondary Products and Contaminants

        The remainder comprises natural secondary products, which are present
in varying amounts depending on the origin and the method of production of the
salt, and which are composed mainly of calcium, potassium, magnesium and sodium
sulphates, carbonates, bromides, and of calcium, potassium, magnesium chlorides as
well. Natural contaminants may also be present in amounts varying with the origin
and the method of production of the salt.

3.3   Use as a Carrier

        Food grade salt shall be used when salt is used as a carrier for food
additives or nutrients for technological or public health reasons. Examples of
such preparations are mixtures of salt with nitrate and/or nitrite (curing salt)
and salt mixed with small amounts of fluoride, iodide, iron, vitamins, etc., and
additives used to carry or stabilize such additions.

4.   FOOD ADDITIVES

4.1   All Additives used shall be of food grade quality.

4.2   Anticaking Agents

                                                                     Maximum Level
                                                                     in the
                                                                     Final Product

4.2.1   Coating agents; Carbonates, calcium and/or   )
              magnesium;   )
              Magnesium oxide; Phosphate, tricalcium;   )

	Silicon dioxide, amorphous; Silicates, calcium, magnesium, sodium alumino, or sodium calcium alumino	))))	20 g/kg singly or in combination
4.2.2	Coating hydrophobic agents; aluminium, calcium magnesium, potassium or sodium salts of myristic, palmitic or stearic acids	))))	
4.2.3	Crystal modifiers: ferrocyanides, calcium, potassium* or sodium*	))	10 mg/kg* singly or in combination expressed as $[Fe\ (CN_6)]^{3-}$

4.3   <u>Emulsifiers</u>

       Polysorbate 80   10 mg/kg

4.4   <u>Processing Aid</u>

       Dimethylpolysiloxane   10 mg of
                                       residue/kg

5.   <u>**CONTAMINANTS**</u>

Food grade salt may not contain contaminants in amounts and in such form that may be harmful to the health of the consumer. In particular the following maximum limits shall not be exceeded:

5.1   Arsenic   - not more than 0.5 mg/kg expressed as As
5.2   Copper   - not more than 2   mg/kg expressed as Cu
5.3   Lead   - not more than 2   mg/kg expressed as Pb
5.4   Cadmium   - not more than 0.5 mg/kg expressed as Cd
5.5   Mercury   - not more than 0.1 mg/kg expressed as Hg

6.   <u>**HYGIENE**</u>

In order to ensure that proper standards of food hygiene are maintained until the product reaches the consumer, the method of production, packaging, storage and transportation of food grade salt shall be such as to avoid any risk of contamination.

7.   <u>**LABELLING**</u>

In addition to the requirements of the Codex General Standard for the Labelling of Prepackaged Foods (CODEX STAN 1-1985) the following specific provisions apply:

7.1   <u>The Name of the Product</u>

7.1.1   The name of the product, as declared on the label shall be "salt".

7.1.2   The name "salt" shall have in its close proximity a declaration of either "Food Grade" or "Cooking Salt" or "Table Salt".

---

   * Sodium and potassium ferrocyanides, maximum level may be 20 mg/kg when used in the preparation of "dendritic" salt.

7.1.3   Only when salt contains one or more ferrocyanide salts, added to the brine during the crystallization step, the term "dendritic" could be included accompanying the name.

7.1.4   Where salt is used as a carrier for one or more nutrients, and sold as such for public health reasons, the name of the product shall be declared properly on the label, for example "salt fluoridated", "salt iodated", "salt iodized", "salt fortified with iron", "salt fortified with vitamins" and so on, as appropriate.

7.1.5   An indication of either the origin, according to the description on Section 2, or the method of production may be declared on the label, provided such indication does not mislead or deceive the consumer.

7.2   Labelling of Non-Retail Containers

Information for non-retail containers shall either be given on the container or in accompanying documents, except that the name of the product, lot identification and name and address of the manufacturer or packer shall appear on the container. However, lot identification and the name and address of the manufacturer or packer may be replaced by an identification mark, provided that such mark is clearly identifiable with the accompanying documents.

8.   **METHODS OF ANALYSIS AND SAMPLING**

8.1   Sampling

See Appendix

8.2   Determination of Sodium Chloride Content

This method allows the calculation of sodium chloride content, as provided for in Section 3.1, on the basis of the results of the determinations of sulphate (Method 8.4), halogens (Method 8.5), calcium and magnesium (Method 8.6), potassium (Method 8.7) and loss on drying (Method 8.8). Convert sulphate to $CaSO_4$ and unused calcium to $CaCl_2$, unless sulphate in sample exceeds the amount necessary to combine with calcium, in which case convert calcium to $CaSO_4$ and unused sulphate first to $MgSO_4$ and any remaining sulphate to Na_2SO_4. Convert unused magnesium to $MgCl_2$. Convert potassium to Kcl. Convert unused halogens to NaCl. Report the NaCl content on a dry matter basis, multiplying the percentage NaCl by 100/100-P, where P is the percentage loss on drying.

8.3   Determination of Insoluble Matter

According to ISO 2479-1972 "Determination of matter insoluble in water or in acid and preparation of principal solutions for other determinations".

8.4   Determination of Sulphate Content

According to ISO 2480-1972 "Determination of sulphate content. Barium sulphate gravimetric method".

8.5   <u>Determination of Halogens</u>[1]

According to ISO 2481-1973 "Determination of halogens, expressed as chlorine. Mercurimetric method" (for the recovery of mercury from the laboratory waste, see Annex of ECSS/SC 183-1979).

8.6   <u>Determination of Calcium and Magnesium Contents</u>

According to ISO 2482-1973 "Determination of calcium and magnesium contents. EDTA complexometric methods".

8.7   <u>Determination of Potassium Content</u>

According to ECSS/SC 183-1979 "Determination of potassium content by sodium tetraphenylborate volumetric method" or alternatively according to ECSS/SC 184-1979 "by flame atomic absorption spectrophotometric method".

8.8   <u>Determination of the Loss on Drying (Conventional Moisture)</u>

According to ISO 2483-1973 "Determination of the loss of mass at 110°C".

8.9   <u>Determination of Copper Content</u>

According to ECSS/SC 144-1977 "Determination of copper content, Zinc dibenzyldithiocarbamate photometric method".

8.10   <u>Determination of Arsenic Content</u>

According to method ECSS/SC 311-1982 "Determination of arsenic content. Silver diethyldithiocarbamate photometric method".

8.11   <u>Determination of Mercury Content</u>

According to method ECSS/SC 312-1982 "Determination of total mercury content. Cold vapour atomic absorption spectrometric method".

8.12   <u>Determination of Lead Content</u>

According to method ECSS/SC 313-1982 "Determination of total lead content. Flame atomic absorption spectrometric method".

8.13   <u>Determination of Cadmium Content</u>

According to method ECSS/SC 314-1982 "Determination of total cadmium content. Flame atomic absorption spectrometric method".

---

[1] An alternative method for the determination of halogens by using silver nitrate is being studied.

CODEX STANDARD FOR FOOD GRADE SALT
(World-wide Standard)

METHOD FOR SAMPLING OF FOOD GRADE SALT FOR DETERMINATION OF SODIUM CHLORIDE

1.   SCOPE

        This method specifies the sampling procedure to be applied when determining the main component in order to assess the food grade quality of sodium chloride (salt) as provided for in the Codex Standard for Food Grade Salt, Section 3: "Essential Composition and Quality Factors".

        The criterion to be used for acceptance or rejection of a lot or consignment on the basis of this sample is also provided.

2.   FIELD OF APPLICATION

        This method is applicable to the sampling of any type of salt intended for use as food, either prepacked or in bulk.

3.   PRINCIPLE

        This method represents a variables sampling procedure for mean quality: blended bulk sample analysis.

        A blended bulk sample is produced in such a way that it is representative of the lot or consignment. It is composed of a proportion of items drawn from the lot or consignment to be analyzed.

        Acceptance criterion is on the basis that the mean value obtained from analyses of those blended bulk samples must comply with the provision in the Standard.

4.   DEFINITIONS

        The terms used in this sampling method refer to those in the "Instructions on Codex Sampling Procedures" (CX/MAS 1-1987).

5.   EQUIPMENT

        The sampling equipment used should be adapted to the nature of the tests to be carried out (for example: sampling by borer, sampling equipment made of chemically inert material, etc.). The containers used for collecting the samples should be made of a chemically inert material and should be air-tight.

6.   PROCEDURE

6.1   Prepacked Salt

        Sampling may be carried out by "random sampling" or by "systematic sampling". The choice of the method to be used depends on the nature of the lot (for example: if the packages are marked with successive numbers, systematic sampling may be suitable).

6.1.1   Random sampling

Draw the n items from the lot in such a way that each item in the lot has the same chance of being selected.

6.1.2   Systematic sampling

If the N units in the lot have been classified and can be numbered from 1 to N, the 1-in-k systematic sampling of n items can be obtained as follows:

a)   Determine the k value as $k = N/n$. (If k is not an integer, then round to the nearest integer).

b)   From the first k items in the lot take one at random and then make every k^{th} item thereafter.

6.2   <u>Salt in Bulk</u>

Here, the lot is fictitiously divided into items (strata); a lot with a total mass of m kg is considered to be composed of m/100 items. In this case, it is necessary to draw up a "stratified sampling" plan appropriate to the lot dimension. The samples are selected from all the strata in proportion to the stratum sizes.

<u>Note</u>: <u>Stratified sampling</u> of a population which can be divided into different subpopulations (called strata) is carried out in such a way that specified proportions of the sample are drawn from the different strata.

6.3   <u>Constitution of the Sample</u>

6.3.1   The size and the number of the items forming the sample depend on the type of salt and the lot magnitude. The minimum size to be taken into account should be in accordance with one of the following specifications according to the circumstances:

-       250 g of salt in bulk or prepacked in more than 1 kg packages;

-       one package for prepacked salt in 500 g or 1 kg packages.

Concerning the number of samples to be drawn from the lot, an example of minimum sample number that would be picked up, can be found in the document CX/MAS 1-1987, Appendix V, Table 3, taking into account the magnitude of the lot and appropriate inspection level, in this case generally level 4 (see paragraph 8.4 in the same document).

6.3.2   Combine and mix well the different items drawn from the lot. This blended bulk sample constitutes the laboratory sample. More than one laboratory sample may be composed in such a manner.

7.   <u>ACCEPTANCE CRITERION</u>

7.1   Determine the NaCl content (%) of at least two test portions of the laboratory sample.

7.2   Calculate the average of the results obtained for the n test portions of the laboratory sample using:

$$\bar{x} = \frac{\Sigma x}{n} \ (n \geq 2)$$

7.3   In accordance with the provision for the relevant NaCl content (%), a lot or a consignment shall be considered acceptable if the following condition is verified:

- $\geq$ minimum level specified

8.   **SAMPLING REPORT**

The sampling report should contain the following information:

a)   type and origin of the salt;
b)   alterations of state of the salt (e.g. presence of foreign matter);
c)   date of sampling;
d)   lot or consignment number;
e)   method of packing;
f)   total mass of lot or consignment;
g)   number, unit mass of packages and whether the mass is given net or gross;
h)   number of items sampled;
i)   number, nature and initial position of sampled items;
j)   number, composition and mass of the bulk sample(s); and the method used to obtain and conserve it (them);
k)   names and signature of people who have carried out the sampling.

9.   **BASIC REFERENCE**

Document CX/MAS 1-1987.

10.   **REMARK**

"Laboratory sample" is the "blended bulk sample" described in CX/MAS 1-1987, Appendix IV, paragraph 4-B.

SECTION 5.6

GENERAL REQUIREMENTS FOR NATURAL FLAVOURINGS

INTRODUCTION

The General Requirements for Natural Flavourings were adopted by the Codex Alimentarius Commission in 1985 by the 16th Session. The have been sent to all Member Nations and Associate Members of FAO and WHO as an advisory text, and it is for individual governments to decide what use they wish to make of the Code. The Commission has expressed the view that the General Requirements might provide useful checklists of requirements for national food control or enforcement authorities.

GENERAL REQUIREMENTS FOR
NATURAL FLAVOURINGS

1.   DEFINITIONS

1.1   Natural Flavourings

Natural flavourings are products used to impart flavour to a food or beverage - with the exception of only salty, sweet or acid tastes. Their aromatic part consists exclusively of "natural flavours" and/or "natural flavouring substances" and they may or may not contain adjuncts. They are not intended to be consumed as such.

1.2   Natural Flavours

Natural Flavours and Natural Flavouring Substances are preparations and single substances respectively, acceptable for human consumption, obtained exclusively by physical, microbiological or enzymatic processes from material of vegetable or animal origin either in the raw state or after processing for human consumption by traditional food preparation processes (including drying, roasting and fermentation).

1.3   Adjuncts

Adjuncts are foodstuffs and food additives which are essential in the manufacture and use of "natural flavourings".

1.4   Natural Aromatic Raw Materials

Natural aromatic raw materials are vegetable or animal raw materials suitable for use in the preparation of "natural flavours". These raw materials include foods, spices and herbs and other vegetable source[1] which are appropriate for use in the intended application.

2.   FOOD ADDITIVES

Natural flavourings may contain food additives (including carriers) as far as these are necessary for the production, storage and application of the flavourings and as far as these are present in amounts which would not perform a technological function in the finished food.

3.   BIOLOGICALLY ACTIVE SUBSTANCES

With the exception of quinine and quassine, the following biologically active substances should not be added as such to food and beverages. They may only be contributed through the use of natural flavourings to foods and beverages, provided that the maximum levels specified below in mg/kg of the final product ready for consumption are not exceeded.

---

[1] For information concerning appropriate aromatic raw materials for use in foods and beverages, see list of references in Appendix A.

Biologically active substance	Food Commodity	Beverage	Exceptions
3.1 Agaric acid	20	20	100 mg/kg in alcoholic beverages and in food containing mushrooms
3.2 Aloin	0.1	0.1	50 mg/kg in alcoholic beverages
3.3 beta-Azarone	0.1	0.1	1 mg/kg in alcoholic beverages 1 mg/kg when seasoning used at low levels in food
3.4 Berberine	0.1	0.1	10 mg/kg in alcoholic beverages only
3.5 Cocaine	cocaine-free by agreed test		
3.6 Coumarin	2	2	10 mg/kg in special caramels and in alcoholic beverages
3.7 Total hydro-cyanic acid (free and combined)	1	1	25 mg/kg in confectionery 50 mg/kg in marzipan 5 mg/kg in stone fruit juices 1 mg/kg per % volume in alcoholic beverages
3.8 Hypericine	0.1	0.1	1 mg/kg in pastilles (lozenges) 2 mg/kg in alcoholic beverages
3.9 Pulegone	25	100	250 mg/kg in peppermint ormint flavoured beverages 350 mg/kg in mint confectionery (higher levels are to be found in special strong mint)
3.10 Quassine	5	5	10 mg/kg in pastilles (lozenges) 50 mg/kg in alcoholic beverages
3.11 Quinine	0.1	85	300 mg/kg in alcoholic beverages 40 mg/kg in fruit curds
3.12 Safrole	1	1	2 mg/kg in alcoholic beverages containing less than 25% vol. 5 mg/kg in alcoholic beverages above 25% vol.

Biologically active substance	Food Commodity	Beverage	Exceptions
			15 mg/kg in food containing mace and nutmeg
3.13 Santonin	0.1	0.1	1 mg/kg in alcoholic beverages above 25% vol.
3.14 Thujones (α and β)	0.5	0.5	10 mg/kg in alcoholic beverages above beverages above 25% vol.
			5 mg/kg in alcoholic beverages containing less than 25% vol.
			35 mg/kg in bitters
			25 mg/kg in food containing sage
			250 mg/kg in sage stuffings

4.   **HYGIENE** (subject to endorsement by the CCFH)

4.1   It is recommended that "natural flavourings" be prepared in accordance with the appropriate sections of the General Principles of Food Hygiene recommended by the Codex Alimentarius Commission (CAC/RCP 1-1969, Rev.2 (1985))

4.2   When tested by appropriate methods of sampling and examination, the natural flavourings:

(a)   should be free from micro-organisms of public health significance capable of development under normal conditions of storage of the natural flavourings of the food commodity and of the beverage; and

(b)   should not contain any substances originating from micro-organisms in amounts which may represent a hazard to health.

5.   **METHODS OF ANALYSIS**

          References to methods of analysis:

5.1   **General Methods, recommended by IOFI:**

Analytical Procedure for a General Headspace Method. Recommended Method 1 (1973). Int. Flav. Food Add., 6(2), 128 (1975)

Analytical Procedure for a General Method for Gas Chromatography. Recommended Method 4 (1974). Int. Flav. Add., 7(2), 55-56 (1976)

Analytical Procedure for a General Method for High Pressure - (high performance) Liquid Chromatography. Recommended Method 17 (1980). Z. Lebensm.-Unters. Forsch.174, 396-398 (1982)

Analytical Procedure for a General Method for Gas Chromatography on Capillary Columns. Recommended Method 18 (1980) Z. Lebensm.-Unters. Forsch.174, 399-400 (1982)

5.2   **Specific Methods, recommended by IOFI:**

Quinine-Spectrophotometric Determination. Recommended Method 2 (1973). Int.
Flav. Food Add., 6(3), 184 (1975)

Safrole and Isosafrole - Gas Chromatographic Determination.   Recommended
method 5 (1976). Int. flav. Food Add., 8(1), 27 (1977)

Thujone - Gas Chromatographic Determination. Recommended Method 6 (1976).
Int. Flav. Food Add., 8(1), 28(1977)

Pulegone - Gas chromatographic Determination. Recommended Method 7 (1976).
Int. Flav. Food Add., 8(4), 161 (1977)

Coumarin in Certain Foods - Isolation by Extraction. Recommended Method 8
(1978) Int. Flav. Food Add., 9(5), 223(1978)

Coumarin - Gas chromatographic Determination. Recommended Method 9 (1978).
Int. Flav. Food Add., 9(5), 223, 228 (1978)

Beta-Azarone - Gas chromatographic Determination.   Recommended Method 10
(1978). Int. flav. Food Add., 9(5), 228 (1978)

Quassine - Gas Chromatographic Determination. Recommended Method 11 (1978).
FFIP, 1 (1), 24 (1979)

Coumarin in Certain Foods - Isolation by Steam Distillation. Recommended
Method 12 (1979) Revised version. FFIP, 1 (2) 93 (1979)

Hydrocyanic Acid - Photometric Determination. Recommended Method 13 (1979).
FFIP, 1 (3), 140 (1979)

Agaric Acid - Gas chromatographic Determination. Recommended Method 14
(1979) FFIP, 1(4), 193 (1979)

5.3   **Specific Methods, recommended by FIVS:**

Détection et dosage de quatre composés (thujone, safrole, β-azarone et
coumarine) dans les boissons alcooliques. P.A.P. Liddle c.s., Ann. Fals. Exp.
Chim. 69, 857-864 (1976)

Dosage de l'acide agarique dans les boissons alcooliques. P.A.P. Liddle
c.s., Ann. Fals. Exp. Chim. 72, 125-132 (1979)

La determinazione del safrolo nelle bevande alcoliche aromatizzate, L.
Ussegli-Tommaset & G. Mazza, Riv. Viticolt. e Enol. Conegl. 33, 435-452
(1980)

La determinazione della cumarine nelle bevande alcoliche aromatizzate, ibid.
33, 247-256 (1980)

La determinazione della cumarine mediante HPLC.G. Mazza, ibid. 37, 316-323
(1984)

La determinazione del safrolo mediante HPLC. G. Mazza,Riv. Soc. Ital. Sc.
aliment. 12, 159-166 (1983)

Dosage de la β-azarone par HPLC.G. Mazza, Sciences des aliments 4, 233-245 (1984)

5.4   Specific Methods recommended by ISO

ISO 7355-1985 Determination of safrole and cis- and trans-isosafrole.in oils of sassafras and nutmeg by GLC

ISO 7356-1986 Determination of α- and β-thujone in oils of artemisia and sage by GLC

ISO 7357-1985 Determination of cis-β-azarone in oil of calamus by GLC

Appendix A

REFERENCES TO LISTS OF AROMATIC RAW MATERIALS
SUITABLE FOR THE PREPARATION OF NATURAL FLAVOURS[1],[2]

1. Flavouring Substances and Natural Sources of Flavourings, Council of Europe, 3rd ed. 1981.

2. International Standard ISO 676 Spices and condiments. 1st List.

3. United States of America Code of Federal Regulations (Revised as of April 1, 1986), Title 21, Parts 172.510, 182 and 184.

4. Canada, Food and Drugs Regulations Part B, Division 10.

5. AFNOR Norme Française NF V00-001

6. Payom Tuntiwat, 1984, Creungthate, Mahidol University, Bangkok, Thailand.

7. Fenaroli's Handbook of Flavour Ingredients (Volume I) by CRC Press Inc., Cleveland, Ohio.

8. Tanaka's Cyclopedia of Edible Plants of the World by Tyôzaburô, Tanaka Keigaku Publishing co., Tokyo, 1976.

9. Reports of the Flavor and Extract Manufacturers' Association of the United States (FEMA) Expert Panel's publications on generally recognized as safe (GRAS) status:

Food Technology	19(2) :	151-197, 1965
" "	24(5) :	25-28, 30-32 & 34, 1970
" "	26(5) :	35-42, 1972
" "	27(1) :	64-67, 1973
" "	27(11):	56-57, 1973
" "	28(9) :	76-80, 1974
" "	29(1) :	70-72, 1975
" "	31(1) :	65-67, 70, 72 & 74, 1977
" "	32(2) :	60-62, 64-66, 68-70, 1978
" "	33(7) :	65-73, 1979
" "	38(10):	70-72, 74, 76-78, 80-85 & 88-89, 1984
" "	39(11):	108, 110, 112, 114 & 116-117, 1985

---

[1] It should be understood that the references contain potential sources for natural flavours without reference to the safety or acceptability for human consumption of any specific source.

[2] This list is not exhaustive and will be up-dated from time to time.

SECTION 5.7

INVENTORY OF PROCESSING AIDS

INTRODUCTION

The Inventory of Processing Aids was adopted by the Codex Alimentarius commission at its 18th Session in 1989. It has been sent to all Member Nations and Associate Members of FAO and WHO as an advisory text, and it is for individual governments to decide what use they wish to make of the Inventory.

INVENTORY OF PROCESSING AIDS

INTRODUCTION

This Inventory of Processing Aids was prepared by the Codex Committee on Food Additives and Contaminants. The objectives of the Committee are: (1) to develop information on substances used as processing aids and (2) to identify processing aids whose safety should be evaluated by the Joint FAO/WHO Expert Committee on Food Additives (JECFA). The Inventory of Processing Aids catalogues substances that are used in food solely as processing aids as defined by the Codex Alimentarius Commission (see Part 2, page 2.3). The Committee notes that the character of the Inventory is not intended to be complete or a "positive list" of permitted aids.

The Inventory is arranged in tabular format for presentation of information that will be necessary for the Committee to select substances for JECFA evaluation. The following information is provided:

- Category - the functional effect classification.

- Processing Aid - the chemical name or description of the substance used as a processing aid.

- Area of Utilization - the foods or food processing procedures in which the processing aid is utilized.

- Level of Residues - the level of processing aid remaining in food after processing. The levels should be designated with respect to those: (1) directly measured by analysis or (2) estimated by other means. Values are in mg/kg and values at the detection limit of available analytical procedures are reported as "less than" (<).

- Interaction with Food - describes the degree of chemical interaction with food components. Provides data on levels of interaction products in food.

- JECFA Evaluation - if the processing aid substance has been reviewed or considered by a JECFA, then the number of the JECFA meeting is reported. The reference is to the latest JECFA evaluation, for either toxicological or specifications review. Additionally, the reference pertains to JECFA consideration of a substance and does not necessarily mean that JECFA reviewed the processing aid use(s) of this substance nor that JECFA assigned an ADI to the substance.

Appendix A to this inventory catalogues all substances that are used as processing aids. The substances are annotated according to the following system:

1. indicates a processing aid that clearly fits the definition of "processing aid" above.

2. indicates those materials that are both food additives (see definition below) and processing aids (i.e. the substance functions as a processing aid in one food but may have a different function in another food).

3.   indicates those compounds that because of carry-over residues, would seem to usually be considered only as food additives (see section 5.2).

4.   indicates those materials that might actually have simultaneous function as processing aids and functionality in the finished food.

The Committee recognizes that any food additive, even if not included in the inventory or the appendix, may be used as a processing aid and is eligible for addition to the appendix. In some cases, however, the processing aid use of the food additive may require a separate JECFA evaluation.

Appendix B reproduces the Microbial Enzyme Preparation section of the inventory but arranges the enzymes by source organism rather than by function.

CATEGORY	Areas of Use	Residues (mg/kg)	Interaction with Food	JECFA Evaluation
ANTIFOAM AGENTS				
Alkylene oxide adduct	Juice-making			
Coconut oil	Juice-making			
Dimethylpolysiloxane	Beer, Fats & Oils			
Ethylene oxide-propylene oxide copolymers	Juice-making			
Fatty acid methyl ester				
Fatty acid polyakylene glycol ester (1-5 moles ethylene oxide or propylene oxide)	Juice-making			
Fatty alcohol-glycol ether				
Fatty alcohols (C8-C30)				
Formaldehyde	Sugar beet processing	< 0.05	None	
	Yeast processing	< 0.05	None	
	Confectionery	5-15		
Hydrogenated coconut oil	Juice-making			
Hydrophillic fatty acyl esters, linked to a neutral carrier	Juice-making			
alpha-methylglycoside water	Juice-making			
Mixture of ethylene and propylene oxides, copolymers and esters, castor oil and polyethylene glycol ester	Juice-making			
Mixture of naturally occurring and synthetic fatty acyl derivatives, with added emulgators	Juice-making			
Non-ionogenic alkylene oxide adduct with emulgator	Juice-making			
Oxoalcohols C9-C30				

CATEGORY	Areas of Use	Residues (mg/kg)	Interaction with Food	JECFA Evaluation
Polyalkylene oxide, in combination with special fatty alcohols	Juice-making			
Polyethoxylated alcohols, modified	Juice-making			
Polyglycol copolymer	Juice-making			
Polyoxyethylene esters of C8-C30 fatty acids				
Polyoxypropylene esters of C8-C30 fatty acids				
Polyoxyethylene esters of C9-C30 oxoalcohols				
Polyoxypropylene esters of C9-C30 oxoalcohols				
Methylglycoside coconut oil ester	Juice-making			
Mixtures of polyoxyethylene and polyoxypropylene esters of C8-C30 fatty acids				
Modified higher alcohol	Juice-making			
Mono- and diglycerides of fatty acids from feed fat (E471)	Juice-making			
Mono- and diglycerides of fatty acids from feed fat, esterified with acetic acid, lactic acid and citric acid (E472a, b, c)	Juice-making			
Polypropylene-polyethylene block polymer	Juice-making			
Sorbitan-fatty acyl esters and poly-oxyethylene-20-sorbitan fatty acyl esters	Juice-making			
Surface-active esters with neutral carriers	Juice-making			
Vegetable fatty acid esters	Juice-making			
Vegetable fatty acyl (hydrophillic)	Juice-making			

CATEGORY	Areas of Use	Residues (mg/kg)	Interaction with Food	JECFA Evaluation
CATALYSTS				
Alloys of 2 or more listed metals	Hydrogenated food oils			
Alluminium				
Chromium	Hydrogenated food oils	< 0.1		
Copper	Hydrogenated food oils	< 0.1		26
Copper chromate				
Copper chromite				
Manganese	Hydrogenated food oils	< 0.4		
Magnesium oxide				
Molybdenum	Hydrogenated food oils	< 0.1		
Nickel	sugar alcohols Hardened oil mfg. Hydrogenated food oils	< 1 < 0.8 0.2 to 1		
Palladium	Hydrogenated food oils	< 0.1		
Platinum	Hydrogenated food oils	< 0.1		
Potassium metal	Interesterified food oils	< 1		
Potassium methylate (methoxide)	Interesterified food oils	< 1		

CATEGORY	Areas of Use	Residues (mg/kg)	Interaction with Food	JECFA Evaluation
Potassium ethylate (ethoxide)	Interesterified food oils	< 1		
Silver	Hydrogenated food oils	< 0.1		
Sodium amide	Interesterified food oils	< 1		
Sodium ethylene (sodium ethylate)	Interesterified food oils	< 1		
Sodium metal	Interesterified food oils	< 1		
Sodium methylate (methoxide)	Interesterified food oils	< 1		
Trifluoromethane sulfonic acid	Cocoa butter substitute	< 0.01	None	
Various metal oxides	Hydrogenated food oils	< 0.1		
Zirconium				
CLARIFYING AGENTS/FILTRATION AIDS				
Absorbent clays (bleaching, natural, or activated earths)	Starch hydrolysis Sugars Edible vegetable oil			
Active carbon	Sugars			22
Albumin				
Asbestos				
Bentonite	Starch hydrolysis			
Chitin/Chitosan				

CATEGORY	Areas of Use	Residues (mg/kg)	Interaction with Food	JECFA Evaluation
Chloromethylated aminated styrene-divinylbenzene resin	Sugar processing	< 1	None	
Calcium oxide	Sugar			
Diatomaceous earth	Fruit juices Starch hydrolysis general use			
Divinylbenzene-ethylvinylbenzene copolymer	Aqueous foods (excluding carbonated beverages)	0.00002 (extractives from copolymer)	None	
Fuller's earth	Starch hydrolysis			
Ion exchange resins (see ION EXCHANGE RESINS)				
Isinglass				
Kaolin				
Magnesium acetate				
Perlite	Starch hydrolysis			
Polymaleic acid and sodium polymaleate	Sugar processing	< 5	None	
Tannin (to be specified)				
Vegetable carbon (activated)	Starch hydrolysis			
Vegetable carbon (unactivated)	Starch hydrolysis			
CONTACT FREEZING AND COOLING AGENTS				
Dichlorofluoromethane	frozen food	100		
Freon (to be specified)				
Nitrogen				

CATEGORY	Areas of Use	Residues (mg/kg)	Interaction with Food	JECFA Evaluation
DESICCATING AGENT/ANTICAKING AGENTS				
Aluminum stearate				
Calcium phosphate				26
Calcium stearate				
Magnesium stearate				
Octadecylammonium acetate (in ammonium chloride)				
Potassium aluminum silicate				
Sodium calcium silicoaluminate				
DETERGENTS (WETTING AGENTS)				
Dioctyl sodium sulfosuccinate	Fruit drinks	< 10		24
Methyl glucoside of coconut oil ester	Molasses	320		
Quaternary ammonium compounds				
Sodium lauryl sulphate	Food fats & oils	< 1		
Sodium xylene sulphonate	Food fats & oils	< 1		
ENZYME IMMOBILIZATION AGENTS AND SUPPORTS				
Polyethylenimine				29
Glutaraldehyde				25
Glass	Starch hydrolysis			
Diatomaceous earth				
Ceramics	Starch hydrolysis			
Diethylaminoethyl cellulose				
Ion exchange resins				

CATEGORY	Areas of Use	Residues (mg/kg)	Interaction with Food	JECFA Evaluation
ENZYME PREPARATIONS (INCLUDING IMMOBILIZED ENZYMES)				
Animal-Derived Preparations:				
Alpha-amylase (hog or bovine pancreas)				15
Catalase (bovine or horse liver)				37
Chymosin (Calf, kid, or lamb abomasum)				
Chymosin A from Eschorichia Coli K-12 containing calf prochymosin A gene.	milk clotting in cheese and other milk-derived products			15
Chymosin B produced from *Aspergillus niger* var. *awamori* containing calf prochymosin B gene.				
Chymosin B produced from *Kluyveromyces lactis* containing calf prochymosin B gene.				
Lipase (bovine stomach) (salivary glands or forestomach of calf, kid, or lamb) (hog or bovine pancreas)				15
Lysozyme (egg whites)	Cheese			15
Pepsin (hog stomach)				20
Pepsin, avian (proventicum of poultry)				
Phospholipase (pancreas)	baking, starch processing			15
Rennet (bovine, calf, goat, kid, or sheep, lamb stomach)				15
Typsin (porcine or bovine pancreas)				15
Plant-Derived Preparations:				
Bromelain (*Ananas spp.*)				15
Chymopapain (*Carica papaya*)				23

CATEGORY	Areas of Use	Residues (mg/kg)	Interaction with Food	JECFA Evaluation
Ficin (*Ficus spp.*)				15
Liposydase (soya)	baking			15
Malt carbohydrases (malted barley & barley) (alpha- and beta-amylase)	Beer			15
Papain (*Carica papaya*)	Starch hydrolysis			15
Alcohol dehydrogenase (*Saccharomyces cerevisiae*)				15
Alpha amylase				
(*Aspergillus niger*)	Bakery products			
(*Aspergillus oryzae*)	Glucose syrups			25
(*Bacillus licheniformis*)	Fruit & vegetable			25
(*Bacillus stearothermophilus*)				
(*Bacillus subtilis*)	Beer			
(*Rhizopus delemar*)	Cereals			
(*Rhizopus oryzae*)				15
Alpha galactosidase				
(*Aspergillus niger*)				15
(*Mortierella vinacea sp.*)				
(*Saccharomyces carlsbergensis*)				
Arabinofuranosidease				
(*Aspergillus niger*)				15
Beta amylase				
(*Bacillus cereus*)				
(*Bacillus megaterium*)				15
(*Bacillus subtilis*)				
Beta glucanase				
(*Aspergillus niger*)				15
(*Bacillus subtilis*)				15
(*Trichoderma harzianum*)				

CATEGORY	Areas of Use	Residues (mg/kg)	Interaction with Food	JECFA Evaluation
Catalase				
(Aspergillus niger)	Egg products			25
(Micrococcus lysodeicticus)	Milk products			25
Cellobiase				
(betaglucosidase):				
(Aspergillus niger)				25
(Trichoderma harzianum)				20
(Trichoderma reesei)				
Cellulase				
(Aspergillus niger)	Juices fruit and			15
(Aspergillus oryzae)	vegetable			15
(Rhizopus delemar)	processing, baking,			
(Rhizopus oryzae)	beer, extractions			15
(Sporotrichum dimorphosporum)	(coffee, tea,			
(Trichoderma reesei)	spices), starch			
(Thielavia terrestris)	processing			
Dextranase				
(Aspergillus sp.)				
(Bacillus subtilis)				
(Klebsiella aerogenes)				15
(Penicillium funiculosum)				
(Penicillium lilacinum)				
Endo-beta glucanase				
(Aspergillus niger)				15
(Aspergillus oryzae)				15
(Bacillus circulans)				
(Bacillus subtilis)				
(Disporotrichum dimorphosphorum)	Beer			15
(Penicillium emersonii)				
(Rhizopus delemar)				
(Rhizopus oryzae)				
(Trichoderma reesei)				15

CATEGORY	Areas of Use	Residues (mg/kg)	Interaction with Food	JECFA Evaluation

Esterase
  (Mucor miehei)
  (Aspergillus niger, Trichoderma reesei)
				15

Exo-alpha glucosidase *(Aspergillus niger)*				
Exo-alpha glucosidase (immobilized) (same sources as above) no more than 10 mg/kg glutaraldehyde				

Glucoamylase or amyloglucosidase:
  (Aspergillus amaurii)
  (Aspergillus awamori)
  (Aspergillus niger)
  (Aspergillus oryzae)
  (Rhizopus arrhizus)
  (Rhizopus delemar)
  (Rhizopus niveus)
  (Rhizopus oryzae)
  (Trichoderma reesei)
	Starch hydrolysis
	
	Glucose syrups
				22
				
				25
				
				15

Glucose isomerase:
  (Actinoplanes missouriensis)
  (Arthrobacter sp.)
  (Bacillus coagulans)
  (Streptomyces albus)
  (Streptomyces olivaceus)
  (Streptomyces olivochromogenes)
  (Streptomyces rubiginosus)
  (Streptomyces sp.)
  (Streptomyces violaceoniger)
	Isomerized
	glucose syrups
		None detected		28
				15
				28
				28
				28
				28
				25
				15
				28

Glucose isomerase (immobilized) (same sources as above) not more than 10 mg/kg glutaraldehyde				

CATEGORY	Areas of Use	Residues (mg/kg)	Interaction with Food	JECFA Evaluation
Glucose oxidase (Aspergillus niger)	Egg powder, baking, Beverages, mayonnaise, fish and meat products, Canned foods, cheese			25
Hemicellulase (Aspergillus niger) (Aspergillus oryzae) (Bacillus subtilis) (Rhizopus delemar) (Rhizopus oryzae) (Sporotrichum dimorphosporum) (Trichoderma reesei)	Juices, fruit and vegetable processing, baking, beer, extractions (coffee, tea, spices)			15 15 15 15
Inulinase (Aspergillus niger) (Kluyveromyces fragilis) (Soporotrichum dimorphosporum) (Streptomyces sp.)				15 15
Invertase (Aspergillus niger) (Bacillus subtilis) (Kluyveromyces fragilis) (Saccharomyces carlsbergensis) (Saccharomyces cerevisiae) (Saccharomyces sp.)				15 15 15 15 15
Isoamylase (Bacillus cereus)				

CATEGORY	Areas of Use	Residues (mg/kg)	Interaction with Food	JECFA Evaluation
Lactase (Betagalactosidase):				
(*Aspergillus niger*)	Milk products			15
(*Aspergillus oryzae*)				15
(*Kluyveromyces fragilis*)				
(*Kluyveromyces lactis*)	Infant formula			15
(*Saccharomyces sp.*)				
Lactoperoxidase				
Lipase				15
(*Aspergillus flavus*)				
(*Aspergillus niger*)				
(*Aspergillus oryzae*)				
(*Brevibacterium lineus*)				
(*Candida lipolytica*)				
(*Mucor javanicus*)				
(*Mucor miehei*)				
(*Mucor pusillus*)				
(*Rhizopus arrhizus*)				
(*Rhizopus delemar*)				
(*Rhizopus nigrican*)				
(*Rhizopus niveus*)				
Malic acid decarboxylase				
(*Leuconostoc oenos*)				
Maltase or alphaglucosidase				
(*Aspergillus niger*)				15
(*Aspergillus oryzae*)				15
(*Rhizopus oryzae*)				15
(*Trichoderma reesei*)				
Melibiase (alpha galactosidase):				
(*Mortierella vinacea sp.*)				15
(*Saccharomyces carlsbergensis*)				
Nitrate reductase				
(*Micrococcus violagabriella*)				

CATEGORY	Areas of Use	Residues (mg/kg)	Interaction with Food	JECFA Evaluation
Pectinase	Fruit & vegetable juices, Cereal processing, extractions (coffee, tea, spices)			
(Aspergillus awamora)				
(Aspergillus awamori)				
(Aspergillus foetidus)				
(Aspergillus niger)				15
(Aspergillus oryzae)				15
(Pencillium simplicissium)				
(Rhizopus oryzae)				15
(Trichoderma reesei)				
Pectin esterase				
(Aspergillus niger)				15
Pectinlyase				
(Aspergillus niger)				15
Polygalacturonase				
(Aspergillus niger)				15
Protease (including milk clotting enzymes):				
(Aspergillus melleus)				
(Aspergillus niger)				
(Aspergillus oryzae)				
(Bacillus cereus)				25
(Bacillus licheniformis)				28
(Bacillus subtilis)				
(Brevibacterium lineus)	Bakery products			15
(Endothia parasitica)				
(Lactobacillus casei)	Cheese			28
(Micrococcus caseolyticus)				
(Mucor miehei)				
(Mucor pusillus)	Cheese			28
(Streptococcus cremoris)	Cheese			28
(Steptococcus lactis)				
	Starch hydrolysis, Glucose syrups, Maltose syrups			

CATEGORY	Areas of Use	Residues (mg/kg)	Interaction with Food	JECFA Evaluation
Pullulanase (Bacillus acidopullulyticus) (Bacillus subtilis) (Klebsiella aerogenes)	—			25
Serine proteinase (Streptomyces fradiae) (Bacillus licheniformis)				28
Tannase (Aspergillus niger) (Aspergillus oryzae)				
Xylanase (Aspergillus niger) (Sporotrichum dimorphosporum) (Streptomyces sp.) (Trichoderma reesei)	baking, cereal processing, brewing, starch processing, juice, wine			
Beta-xylosidase (Trichoderma reesei)	baking			
FLOCCULATING AGENTS				
Acrylate-acrylamide resin	Sugar	(10 in sugar liquor)		
Chitin/Chitosan				
Complexes of soluble aluminum salt and phosphoric acid	Drinking water			
Dimethylamine-epichlorohydrin copolymer	Sugar processing	< 5	None	
Fuller's earth (calcium analogue of sodium montmorillonite)				
Isinglass				
Dried and powdered blood plasma				

CATEGORY	Areas of Use	Residues (mg/kg)	Interaction with Food	JECFA Evaluation
Modified acrylamide resin	Sugar, boiler water			
Polyacrylic acid	Sugar			
Polyacrylamide	Sugar (beet)			
Sodium polyacrylate	Sugar (beet)			
Trisodium diphosphate				
Trisodium orthophosphate				

ION EXCHANGE RESINS, MEMBRANES AND MOLECULAR SIEVES

CATEGORY	Areas of Use	Residues (mg/kg)	Interaction with Food	JECFA Evaluation
Resins:	Enzyme immob. Starch hydrolysis	< 1 (Calculated at Total Organic Carbon)		
Completely hydrolyzed copolymers of methyl acrylate and divinylbenzene				
Completely hydrolyzed terpolymers of methyl acrylate, divinylbenzene and acrylonitrile				
Cross-linked phenol-formaldehyde activated with one or both of the following: Triethylenetetramine Tetraethylenepentamine				
Cross-linked polystyrene, first chloromethylated then aminated with trimethylamine, dimethylamine, diethylenetriamine or dimethylethanolamine				
Diethylenetriamine, triethylenetetramine, tetraethylenepentamine cross-linked with epichlorohydrin				
Epichlorohydrin cross-linked with ammonia				

CATEGORY	Areas of Use	Residues (mg/kg)	Interaction with Food	JECFA Evaluation
Epichlorohydrin cross-linked with ammonia and then quaternized with methyl chloride to contain not more than 18 percent strong base capacity by weight of total exchange capacity	Water used in food processing	None		
Methacrylic acid-divinylbenzene copolymer				
Methacrylic acid-divinylbenzene copolymer with RCOO active groups				
Methyl acrylate-divinylbenzene copolymer containing not less than 2 percent by weight of divinylbenzene, aminolyzed with dimethylaminopropylamine				
Methyl acrylate-divinylbenzene copolymer containing not less than 3.5 percent by weight of divinylbenzene, aminolyzed with dimethylaminopropylamine				
Methyl acrylate-divinylbenzenediethylene glycol divinyl ether terpolymer containing not less than 3.5 percent by weight of divinylbenzene and not more than 0.6 percent by weight of diethylene gycol divinyl ether, aminolyzed with dimethylaminopropylamine				
Methyl acrylate-divinylbenzene-diethylene glycol divinyl ether terpolymer containing not less than 7 percent by weight of divinylbenzene and not more than 2.3 percent by weight of diethylene glycol divinyl ether, aminolyzed with dimethylaminopropylamine and quaternized with methyl chloride	Sugar processing	0.015 (extractives from resin)	None	
Polystyrene-divinylbenzene reticulum with trimethylammonium groups	Sugar, distilled liquors	Migrants from resin < 1		

CATEGORY	Areas of Use	Residues (mg/kg)	Interaction with Food	JECFA Evaluation
Reaction resin of formaldehyde, acetone and tetraethylenepentamine				
Styrene-divinylbenzene cross-linked copolymer, first chloromethylated then aminated with dimethylamine and oxidized with hydrogen peroxide whereby the resin contains not more than 15 percent by weight of vinyl N,N-dimethyl-benzylamine-N-oxide and not more than 6.5 percent by weight of nitrogen				
Sulfite-modified cross-linked phenol-formaldehyde, with modification resulting in sulfonic acid groups on side chains				
Sulfonated anthracite coal meeting the requirements of American Society for Testing and Materials D388-38, Class I, Group 2				
Sulfonated copolymer of styrene and divinylbenzene				
Sulfonated terpolymers of styrene, divinylbenzene and acrylonitrile or methyl acrylate				
Sulfonated tetrapolymer of styrene, divinylbenzene, acrylonitrile and methyl acrylate derived from a mixture of monomers containing not more than a total of 2 percent by weight of acrylonitrile and methyl acrylate				

CATEGORY	Areas of Use	Residues (mg/kg)	Interaction with Food	JECFA Evaluation

Counter ions for resins:
   Aluminum
   Bicarbonate
   Calcium
   Carbonate
   Chloride
   Hydronium
   Hydroxyl
   Magnesium
   Potassium
   Sodium
   Strontium
   Sulfate
 	
 Membranes:
 	
 Polyethylene - polystyrene base modified by reaction with chloramethyl ether and subsequent amination with trimethylamine, diethylenetriamine or dimethylethanolamine
 	
 Polymers and copolymers containing the following components: cellulosics (such as cellulose diacetate, cellulose triacetate, cellulose ethers, cellulose), Polysulfone-sulfonated polysulfone, Polyethersulfone, sulfonated polyethersulfone, Fluoropolymers (such as polyvinylidene fluoride, chlorotrifluorethylene-vinylidenefluoride copolymer, polytetrafluoroethylene), Polysulfonamides, aliphatic/aromatic polyamide and copolyamides (such as polypiperazineamides, m-phenylenediamine trimesamide polymer), Polyesters (such as				

CATEGORY	Areas of Use	Residues (mg/kg)	Interaction with Food	JECFA Evaluation
polyethyleneterephalate), Polyolefins (such as polypropylene, polyethylene), Polyamide-imide polymers, Polyimides, Polyacrylonitriles, Polyvinylpyrrolidone, Polystyrene-sulfonated polystyrene, chitin/chitosan and derivatives, polyureas-polyurethanes, Polyethers, and Polyamines				
Molecular Sieves:				
Calcium aluminum silicate				18
Sodium aluminum silicate				17
LUBRICANTS, RELEASE AND ANTI-STICK AGENTS, MOULDING AIDS				
Bentonite	Confectionery			
Dimethylpolysiloxane	Confectionery			26
Kaolin	Confectionery			17
MICRO-ORGANISM CONTROL AGENTS				
Chlorine dioxide	Flour			7
Dimethyl dicarbonate	Wine	None		
Formaldehyde	Sugar			
Hydrogen peroxide	Sugar, fruit and vegetable juice			24
Hypochlorite	Food oils			
Iodophors	Food oils			
Peracetic acid	Food oils			
Quaternary ammonium compounds				
Salts of sulfurous acid	Corn milling Starch hydrolysis	< 100		

CATEGORY	Areas of Use	Residues (mg/kg)	Interaction with Food	JECFA Evaluation
Lactoperoxidase system (lactoperoxidase, glucose oxidase, thiocyanate salt)				
PROPELLANT AND PACKAGING GASES				
Air				
Argon				
Carbon dioxide				
Chloropentafluoroethane				
Combustion product gas [a variable mixture of gases produced by controlled combustion of butane, propane, or natural gas. The principal components are nitrogen and carbon dioxide, with lesser amounts of hydrogen, oxygen, carbon monoxide (not to exceed 4.5%), and traces of other inert gases]				
Dichlorodifluoromethan (F 12)				
Helium				
Hydrogen				
Nitrous oxide				28
Nitrogen				26
Octafluorocyclobutane				
Propane				23
Trichlorofluoromethane (F 11)				
SOLVENTS, EXTRACTION AND PROCESSING				
Acetone (dimethyl ketone)	Flavourings, colours, food oils	< 30, 2, & 0.1		14
Amyl acetate	Flavourings, colours			

CATEGORY	Areas of Use	Residues (mg/kg)	Interaction with Food	JECFA Evaluation
Benzyl alcohol	Flavourings, colours, fatty acids			
Butane	Flavourings, food oils	< 1, 01		23
Butane-1,3-diol	Flavourings			23
Butan-1-ol	Fatty acids, flavourings, colours	< 1000		28
Butan-2-ol	Flavourings	1		
Butyl acetate				
Carbon dioxide				
Cyclohexane	Flavourings, food oils	< 1		23
Dibutyl ether	Flavourings	< 2		
1,2-Dichlororethane (Dichloroethane)	Decaf. coffee	< 5		23
Dichlorodifluoromethane	Flavourings, colours	< 1		19
Dichlorofluoromethane	Flavourings	< 1		
Dichloromethane	Flavourings, colours, decaf. coffee, food oils	< 2, 5, 10		27
Dichlorotetrafluoroethane	Flavourings	< 1		
Diethyl citrate	Flavourings, colours			27
Diethyl ether	Flavourings, colours	< 2		
Di-isopropylketone				
Ethanol				
Ethyl acetate				
Nitrous oxide				29

CATEGORY	Areas of Use	Residues (mg/kg)	Interaction with Food	JECFA Evaluation
n-Octyl alcohol	Citric acid			
Pentane	Flavourings, food oils	< 1		25
Petroleum ether (light petroleum)	Flavourings, food oils	< 1		
Propane	Flavourings, food oils	< 1, 0.1		28
Propane-1,2-diol	Fatty acids, flavourings, colours			
Propane-1-ol	Fatty acids, flavourings, colours			
Tertiary butyl alcohol				
1,1,2-Trichloroethylene	Flavourings, food oils	< 2		27
Trichlorofluoromethane	Flavourings	< 1		
Tridodecylamine	Citric acid			
Toluene	Flavourings	< 1		
Ethylmethylketone (butanone)	Fatty acids, flavourings, colourings. Decaffeination of coffee, tea	< 2		28
Glycerol tributyrate	Flavourings, colours			
Glycerol tripropionate	Flavourings, colours			
Heptane	Flavourings, food oils	< 1		14
Hexane	Flavourings, food oils	< 0.1		14

CATEGORY	Areas of Use	Residues (mg/kg)	Interaction with Food	JECFA Evaluation
Isobutane	Flavourings	< 1		
Isoparaffinic petroleum hydrocarbons	Citric acid			
Isopropyl myristate	Flavourings, colours			
Methylene chloride (dichloromethane)	Food oils	< 0.02		28
Methyl acetate	Coffee decaffeination, flavouring, Sugar refining	20 1		
Methyl propanol-1	flavourings	1		
WASHING AND PEELING AGENTS				
A mixture of alklene oxide adducts of alkyl alcohol and phosphate esters of alkylene oxide adducts of alkyl alcohols consisting of alpha-alkyl(C12-C18)-omega-hydroxy-poly(oxethylene)(7.5-8.5 moles) poly(oxypropylene) block copolymer having an average molecular weight of 810, alpha-alkyl-(C12-C18)-omega-hydroxy-poly(oxyethylene) (3.3-3.7 moles) polymer having an average molecular weight of 380, and subsequently esterified with 1.25 moles phosphoric anhydride; and alpha-alkyl (C10-C12)-omega-hydroxy poly(oxyethylene) (11.9-12.9 moles)/poly(oxypropylene) copolymer having an average molecular weight of 810 and subsequently esterified with 1.25 moles phosphoric anhydride	Fruits and vegetables	< 0.001 up to 0.01	None	
Alkylene oxide adducts of alkyl alcohols and fatty acids	Sugar beets	No information available		

CATEGORY	Areas of Use	Residues (mg/kg)	Interaction with Food	JECFA Evaluation
Aliphatic acid mixture consisting of valeric, caproic, enanthic, caprylic, and pelargonic acids	Fruits and vegetables	0.04-0.11	None	
Alpha-alkyl-omega-hydroxy-poly(oxyethylene)	Sugar beets	0.001 in sugar beets 0 in sugar	None	
Ammonium chloride, quaternary	Sugar beets			
Ammonium orthophosphate	Fruits and vegetables			
Calcium chloride	Fruits and vegetables			
Calcium hydroxide	Sugar beets			
Calcium oxide	Sugar beets			
Carbamate	Sugar beets			
Dialkanolamine	Sugar beets	0.001 in sugar beets 0 in sugar	None	
Diammonium orthophosphate	Fruits and vegetables for canning			
Diammonium orthophosphate, (5% aqueous solution)	Fruits and vegetables for canning			
Dithiocarbamate	Sugar beets			
Ethylene dichloride	Sugar beets	0.00001 in sugar beets, 0 in sugar	None	23
Ethylene glycol monobutyl ether	Sugar beets	0.00003 in sugar beets, 0 in sugar	None	

CATEGORY	Areas of Use	Residues (mg/kg)	Interaction with Food	JECFA Evaluation
Hydrogen peroxide		No information available		24
Linear undecylbenzenesulfonic acid	Sugar beets	0.001 in sugar beets, 0 in sugar	None	
Monoethanolamine	Fruits and vegetables, sugar beets	100		
Monoethanolamine	Sugar beets	0.0001 in sugar beets, 0 in sugar	None	
Monoethanolamine (8%)	Fruits and vegetables for canning	1		
Organophosphates	Sugar beets			
Polyacrylamide	Fruits and vegetables, sugar beets	< 1	None	
Potassium bromide	Fruits and vegetables	No information available		
Sodium dodecylbenzenesulfonate (akyl group predominantly C12 and not less than 95 percent C10-C16)	Fruits and vegetables, meat and poultry	< 2	None	
Sodium 2-ethylhexyl sulphate	Fruits and vegetables	< 20	None	
Sodium carbonate				
Sodium hydroxide	Fruits and vegetables, sugar beets			

CATEGORY	Areas of Use	Residues (mg/kg)	Interaction with Food	JECFA Evaluation
Sodium hydroxide (10%, max.)	Fruits and vegetables for canning			
Sodium hydroxide (2%)	Mackerel for canning			
Sodium hypochlorite	Fruits and vegetables	No information available		
Sodium mono- and di-methyl naphthalene-sulfonates (mol. wt. 245-260)	Fruits and vegetables	< 0.2	None	
Sodium n-alkylbenzenesulfonate (alkyl group predominantly C12 and C13 and not less than 95 percent C10-C16)	Fruits and vegetables	Same as sodium dodecylbenzene-sulfonate	None	
Sodium tripolyphosphate				
Tetrapotassium pyrophosphate	Sugar beets	0.00002 in sugar beets 0 in sugar	None	26
Tetrasodium ethylenediaminetetraacetate	Sugar beets	0.000003 in sugar beets 0 in sugar	None	17
Triethanolamine	Sugar beets	0.00005 in sugar beets 0 in sugar	None	
OTHER PROCESSING AIDS				
Aluminum oxide				
Aluminum potassium sulfate				22
Ammonium nitrate				
Calcium tartrate				
Erythorbic acid				17
Ethyl parahydroxybenzoate				17

CATEGORY	Areas of Use	Residues (mg/kg)	Interaction with Food	JECFA Evaluation
Gibberellic acid				
Glycerol ester of adipic acid				
Hydrogen				
Magnesium tartrate				
Polyvinyl polypyrrolidone	Beverages			27
Potassium gibberellate				
Propyl parahydroxybenzoate				17
Sodium				
Sodium hypochlorite				
Sodium silicates				

CODEX INVENTORY OF ALL COMPOUNDS USED AS PROCESSING AIDS
-includes substances that may serve other functions-

ANTIFOAM AGENTS

- (2) Aluminum stearate
- (2) Butyl stearate
- (3) Butylated hydroxyanisole (as antioxidant in defoamers)
- (3) Butylated hydroxytoluene (as antioxidant in defoamers)
- (2) Calcium stearate
- (2) Dimethylpolysiloxane
- (2) Fatty acids
- (1) Fatty acid methyl ester
- (1) Fatty acid polyalkylene glycol ester (1-5 moles ethylene oxide or propylene oxide)
- (1) Fatty alcohols (C8-C30)
- (1) Formaldehyde
- (1) Hydrogenated coconut oil
- (2) Hydroxylated lecithin
- (2) Magnesium stearate
- (3) Margarine
- (2) Mineral oil
- (2) Mono- and diglycerides of fatty acids
- (2) n-Butoxypolyoxyethylene polyoxypropylene glycol
- (2) Odourless light petroleum hydrocarbons
- (2) Oleic acid from tall oil fatty acids
- (1) Oxoalcohols C9-C30
- (2) Oxystearin
- (2) Petroleum wax
- (2) Petroleum wax (synthetic)
- (2) Petrolatum
- (2) Polyacrylic acid, sodium salt
- (2) Polyethylene glycol
- (2) Polyethylene glycol (400) dioleate
- (2) Polyethylene glycol (600) dioleate
- (2) Polyglycerol esters of fatty acids
- (2) Polyoxyethylene 40 monostearate
- (1) Polyoxyethylene esters of C8-C30 fatty acids
- (1) Polyoxypropylene esters of C8-C30 fatty acids
- (1) Polyoxyethylene esters of C9-C30 oxoalcohols
- (1) Polyoxypropylene esters of C9-C30 oxoalcohols
- (1) Mixtures of polyoxyethylene and polyoxypropylene esters of C8-C30 fatty acids
- (2) Polypropylene glycol
- (2) Polysorbate 60
- (2) Polysorbate 65
- (2) Polysorbate 80
- (2) Potassium stearate
- (2) Propylene glycol alginate
- (2) Propylene glycol mono- and di-esters of fats and fatty acids
- (2) Silicon dioxide
- (2) Sorbitan monolaurate
- (2) Sorbitan monostearate
- (2) Soybean oil fatty acids
- (2) Tallow

(2) Tallow, hydrogenated, oxidized or sulphated
(2) Tallow alcohol, hydrogenated
(3) Vegetable oil

CATALYSTS

(1) Alloys of 2 or more listed metals
(1) Aluminum
(2) Ammonia
(2) Ammonium bisulfite
(2) Calcium chloride
(1) Chromium
(1) Copper
(1) Copper chromate
(1) Copper chromite
(2) Ferrous sulfate
(1) Manganese
(1) Magnesium oxide
(1) Molybdium
(1) Nickel
(1) Palladium
(1) Platinum
(1) Potassium metal
(1) Potassium methylate (methoxide)
(1) Potassium ethylate (ethoxide)
(1) Silver
(1) Sodium amide
(2) Sodium chloride
(1) Sodium ethylate
(2) Sodium hydroxide
(2) Sodium metabisulfite
(1) Sodium metal
(1) Sodium methylate (methoxide)
(2) Sulfur dioxide
(1) Trifluoromethane sulfonic acid
(1) Various metal oxides
(1) Zirconium

CLARIFYING AGENTS/FILTRATION AIDS

(1) Absorbent clays (bleaching, natural, or activated earths)
(2) Acacia
(1) Active carbon
(2) Agar
(1) Albumin
(1) Asbestos
(1) Bentonite
(1) Calcium oxide
(2) Carbon dioxide
(2) Carrageenan/Furcelleran
(2) Casein
(2) Cellulose
(2) Cellulose powder
( ) Chloromethylated aminated styrene-divinylbenzene resin
(2) Citric acid
(1) Diatomaceous earth
( ) Divinylbenzene-ethylvinylbenzene copolymer

(1) Fuller's earth
(2) Gelatin (edible)
(1) Ion exchange resins (see ION EXCHANGE RESINS)
(1) Isinglass
(1) Kaolin
(1) Magnesium acetate
(1) Perlite
(2) Phosphoric acid
( ) Polyacrylamide/polysodium acrylate copolymer
( ) Polymaleic acid and sodium polymaleate
(2) Polyvinylpyrrolidone
(2) Polyvinylpolypyrrolidone
(2) Potassium ferrocyanide
(2) Silicon dioxide amorphous - silica hydrogel
(2) Sodium alginate
(2) Stabilized aqueous silica sol
(2) Sulfur dioxide
(2) Tannic acid
(1) Tannin (to be specified)
(1) Vegetable carbon (activated)
(1) Vegetable carbon (unactivated)
(2) Wood flour/Sawdust

COLOUR STABILIZERS

(2) Dextrose
(2) Sodium acid pyrophosphate
(2) Sulphur dioxide

CONTACT FREEZING AND COOLING AGENTS

(2) Brine (eg. salt brine)
(2) Carbon dioxide
( ) Dichlorodifluoromethane
(1) Dichlorofluoromethane
(1) Freon (to be specified)
(2) Glycerol
(1) Nitrogen

DESICCATING AGENT/ANTICAKING AGENTS

( ) Aluminum stearate
(2) Calcium aluminum silicate
(1) Calcium phosphate
(2) Calcium silicate
( ) Calcium stearate
(2) Magnesium carbonate, heavy
(2) Magnesium carbonate, light
(2) Magnesium oxide, heavy
(2) Magnesium oxide, light
(2) Magnesium silicate, synthetic
( ) Magnesium stearate
(2) Magnesium trisilicate
(1) Octadecylammonium acetate (in ammonium chloride)
(1) Potassium aluminum silicate : change to category (2),Ref. 57
(2) Silicon dioxide

(2) Silicon dioxide amorphous - silica gel
(2) Sodium aluminum silicate
( ) Sodium calcium silicoaluminate
(2) Tricalcium diorthophosphate

DETERGENTS (wetting agents)

(1) Dioctyl sodium sulfosuccinate (10 ppm in fruit drinks)
(1) Methyl glucoside of coconut oil ester (320 ppm in molasses)
(1) Quaternary ammonium compounds
(1) Sodium lauryl sulphate
(1) Sodium xylene sulphonate

ENZYME IMMOBILIZATION AGENTS AND SUPPORTS

(1) Glutaraldehyde
(1) Glass
(1) Diatomaceous earth
(2) Carrageenan (including Furcelleran)
(1) Ceramics
(1) Diethylaminoethyl cellulose
(2) Gelatin
(1) Ion exchange resins
(1) Polyethylenimine
(2) Sodium alginate

ENZYME PREPARATIONS (Including immobilized enzymes)

Animal-Derived Preparations

(1) Alpha-amylase   (hog or bovine pancreas)
(1) Catalase   (bovine or horse liver)
(1) Chymosin   (calf, kid, or lamb abomasum)
(1) Lipase   (bovine stomach) (salivary
                         (glands or forestomach
                         of calf, kid, or lamb)
                         (hog or bovine pancreas)
(1) Lysozyme   change to category 2 (ref 57)
                         (chicken egg whites)
(1) Pepsin   (hog stomach)
(1) Pepsin, avian   (proventicum of poultry)
( ) Phospholipase   (pancrease)
(1) Rennet   (bovine, calf, goat, kid, or
                         sheep, lamb stomach)
(1) Trypsin   (porcine or bovine pancreas)

Plant-Derived Preparations

(1) Bromelain   (Ananas spp.)
(1) Chymopapain   (Carica papaya)
(1) Ficin   (Ficus spp.)
( ) Liposydase   (soya)
(1) Malt carbohydrases   (malt barley and barley)
(1) Papain   (Carica papaya)

Microbiological Origin (see Appendix B for list by microbial source)

(1)	Alcohol dehydrogenase	*(Saccharomyces cerevisiae)*
(1)	Alpha amylase	*(Aspergillus niger)*
		(Aspergillus oryzae)
		(Bacillus licheniformis)
		(Bacillus stearothermophilus)
		(Bacillus subtilis)
		(Rhizopus delemar)
		(Rhizopus oryzae)
(1)	Alpha galactosidase	*(Aspergillus niger)*
		(Mortierella vinacea sp.)
		(Saccharomyces carlsbergensis)
(1)	Arabino-furanosidease	*(Aspergillus niger)*
(1)	Beta amylase	*(Bacillus cereus)*
		(Bacillus megaterium)
		(Bacillus subtilis)
(1)	Beta glucanase	*(Aspergillus niger)*
		(Bacillus subtilis)
		(Trichoderma harzianum)
(1)	Beta glucosidase	*(Trichoderma harzianum)*
(1)	Catalase	*(Aspergillus niger)*
		(Micrococcus lysodeicticus)
(1)	Cellobiase	*(Aspergillus niger)*
	or betaglucosidase	*(Trichoderma reesei)*
(1)	Cellulase	*(Aspergillus niger)*
		(Aspergillus oryzae)
		(Rhizopus delemar)
		(Rhizopus oryzae)
		(Sporotrichum dimorphosporum)
		(Trichoderma reesei)
		(Thielavia terrestris)
(1)	Dextranase	*(Aspergillus species)*
		(Bacillus subtilis)
		(Klebsiella aerogenes)
		(Penicillium funiculosum)
		(Penicillium lilacinum)
(1)	Endo-beta glucanase	*(Aspergillus niger)*
		(Aspergillus oryzae)
		(Bacillus circulans)
		(Bacillus subtilus)
		(Penicillium emersonii)
		(Rhizopus delemar)
		(Rhizopus oryzae)
		(Trichoderma reesei)
		(Disporotrichum dimorphosphorum)
(1)	Esterase	*(Mucor miehei)*
(1)	Exo-alpha glucosidase	*(Aspergillus niger)*
(1)	Exo-alpha glucosidase (immobilized)	(same sources as above)
(1)	Glucoamylase or amyloglucosidase	*(Aspergillus awamori)*
		(Aspergillus niger)
		(Aspergillus oryzae)
		(Rhizopus arrhizus)
		(Rhizopus delemar)
		(Rhizopus niveus)

	(Rhizopus oryzae)
	(Trichoderma reesei)
(1) Glucose isomerase	*(Actinoplanes missouriensis)*
	(Arthrobacter sp.)
	(Bacillus coagulans)
	(Streptomyces albus)
	(Streptomyces olivaceus)
	(Streptomyces olivochromogenes)
	(Streptomyces rubiginosus)
	(Streptomyces sp.)
	(Streptomyces violaceoniger)
(1) Glucose isomerase (immobilized)	(same sources as above)
(1) Glucose oxidase	*(Aspergillus niger)*
(1) Hemicellulase	*(Aspergillus niger)*
	(Aspergillus oryzae)
	(Bacillus subtilis)
	(Rhizopus delemar)
	(Rhizopus oryzae)
	(Sporotrichum dimorphosporum)
	(Trichoderma reesei)
(1) Inulinase	*(Aspergillus niger)*
	(Kluyveromyces fragilis)
	(Sporotrichum dimorphosporum)
	(Streptomyces sp.)
(1) Invertase	change to category (2), Ref. 57
	(Aspergillus niger)
	(Bacillus subtilis)
	(Kluyveromyces fragilis)
	(Saccharomyces carlsbergensis)
	(Saccharomyces cerevisiae)
	(Saccharomyces sp.)
(1) Isoamylase	*(Bacillus cereus)*
(1) Lactase (Beta-galactosidase)	*(Aspergillus niger)*
	(Aspergillus oryzae)
	(Kluyveromyces fragilis)
	(Kluyveromyces lactis)
	(Saccharomyces sp.)
(1) Lactoperoxidase	change to category (2), Ref. 57
(1) Lipase	change to category (2), Ref. 57
	(Aspergillus flavus)
	(Aspergillus niger)
	(Aspergillus oryzae)
	(Brevibacterium lineus)
	(Candida lipolytica)
	(Mucor javanicus)
	(Mucor miehei)
	(Mucor pusillus)
	(Rhizopus arrhizus)
	(Rhizopus delemar)
	(Rhizopus nigrican)
	(Rhizopus niveus)
(1) Malic acid decarboxylate	*(Leuconostoc oenos)*
(1) Maltase or alphaglucosidase	*(Aspergillus niger)*
	(Aspergillus oryzae)
	(Rhizopus oryzae)
	(Trichoderma reesei)

(1) Melibiase	*(Mortierella vinacea sp.)*
(alphagalactosidase)	*(Saccharomyces carlsbergensis)*
(1) Nitrate reductase	*(Micrococcus violagabriella)*
(1) Pectinase	*(Aspergillus awamori)*
	(Aspergillus foetidus)
	(Aspergillus niger)
	(Aspergillus oryzae)
	(Penicillium simplicissium)
	(Rhizopus oryzae)
	(Trichoderma reesei)
(1) Pectin esterase	*(Aspergillus niger)*
(1) Pectinlyase	*(Aspergillus niger)*
(1) Polygalacturonase	*(Aspergillus niger)*
(1) Protease	*(Aspergillus melleus)*
	(Aspergillus niger)
	(Aspergillus oryzae)
	(Bacillus cereus)
	(Bacillus licheniformis)
	(Bacillus subtilis)
	(Brevibacterium lineus)
	(Endothia parasitica)
	(Lactobacillus casei)
	(Micrococcus caseolyticus)
	(Mucor miehei)
	(Mucor pusillus)
	(Streptococcus cremoris)
	(Streptococcus lactis)
	(Bacillus acidopullulyticus)
(1) Pullulanase	*(Bacillus subtilis)*
	(Klebsiella aerogenes)
(1) Serine proteinase	*(Streptomyces fradiae)*
	(Bacillus licheniformis)
(1) Tannase	*(Aspergillus niger)*
	(Aspergillus oryzae)
(1) Xylanase	*(Aspergillus niger)*
	(Sporotrichum dimorphosporum)
	(Streptomyces sp.)
	(Trichoderma reesei)
( ) β-xylosidase	*(Trichoderma reesei)*

SOLVENTS (extraction and processing)

(1) Acetone (dimethyl ketone)
(2) Ammonia in methanol/ethanol
(1) Amyl acetate
(1) Benzyl alcohol
(2) Benzyl benzoate
(1) Butane
(1) Butane-1,3-diol
(1) Butan-1-ol
(2) Butan-2-ol
(2) Butyl acetate
(2) Carbon dioxide
(2) Castor oil
(1) Cyclohexane
(1) Dibutyl ether

    (1) 1,2-Dichlororethane (Dichloroethane)
    (1) Dichlorodifluoromethane
    (1) Dichlorofluoromethane
    (1) Dichloromethane
    (1) Dichlorotetrafluoroethane
    (1) Diethyl citrate
    (1) Diethyl ether
    (2) Diethyl tartrate
    (1) Di-isopropylketone
    (2) Ethanol
    (2) Ethyl acetate
    (2) Ethyl lactate
    (1) Ethylmethylketone (butanone)
    (2) Glycerol
    (2) Glycerol mono- di- and triacetate
    (1) Glycerol tributyrate
    (1) Glycerol tripropionate
    (1) Heptane
    (1) Hexane
    (1) Isobutane
    ( ) Isobutanol (2-methylpropan-1-ol)
    (1) Isoparaffinic petroleum hydrocarbons
    (2) Isopropyl alcohol
    (1) Isopropyl myristate
    (2) Methanol
    (2) Methyl acetate
    (1) Methylene chloride (dichloromethane)
    ( ) Methyl propanol-1
    (2) Nitric acid
    (1) Nitrous oxide
    (1) 2-Nitropropane
    (1) n-Octyl alcohol
    (1) Pentane
    (1) Petroleum ether (light petroleum)
    (1) Propane
    (1) Propane-1,2-diol
    (1) Propane-1-ol
    (2) Propane-2-ol (isopropyl alcohol)
    (1) Tertiary butyl alcohol
    (1) 1,1,2-Trichloroethylene
    (1) Trichlorofluoroethylene
    ( ) Trichlorofluoromethane
    (1) Tridodecylamine
    (1) Toluene
    (2) Water

FAT CRYSTAL MODIFIERS

    (4) Lecithin
    (4) Oxystearin
    (4) Polyglycerol esters of fatty acids
    (4) Polysorbate 60
    (4) Sodium dodecylbenzene sulphonate
    (4) Sodium lauryl sulphate
    (4) Sorbitan monostearate
    (4) Sorbitan tristearate

FLOCCULATING AGENTS

( ) Acrylamide resins
(1) Acrylate-acrylamide resin
(2) Aluminum ammonium sulfate
(2) Aluminum sulfate
(2) Citric acid
(1) Complexes of soluble aluminum salt and phosphoric acid
( ) Dimethylamine-epichlorohydrin copolymer
(1) Fuller's earth (calcium analogue of sodium montmorillonite)
(2) Gelatin
(1) Isinglass
(1) Dried and powdered blood plasma
(1) Modified acrylamide resin
(1) Polyacrylic acid
(2) Polyacrylic acid, sodium salt
(1) Polyacrylamide
(2) Silica
(2) Sodium alginate
(1) Sodium polyacrylate
(1) Trisodium diphosphate
(1) Trisodium orthophosphate

ION EXCHANGE RESINS, MEMBRANES, AND MOLECULAR SIEVES

RESINS:

(1) Completely hydrolyzed copolymers of methyl acrylate and
    divinylbenzene.
(1) Completely hydrolyzed terpolymers of methyl acrylate, divinylbenzene
    and acrylonitrile.
(1) Cross-linked phenolformaldehyde activated with one or both of the
    following:

    Triethylenetetramine
    Tetraethylenepentamine

(1) Cross-linked polystyrene, first chloromethylated then aminated with
    trimethylamine, dimethylamine, diethylenetriamine or
    dimethylethanolamine.
(1) Diethylenetriamine, triethylenetetramine, tetraethylenepentamine
    cross-linked with epichlorohydrin.
(1) Epichlorohydrin cross-linked with ammonia.
(1) Methacrylic acid-divinylbenzene copolymer.
(1) Methacrylic acid-divinylbenzene copolymer with RCOO active groups.
(1) Methyl acrylate-divinylbenzene copolymer containing not less than 2
    percent by weight of divinylbenzene, aminolyzed with
    dimethylaminopropylamine.
(1) Methyl acrylate-divinylbenzene copolymer containing not less than 3.5
    percent by weight of divinylbenzene, aminolyzed with dimethyl-amino-
    propylamine.

(1) Methyl acrylate-divinylbenzenediethylene glycol divinyl ether
    terpolymer containing not less than 3.5 percent by weight of
    divinylbenzene and not more than 0.6 percent by weight of diethylene
    glycol divinyl ether, aminolyzed with dimethylaminopropylamine.

Methyl acrylate-divinylbenzene-diethylene glycol divinyl ether terpolymer containing not less than 7 percent by weight of divinylbenzene and not more than 2.3 percent by weight of diethylene glycol divinyl ether, aminolyzed with dimethylaminopropyl-amine and quaternized with methyl chloride.

Polystyrene-divinylbenzene reticulum with trimethylammonium groups.

(1) Reaction resin of formaldehyde, acetone and tetraethylene-pentamine.

(1) Styrene-divinylbenzene cross-linked copolymer, first chloromethylated then aminated with dimethylamine and oxidized with hydrogen peroxide whereby the resin contains not more than 15 percent by weight of vinyl N,N-dimethylbenzylamine-N-oxide and not more than 6.5 percent by weight of nitrogen.

(1) Sulfite-modified cross-linked phenol-formaldehyde, with modification resulting in sulfonic acid groups on side chains.

(1) Sulfonated anthracite coal meeting the requirement of American Society for Testing and Materials D388-38, Class I, Group 2.

(1) Sulfonated copolymer of styrene and divinylbenzene.

(1) Sulfonated terpolymers of styrene, divinylbenzene and acrylonitrile or methyl acrylate.

(1) Sulfonated tetrapolymer or styrene, divinylbenzene, acrylonitrile and methyl acrylate derived from a mixture of monomers containing not more than a total of 2 percent by weight of acrylonitrile and methyl acrylate.

Counter ions:

Aluminum	Hydroxyl
Bicarbonate	Magnesium
Calcium	Potassium
Carbonate	Sodium
Chloride	Sulfate
Hydronium	

MEMBRANES:

(1) Polyethylene - polystyrene base modified by reaction with chloramethyl ether and subsequent amination with trimethylamine, diethylenetriamine or dimethylethanolamine.

(1) Polymers and Polyethylene - polystyrene base modified by reaction with chloramethyl ether and subsequent amination with trimethylamine, diethylenetriamine or dimethylethanolamine.

Polymers and copolymers containing the following components: cellulosics (such as cellulose diacetate, cellulose triacetate, cellulose ethers, cellulose), Polysulfone-sulfonated polysulfone, Polyethersulfone-sulfonated polyethersulfone, Fluoropolymers (such as polyvinylidene fluorid, chlorotrifluoroethylene-vinylidenefluoride copolymer, polytetrafluoroethylene), Polysulfoneamides, aliphatic/aromatic Polyamide

and copolyamides (such as polypiperazineamides, m-phenylenediamine
trimesamide polymer), Polyesters (such as polyethyleneterephalate),
Polyolefins (such as polypropylene, polyethylene), Polyamide-imide
polymers, Polyimides, Polyacrylonitriles, Polyvinylpyrrolidone,
Polystyrene-sulonated polystyrene, chitin/chitosan and derivatives,
polyureas-polyurethanes, Polyethers, and Polyamines.

MOLECULAR SIEVES:

    (1) Calcium aluminum silicate :change to category (2), Ref. 57
    (1) Sodium aluminum silicate :change to category (2), Ref. 57

LUBRICANTS, RELEASE AND ANTI-STICK AGENTS, MOULDING AIDS

    ( ) Acetic acid esters of fatty acid mono- and diglycerides
    (2) Acetylated monoglycerides
    (2) Beeswax
    (1) Bentonite
    (2) Butyl stearate
    (2) Carnauba wax
    (2) Calcium aluminum silicate
    (2) Calcium carbonate
    (2) Calcium phosphates
    (2) Calcium silicate
    (2) Calcium stearate
    (2) Castor oil
    (1) Dimethylpolysiloxane
    (2) Edible bone phosphate
    (2) Ethoxylated mono- and diglycerides
    (2) Fats and waxes of vegetable and animal origin
    (2) Fatty acids of tallow, of cottonseed and of soybean oil
    (2) Hydrogenated sperm oil
    (1) Kaolin
    (2) Lecithin
    (2) Magnesium carbonate
    (2) Magnesium oxide, light and heavy
    (2) Magnesium trisilicate
    (2) Mineral oil based greases (lubricants for pumps)
    (2) Mineral oil/Paraffin oil
    (2) Mineral oils and waxes
    ( ) Mono- and diglycerides of fatty acids
    (2) Oxidatively polymerised soya bean oil
    (2) Paraffin and paraffin oils
    (2) Partially hydrogenated vegetable oil (cottonseed, soy)
    (2) Polyglycerol esters of dimerised fatty acids of soya bean oil
    (2) Polyglycerol polylinoleate
    (2) Polyglycerol polyricinoleate
    ( ) Shellac
    ( ) Silicates (magnesium, potassium, sodium)
    (2) Silicon dioxide
    (2) Sodium aluminum silicate
    (2) Starches
    (2) Stearates (magnesium, calcium, and aluminum)
    ( ) Stearates (potassium and sodium)
    (2) Stearic acid
    (2) Stearins

(2) Talc
(2) Tetrasodium diphosphate
(2) Tri-calcium phosphate
(2) Vegetable triglycerides
(2) Wax
(2) Wax coatings

MICRO-ORGANISM CONTROL AGENTS

(1) Chlorine dioxide :suggest change to category (2), Ref. 57
(3) Disodium cyanodithioamidocarbonate
( ) Disodium ethylene bis dithiocarbamate
( ) Dimethyldicarbonate
(3) Ethylenediamine
(1) Formaldehyde
(1) Hydrogen peroxide
(1) Hypochlorite
(1) Iodophors
(1) Lactoperoxide system (lactoperoxidase, glucose oxidase, thiocyanate
     salt) : suggest change to category (2), Ref.57
(3) N-alkyl (C12-C16) dimethyl benzylchloride
(2) Natamycin
(2) Nitric acid
(1) Peracetic acid
(3) Potassium N-methyldithiocarbamate
(3) Propylene oxide
(1) Quaternary ammonium compounds
(1) Salts of sulfurous acid : suggest change to category (2), Ref. 57
(3) Sodium chlorite
( ) Sodium dimethyldithiocarbamate
(2) Sulfur dioxide

PROPELLANT AND PACKAGING GASES

(1) Air
(1) Argon
(2) Carbon dioxide
(1) Chloropentafluoroethane
(1) Combustion product gas (to be specified)
(2) Dichlorodifluoromethane
(1) Helium
(1) Hydrogen
(1) Nitrous oxide
(1) Nitrogen
(1) Octafluorocyclobutane
(2) Oxygen
(1) Propane
(1) Trichlorofluoromethane

WASHING AND PEELING AGENTS

(1) A mixture of alklene oxide adducts of alkyl alcohols and phosphate
     esters of alkylene oxide adducts of alkyl alcohols consisting of
     alpha-alkyl (C12-C18) -omega -hydroxy -poly(oxyethylene) (7.5-8.5
     moles)/poly(oxypropylene) block copolymer having an average molecular
     weight of 810, alpha-alkyl (C12-C18) -omega-hydroxy-poly(oxyethylene)
     (3.3-3.7 moles) polymer having an average molecular weight of 380, and

subsequently esterified with 1.25 moles phosphoric anhydride; and
alpha-alkyl (C10-C12)-omega-hydroxy-poly(oxy- ethylene) (11.9-12.9
phosphoric anhydride; and alpha-alkyl (C10-C12) -omega-hydroxy-
poly(oxyethylene) (11.9-12.9 moles)/poly(oxypropylene) copolymer
having an average molecular weight of 810 and subsequently esterified
with 1.25 moles phosphoric anhydride.

- (1) Alkylene oxide adducts of alkyl alcohols and fatty acids (1) Aliphatic acid mixture consisting of valeric, caproic, enanthic, caprylic, and pelargonic acids.
- (1) Alpha-alkyl-omega-hydroxy-poly(oxyethylene)
- (2) Ammonium chloride
- ( ) Ammonium orthophosphate
- (2) Calcium chloride
- (2) Calcium hydroxide
- (2) Calcium oxide
- ( ) Carbamate
- (1) Dialkanolamine
- ( ) Diammonium orthophosphate
- ( ) Dithiocarbamate
- (1) Ethylene dichloride
- (1) Ethylene glycol monobutyl ether
- (1) Hydrogen peroxide
- (1) Linear undecylbenzenesulfonic acid
- (1) Monoethanolamine
- (1) Monoethanolamine, 8%
- (1) Nitrogen
- (2) Oleic acid
- ( ) Organophosphates
- (1) Polyacrylamide
- (1) Potassium bromide
- (2) Sodium carbonate
- (1) Sodium dodecylbenzene sulfonate (alkyl group predominantly C12 and not less than 95 percent C10-C16)
- (1) Sodium 2-ethylhexyl sulphate
- (2) Sodium hydroxide
- (2) Sodium hydroxide, 10%
- (2) Sodium hydroxide, 2%
- (1) Sodium hypochlorite
- (1) Sodium mono- and di-methyl naphthalene sulfonates (mol. wt. 245-260)
- (1) Sodium n-alkylbenzene-sulfonate (alkyl group predominately C12 and C13 and not less than 95 percent C10-C16)
- (2) Sodium tripolyphosphate
- (2) Sulfuric acid
- (1) Tetrapotassium pyrophosphate
- (1) Tetrasodium ethylenediaminetetraacetate
- (1) Triethanolamine

YEAST NUTRIENTS

- (3) Ammonium chloride
- (3) Ammonium sulphate
- (3) Ammonium phosphates
- (3) B-Complex vitamins
- (3) Biotin
- (3) Calcium carbonate
- (3) Calcium phosphates

(3) Calcium sulphate
(3) Cupric sulphate
(3) Ferrous ammonium sulphate
(3) Ferrous sulphate
(3) Inositol
(3) Magnesium sulfate
(3) Niacin
(3) Pantothenic acid
(3) Potassium carbonate
(3) Potassium chloride
(3) Potassium hydrogen carbonate
(3) Yeast autolysates
(3) Zinc sulphate

OTHER PROCESSING AIDS

(2) Acetic acid
( ) Acrylic resin with primarily tertiary amino groups
( ) Alkylene oxide adduct
(2) Allyl isothiocyanate
(1) Aluminum oxide   .
(1) Aluminum potassium sulfato
(2) Ammonium bicarbonate
(1) Ammonium nitrate
(2) Amyl acetate
(2) Benzyl alcohol
(2) BHA
(2) BHT
(2) Calcium carbonate
(2) Calcium chloride
(?) Calcium citrate
(2) Calcium hydroxide
( ) Calcium oxide
(2) Calcium phosphates
(2) Calcium sulfate
(1) Calcium tartrate
(2) Caramel flavoring
( ) Carbon dioxide
(2) Citric acid
(2) Coconut oil
(2) Disodium hydrogen phosphate
(1) Erythorbic acid : suggest change to category (2), Refs. 57, 58
(1) Ethyl para hydroxybenzoate
( ) Ethylene oxide-propylene oxide copolymers
(2) Fatty acids of soybean oil
( ) Fatty alcohol-glycol ether
(2) Fractionated soybean oil
(2) Fumaric acid
(1) Gibberellic acid
(1) Glycerol ester of adipic acid
(2) Glycerol tripropionate
(2) Glycine
(1) Hydrogen
(2) Hydrochloric acid
(2) Hydrogenated soybean oil
( ) Hydrophillic fatty acyl esters, linked to a neutral carrier
(2) Isopropyl alcohol

(2) Lactic acid
(2) Lactylated mono esters
(2) Magnesium chloride
(2) Magnesium citrate
( ) Magnesium oxide
(2) Magnesium sulfate
(2) Magnesium hydroxide
(2) Magnesium phosphates
(1) Magnesium tartrate
( ) α-Methyl glycoside water
( ) Methyl glycoside coconut oil ester
(2) Methyl paraben (Methyl parahydroxybenzoate)
(2) Mineral oil
( ) Mixture of ethylene and propylene oxides, copolymers and esters, castor oil
    and polyethylene glycol ester
( ) Mixture of naturally occurring and synthetic fatty acyl derivatives, with
    added emulgators
( ) Modified higher alcohol
( ) Mono- and diglycerides of fatty acids from feed fat (E471)
( ) Mono- and diglycerides of fatty acids from feed fat, esterified with acetic
    acid, lactic acid and citric acid
( ) Non-ionogenic alkylene oxide adduct with emulgator
(2) Oxalic acid
(2) Paraffin
(2) Phosphoric acid
( ) Polyalkylene oxide, in combination with special fatty alcohols
( ) Polyethoxylated alcohol, modified
( ) Polyacrylate
( ) Polyacrylate with carboxyl groups
( ) Polyethylene glycol
( ) Polyglycol copolymer
( ) Polyphosphate
( ) Polypropylene-polyethylene block polymer
(1) Polyvinyl polypyrrolidone
(2) Polyvinylpyrrolidone
(2) Potassium carbonate
(2) Potassium chloride
(2) Potassium citrate
(1) Potassium gibberellate
(2) Potassium nitrate
(2) Potassium phosphates
(2) Potassium sulfate
(2) Potassium tartrate
(2) Propyl gallate
(2) Propan-1-ol
(2) Propane-1,2-diol
(1) Propyl parahydroxybenzoate : suggest change to category (2), Ref. 58
(2) Shellac
(2) Sandarac gum
(1) Sodium
(2) Sodium chloride
(2) Sodium aluminosilicate
(2) Sodium bisulfite
(2) Sodium bicarbonate
(2) Sodium carbonate
(2) Sodium citrate
(2) Sodium hexametaphosphate

(2) Sodium hydroxide
(1) Sodium hypochlorite
(2) Sodium metabisulfite
(2) Sodium phosphate monobasic
(2) Sodium phosphate dibasic
(2) Sodium phosphate tribasic
( ) Sodium polyacrylate
( ) Sodium polyacrylate-acrylamide resin
(1) Sodium silicates
(2) Sodium sulfate
( ) Sodium sulfite
(2) Sodium tartrate
( ) Solution of: anhyd. polyphosphate, polycarboxylic acid salt, polyalkylene glycol, sodium hydroxide
( ) Sorbitan-fatty acyl esters and polyoxyethylene-20-sorbitan fatty acyl esters
(2) Soy lecithin
(2) Sulfuric acid
(2) Sulphur dioxide
( ) Sulphonated copolymer of styrene and divinylbenzene
( ) Surface-active esters with neutral carriers
( ) Tannic acid with quebracho extract
(2) Tartaric acid
(2) TBHQ
( ) Vegetable fatty acid esters
( ) Vegetable fatty acyl (hydrophillic)
(2) Xylose

APPENDIX B

Microbial Enzymes from the
Codex Inventory of Processing Aids
Arranged by Microorganism

(Actinoplanes missouriensis)   (1) Glucose isomerase

(Arthrobacter sp.)   (1) Glucose isomerase

(Aspergillus amaurii)   (1) Glucoamylase or amyloglucosidase

(Aspergillus awamora)   (1) Pectinase

(Aspergillus awamori)   (1) Glucoamylase or amyloglucosidase
                                         (1) Pectinase

(Aspergillus flavus)   (1) Lipase

(Aspergillus foetidus)   (1) Pectinase

(Aspergillus melleus)   (1) Protease

(Aspergillus niger)   (1) Alpha amylase
                                         (1) Alpha galactosidase
                                         (1) Arabino-furanosidease
                                         (1) Beta glucanase
                                         (1) Catalase
                                         (1) Cellobiase or betaglucosidase
                                         (1) Cellulase
                                         (1) Endo-beta glucanase
                                         (1) Esterase
                                         (1) Exo-alpha glucosidase
                                         (1) Glucoamylase or amyloglucosidase
                                         (1) Glucose oxidase
                                         (1) Hemicellulase
                                         (1) Inulinase
                                         (1) Invertase
                                         (1) Lactase
                                         (1) Lipase
                                         (1) Maltase or alphaglucosidase
                                         (1) Melibrase
                                         (1) Pectin esterase
                                         (1) Pectinlyase
                                         (1) Poly-galacturonase
                                         (1) Protease
                                         (1) Tannase
                                         (1) Xylanase
                                         (1) Alpha amylase
                                         (1) Cellulase
                                         (1) Endo-beta glucanase
                                         (1) Glucoamylase or amyloglucosidase
                                         (1) Hemicellulase
                                         (1) Lactase
                                         (1) Lipase

	(1) Maltase or alphaglucosidase
	(1) Pectinase
	(1) Protease
	(1) Tannase
(Aspergillus species)	(1) Dextranase
(Bacillus acidopullulyticus)	(1) Pullulanase
(Bacillus cereus)	(1) Beta amylase
	(1) Isoamylase
	(1) Protease
(Bacillus circulans)	(1) Endo-beta glucanase
(Bacillus coagulans)	(1) Glucose isomerase
(Bacillus licheniformis)	(1) Protease
	(1) Alpha amylase
	(1) Serine proteinase
(Bacillus megaterium)	(1) Beta amylase
(Bacillus stearothermophilus)	(1) Alpha amylase
(Bacillus subtilis)	(1) Alpha amylase
	(1) Beta amylase
	(1) Beta glucanase
	(1) Dextranase
	(1) Endo-beta glucanase
	(1) Hemicellulase
	(1) Invertase
	(1) Protease
	(1) Pullulanase
(Brevibacterium lineus)	(1) Lipase
	(1) Protease
(Candida lipolytica)	(1) Lipase
(Disporotrichum dimorphosphorum)	(1) Beta-glucanase
(Endothia parasitica)	(1) Protease
(Klebsiella aerogenes)	(1) Dextranase
	(1) Pullulanase
(Kluyveromyces fragilis)	(1) Inulinase
	(1) Invertase
	(1) Lactase
(Kluyveromyces lactis)	(1) Lactase
(Lactobacillus casei)	(1) Proetase
(Leuconostoc oenos)	(1) Malic and decarboxylase
(Micrococcus caseolyticus)	(1) Protease

(Micrococcus lysodeicticus)	(1) Catalase
(Mortierella vinacea sp.)	(1) Alpha galactosidase
	(1) Melibrase
(Mucor javanicus)	(1) Lipase
(Mucor miehei)	(1) Esterase
	(1) Lipase
	(1) Protease
(Mucor pusillus)	(1) Lipase
	(1) Protease
(Penicillium emersonii)	(1) Endo-beta glucanase
(Penicillium funiculosum)	(1) Dextranase
(Penicillium lilacinum)	(1) Dextranase
(Penicillium simplicissium)	(1) Pectinase
(Rhizopus arrhizus)	(1) Alpha amylase
	(1) Cellulase
	(1) Endo-beta glucanase
	(1) Glucoamylase or amyloglucosidase
	(1) Hemicellulase
	(1) Lipase
(Rhizopus nigrican)	(1) Lipase
(Rhizopus niveus)	(1) Glucoamylase or amyloglucosidase
	(1) Lipase
(Rhizopus oryzae)	(1) Cellulase
	(1) Endo-beta glucanase
	(1) Glucoamylase or amyloglucosidase
	(1) Hemicellulase
	(1) Maltase or alphaglucosidase
	(1) Pectinase
(Saccharomyces carlsbergensis)	(1) Alpha galactosidase
	(1) Invertase
	(1) Melibrase
(Saccharomyces cerevisiae)	(1) Alcohol dehydrogenase
	(1) Invertase
(Saccharomyces sp.)	(1) Invertase
	(1) Lactase
(Sporotrichum dimorphosporum)	(1) Cellulase
	(1) Hemicellulase
	(1) Inulinase
	(1) Xylanase

(Streptococcus cremoris)	(1)	Protease
(Streptococcus lactis)	(1)	Protease
(Streptomyces albus)	(1)	Glucose isomerase
(Streptomyces olivaceus)	(1)	Glucose isomerase
(Streptomyces olivochromogenes)	(1)	Glucose isomerase
(Streptomyces rubiginosus)	(1)	Glucose isomerase
(Streptomyces violaceoniger)	(1)	Glucose isomerase
(Streptomyces fradiae)	(1)	Serine proteinase
(Streptomyces sp.)	(1)	Glucose isomerase
	(1)	Inulinase
	(1)	Xylanase
(Trichoderma harzianum)	(1)	Beta glucanase
	(1)	Beta glucosidase
(Trichoderma reesei)	(1)	Cellobiase or betaglucosidase
	(1)	Cellulase
	(1)	Endo-beta glucanase
	(1)	Esterase
	(1)	Glucoamylase or amyloglucosidase
	(1)	Hemicellulase
	(1)	Maltase or alphaglucosidase
	(1)	Pectinase
	(1)	Xylanase
	(1)	Beta-xylosidase
(Thielavia terrestris)	(1)	Cellulase

SECTION 6

CONTAMINANTS

INTRODUCTION

Individual Codex Standards list maximum limits for contaminants and should be consulted directly. This section contains only those additional recommendations in relation to contaminants, made by the Codex Alimentarius Commission independently of limits specified in individual standards.

SECTION 6.1

GUIDELINE LEVELS FOR RADIONUCLIDES IN FOODS FOLLOWING ACCIDENTAL NUCLEAR CONTAMINATION FOR USE IN INTERNATIONAL TRADE

CAC/GL 5-1989

INTRODUCTION

The Codex Alimentarius Commission at its 18th Session (Geneva 1989) adopted Guideline Levels for Radionuclides in Foods Following Accidental Nuclear Contamination.   The Guideline Levels which are in this publication remain applicable for one year following a nuclear accident.

The Commission also adopted, as an interim measure, the following definition of Guideline Level:

"Guideline Levels are intended for use in regulating foods moving in international trade.   When the Guideline Levels are exceeded, governments should decide whether and under what circumstances, the food should be distributed within their territory or jurisdiction."

**GUIDELINE LEVELS FOR RADIONUCLIDES IN FOODS
FOLLOWING ACCIDENTAL NUCLEAR CONTAMINATION
FOR USE IN INTERNATIONAL TRADE**

CAC/GL 5-1989

FOODS DESTINED FOR GENERAL CONSUMPTION

DOSE PER UNIT INTAKE FACTOR (Sv/Bq)	REPRESENTATIVE RADIONUCLIDES	LEVEL (Bq/Kg)
10^{-6}	^{241}Am, ^{239}Pu	10
10^{-7}	^{90}Sr	100
10^{-8}	^{131}I, ^{134}Cs, ^{137}Cs	1000

MILK AND INFANT FOODS

DOSE PER UNIT INTAKE FACTOR (Sv/Bq)	REPRESENTATIVE RADIONUCLIDES	LEVEL (Bq/kg)
10^{-5}	^{241}Am, ^{239}Pu	1
10^{-7}	^{131}I, ^{90}Sr	100
10^{-8}	^{134}Cs, ^{137}Cs	1000

NOTES:

These levels are designed to be applied only to radionuclides contaminating food moving in international trade following an accident and not to naturally occurring radionuclides which have always been present in the diet. The Guideline Levels remain applicable for one year following a nuclear accident. By an accident is meant a situation where the uncontrolled release of radionuclides to the environment results in the contamination of food offered in international trade.

As the proposed levels have extensive conservative assumptions built-in, there is no need to add contributions between dose per unit intake groups, and each of the three groups should be treated independently. However, the activity of the accidentally contaminating radionuclides within a dose per unit intake group should be added together if more than one radionuclide is present. Thus the 1000 Bq/kg level for the 10^{-8} Sv/Bq dose per unit intake group is the total of all contaminants assigned to that group. For example, following a power reactor accident, ^{134}Cs and ^{137}Cs could be contaminants of food, and the 1000 Bq/kg refers to the summed activity of both these radionuclides.

These levels are intended to be applied to food prepared for consumption. They would be unnecessarily restrictive if applied to dried or concentrated foods prior to dilution or reconstitution.

Both FAO and WHO have called attention in the expert meeting reports to special consideration which might apply to certain classes of food which are consumed in small quantities, such as spices. Some of the foods grown in the areas affected by the Chernobyl accident fall-out contained very high levels of radionuclides following the accident. Because they represent a very small percentage of total diets and hence would be very small additions to the total dose, application of the Guideline Levels to products of this type may be unnecessarily restrictive. FAO and WHO are aware that policies vary at present in different countries regarding such classes of food.

APPENDIX

Derivation of the Codex Guidelines in Foods
Following Accidental Nuclear Contamination

The approach taken by WHO and FAO in recommending the Guideline Levels to the Codex Alimentarius Commission assumes a reference level of dose (5 mSv), a total average food consumption rate, a dose per unit intake factor for various radionuclides and a pattern of food consumption, and calculates the levels by the following formula:

$$Level = \frac{RLD}{m \times d}$$

where RLD = Reference Level of Dose (Sv)
        m = mass of food consumed (kg)
        d = dose per unit intake factor (Sv/Bq)

Controlling radionuclide contamination of foods moving in international trade requires simple, uniform and easily applied values. This approach is one that can be uniformly applied by government authorities and yet one that achieves a level of public health protection to individuals that is considered more than adequate in the event of a nuclear accident.

In making these joint FAO/WHO recommendations the following assumptions were made in calculating the levels:

1.   5 mSv was adopted as the reference level of dose for an accident. This value, for most radionuclides, is the committed effective dose equivalent resulting from ingestion in the first year after an accident. Owing to the extremely conservative assumptions adopted, it is most unlikely that the application of the following levels will result in a dose to an individual greater than a small fraction of 1 mSv.

2.   550 kg of food is consumed in a year, all of which is contaminated.

3.   Dose per unit intake factors for the radionuclides of concern (^{131}I, ^{137}Cs, ^{134}Cs ^{90}Sr, ^{239}Pu) can be conveniently divided into three classes and applied to the general population:

   (a)   those with a dose per unit intake of 10^{-6} Sv/Bq such as ^{239}Pu and other actinides;

   (b)   those with a dose per unit intake factor of 10^{-7} Sv/Bq such as ^{90}Sr and other beta emitters;   and

   (c)   those with a dose per unit intake factor of 10^{-8} Sv/Bq such as ^{134}Cs, ^{137}Cs, ^{131}I.

For infant foods and milk a dose per unit intake factor of 10^{-5} Sv/Bq was used instead of the 10^{-6} Sv/Bq value and ^{131}I was assigned to the 10^{-7} Sv/Bq class of radionuclides.

Applying these assumptions to the above formula, the level for the general population for the radionuclides in the 10^{-8} Sv/Bq group is:

$$\frac{5 \times 10^{-3}}{550 \times 10^{-8}} = 909 \ Bq/kg$$

which can then be rounded 1000 Bq/kg. For the actinides this value of 10 Bq/kg, as the dose per unit intake factor is 100 times larger, and for the radionuclides in the 10^{-7} Sv/Bq class (such as ^{90}Sr), it is 100 Bq/kg.

It is recognized that the sensitivity of infants may pose a problem if the dose conversion factor for the general population were applied to them indiscriminately. WHO, in its document Derived Intervention Levels for Radionuclides in Food,[1] proposed separate guidelines for infants. The values were based on an infant consumption of milk of 275 L/y and the specific dose conversion factors for infants for ^{90}Sr, ^{131}I, ^{137}Cs.

The resulting WHO Guideline values were:

^{90}Sr	160 Bq/L
^{131}I*	1600 Bq/L
^{137}Cs	1800 Bq/L

* The value for ^{131}I was based on a dose of 50 mSv to the thyroid and a mean life of ingested ^{131}I of 11.5 days.

However, the dose per unit intake factors for infants ingesting alpha-emitting actinides have recently been revised upward and as a prudent measure, a dose per unit intake factor of 10^{-5} Sv/Bq for these radionuclides was applied to infants consuming milk and infant foods.

To reflect the infants's sensitivity, ^{131}I was assigned a dose per unit intake factor of 10^{-7} Sv/Bq, putting it in the same class as ^{90}Sr.

For infant foods and milk the application of these dose per unit intake factors result in a level of 1 Bq/kg for the alpha emitters of the actinide series and any other radionuclide with a dose unit intake factor of 10^{-5} Sv/Bq, and 100 Bq/kg for ^{90}Sr and ^{131}I or any other radionuclides assigned a dose per unit intake of 10^{-7} Sv/Bq.

By infant foods is meant a food prepared specifically for consumption by infants in the first year of life. Such foods are packaged and identified as being for this purpose.

---

[1] DERIVED INTERVENTION LEVELS FOR RADIONUCLIDES IN FOOD. Guidelines for application after widespread radioactive contamination resulting from a major radiation accident. WHO, Geneva, 1988.

SECTION 6.2

GUIDELINE LEVELS FOR METHYLMERCURY IN FISH
CAC/GL 7-1991

Codex Guideline Levels for Methylmercury in Fish were adopted by the Commission at its Nineteenth Session (1991), on the understanding that the levels would be kept under review by the Codex Committee on Food Additives and Contaminants as well as the Codex Committee on Fish and Fishery Products, especially as to the identification of predatory species of fish to which the higher guideline level applies.

Methylmercury	Guideline level
All fish except predatory fish	0.5 mg/kg
Predatory fish (such as shark, swordfish, tuna, pike and others)	1 mg/kg

Note:

The Guideline levels are intended for methylmercury in fresh or processed fish and fish products moving in international trade. Lots should be considered as being in compliance with the proposed guideline levels if the level of methylmercury in the analytical sample, derived from the composite bulk sample, does not exceed the above proposed levels. Where these Guideline levels are exceeded, governments should decide whether and under what circumstances, the food should be distributed within their territory of jurisdiction and what recommendations, if any, should be given as regards restrictions on consumption, especially by vulnerable groups such as pregnant women.

SECTION 6.3

GUIDELINE LEVELS FOR
VINYL CHLORIDE MONOMER AND ACRYLONITRILE
IN FOOD AND PACKAGING MATERIAL
CAC/GL 6-1991

Guideline Levels for Vinyl Chloride Monomer and Acrylonitrile in Food and
Packaging Material were adopted by the Commission at its Nineteenth Session (1991)
on the understanding that the Association of Official Analytical Chemists (AOAC)
and the International Organization for Standardization (ISO) would develop
appropriate sampling plans and methods of analysis.

Vinyl chloride monomer   <u>Guideline level</u>

    Guideline level in food   0.01 mg/kg
    Guideline level in food packaging material   1.0 mg/kg

Acrylonitrile

    Guideline level in food   0.02 mg/kg

SECTION 7

RECOMMENDED INTERNATIONAL CODE OF PRACTICE
GENERAL PRINCIPLES OF FOOD HYGIENE

CAC/RCP 1-1969, Rev. 2 (1985)

INTRODUCTION

The Recommended International Code of Practice on General Principles of Food Hygiene was adopted by the Codex Alimentarius Commission at its 6th Session, 1969 and subsequently revised in 1979 by the 13th Session and in 1985 by the 16th Session. It has been sent to all Member Nations and Associate Members of FAO and WHO as an advisory text, and it is for individual governments to decide what use they wish to make of the Code. The Commission has expressed the view that codes of practice might provide useful checklists of requirements for national food control or enforcement authorities.

RECOMMENDED INTERNATIONAL CODE OF PRACTICE
GENERAL PRINCIPLES OF FOOD HYGIENE
CAC/RCP 1-1969, Rev. 2 (1985)

SECTION I - SCOPE

1.1   This Code recommends general hygienic practices for use in the handling (including growing and harvesting, preparation, processing, packaging, storage, transport, distribution and sale) of food for human consumption in order to ensure a safe, sound and wholesome product.

1.2   It is further intended to provide a basis for establishing codes of hygienic practice for individual commodities or groups of commodities which have specific requirements relating to food hygiene.

SECTION II - DEFINITION

2.   For the purposes of this Code the following expressions have the meaning stated:

2.1   Adequate - sufficient to accomplish the intended purpose of this code.

2.2   Cleaning - the removal of soil, food residues, dirt, grease or other objectionable matter.

2.3   Contamination - the occurrence of any objectionable matter in the product.

2.4   Disinfection - the reduction, without adversely affecting the food, by means of hygienically satisfactory chemical agents and/or physical methods, of the number of micro-organisms to a level that will not lead to harmful contamination of food.

2.5   Establishment - any building(s) or area(s) in which food is handled after harvesting and the surroundings under the control of the same management.

2.6   Food Handling - any operation in the growing and harvesting, preparation, processing, packaging, storage, transport, distribution and sale of food.

2.7   Food Hygiene - all measures necessary to ensure the safety, soundness and wholesomeness of food at all stages from its growth, production or manufacture until its final consumption.

2.8   Packaging Material - any containers such as cans, bottles, cartons, boxes, cases and sacks, or wrapping and covering material such as foil, film, metal, paper, wax-paper and cloth.

2.9   Pests - any animals capable of directly or indirectly contaminating food.

SECTION III - HYGIENE REQUIREMENTS IN PRODUCTION/HARVESTING AREA

3.1   Environmental Hygiene in Areas from which Raw Materials are Derived

3.1.1   Unsuitable growing or harvesting areas

Food should not be grown or harvested where the presence of potentially harmful substances would lead to an unacceptable level of such substances in the food.

3.1.2 Protection from contamination by wastes

3.1.2.1   Raw food materials should be protected from contamination by human, animal, domestic, industrial and agricultural wastes which may be present at levels likely to be a hazard to health. Adequate precautions should be taken to ensure that these wastes are not used and are not disposed of in a manner which may constitute a hazard to health through the food.

3.1.2.2   Arrangements for the disposal of domestic and industrial wastes in areas from which raw materials are derived should be acceptable to the official agency having jurisdiction.

3.1.3 Irrigation control

Food should not be grown or produced in areas where the water used for irrigation might constitute a hazard to health to the consumer through the food.

3.1.4 Pest and disease control

Control measures involving treatment with chemical, physical or biological agents should only be undertaken under direct supervision of personnel who have a thorough understanding of the potential hazards to health. Such measures should only be carried out in accordance with the recommendations of the official agency having jurisdiction.

3.2 Harvesting and Production

3.2.1 Techniques

Methods and procedures associated with harvesting and production should be hygienic and such as not to constitute a potential hazard to health or result in contamination of the product.

3.2.2 Equipment and containers

Equipment and containers used for harvesting and production should be so constructed and maintained as not to constitute a hazard to health. Containers which are re-used should be of such material and construction as will permit easy and thorough cleaning. They should be cleaned and maintained clean and, where necessary, disinfected. Containers previously used for toxic materials should not subsequently be used for holding foods or food ingredients.

3.2.3 Removal of obviously unfit raw materials

Raw materials which are obviously unfit for human consumption should be segregated during harvesting and production. Those which cannot be made fit by further processing should be disposed of in such a place and in such a manner as to avoid contamination of the food and/or water supplies or other food materials.

3.2.4   Protection against contamination and damage

Suitable precautions should be taken to protect the raw materials from being contaminated by pests or by chemical, physical or microbiological contaminants or other objectionable substances. Precautions should be taken to avoid damage.

3.3   Storage at the Place of Production/Harvesting

Raw materials should be stored under conditions which provide protection against contamination and minimize damage and deterioration.

3.4   Transportation

3.4.1   Conveyances

Conveyances for transporting the harvested crop or raw materials from the production area or place of harvest or storage should be adequate for the purpose intended and should be of such material and construction as will permit easy and thorough cleaning. They should be cleaned and maintained clean, and where necessary disinfected and disinfested.

3.4.2   Handling Procedures

All handling procedures should be such as will prevent raw materials from being contaminated. Care should be taken to prevent spoilage, to protect against contamination and to minimize damage. Special equipment - such as refrigeration equipment - should be used if the nature of the product or distances involved so indicate. If ice is used in contact with the product it should be of the quality required in Section 4.4.1.2 of this Code.

SECTION IV - ESTABLISHMENT: DESIGN AND FACILITIES

4.1   Location

Establishments should preferably be located in areas which are free from objectionable odours, smoke, dust or other contaminants and are not subject to flooding.

4.2   Roadways and Areas used by Wheeled Traffic

Such roadways and areas serving the establishment which are within its boundaries or in its immediate vicinity should have a hard paved surface suitable for wheeled traffic. There should be adequate drainage and provision should be made to allow for cleaning.

4.3   Buildings and Facilities

4.3.1   Buildings and facilities should be of sound construction and maintained in good repair. All construction material should be such that they do not transmit any undesirable substances to the food. All construction materials should be such, that when construction is completed, they do not emit toxic vapours.

4.3.2   Adequate working space should be provided to allow for satisfactory performance of all operations.

4.3.3   The design should be such as to permit easy and adequate cleaning and to facilitate proper supervision of food hygiene.

4.3.4   The buildings and facilities should be designed to prevent the entrance and harbouring of pests and the entry of environmental contaminants such as smoke, dust, etc.

4.3.5   Buildings and facilities should be designed to provide separation, by partition, location or other effective means, between those operations which may cause cross-contamination.

4.3.6   Buildings and facilities should be designed to facilitate hygienic operations by means of a regulated flow in the process from the arrival of the raw material at the premises to the finished product, and should provide for appropriate temperature conditions for the process and the product.

4.3.7   In food handling areas:

-   Floors - where appropriate, should be of water-proof, non-absorbent, washable, and non-slip materials, without crevices, and should be easy to clean and disinfect. Where appropriate, floors should slope sufficiently for liquids to drain to trapped outlets.

-   Walls - where appropriate, should be of water-proof, non-absorbent and washable materials sealed and free of insects and should be light-coloured. Up to a height appropriate for the operation, they should be smooth and without crevices, and should be easy to clean and disinfect. Where appropriate angles between walls, between walls and floors, and between walls and ceilings should be sealed and coved to facilitate cleaning.

-   Ceilings should be so designed, constructed and finished as to prevent the accumulation of dirt and minimize condensation, mould development and flaking and should be easy to clean.

-   Windows and other openings should be so constructed as to avoid accumulation of dirt and those which open should be fitted with insect-proof screens. Screens should be easily movable for cleaning and kept in good repair. Internal window sills, if present, should be sloped to prevent use as shelves.

-   Doors should have smooth, non-absorbent surfaces and, where appropriate, be self-closing and close fitting.

-   Stairs, lift cages and auxiliary structures such as platforms, ladders, chutes, should be so situated and constructed as not to cause contamination to food. Chutes should be constructed with inspection and cleaning hatches.

4.3.8   In food handling areas all overhead structures and fittings should be installed in such a manner as to avoid contamination directly or indirectly of food and raw materials by condensation and drip, and should not hamper cleaning operations. They should be insulated where appropriate and be so designed and finished as to prevent the accumulation of dirt and minimize condensation, mould development and flaking. They should be easy to clean.

4.3.9   Living quarters, toilets and areas where animals are kept should be completely separated from and should not open directly on to food handling areas.

4.3.10   Where appropriate, establishments should be so designed that access can be controlled.

4.3.11   The use of material which cannot be adequately cleaned and disinfected, such as wood, should be avoided unless its use would clearly not be a source of contamination.

4.3.12   Water supply

4.3.12.1   An ample supply of water, in compliance with section 7.3 of this Code, under adequate pressure and of suitable temperature should be available with adequate facilities for its storage, where necessary, and distribution, and with adequate protection against contamination.

4.3.12.2   Ice should be made from water, in compliance with section 7.3 of this Code, and should be manufactured, handled and stored so as to protect it from contamination.

4.3.12.3   Steam used in direct contact with food or food contact surfaces should contain no substances which may be hazardous to health or may contaminate the food.

4.3.12.4   Non-potable water used for steam production, refrigeration, fire control and other similar purposes not connected with food should be carried in completely separate lines, identifiable preferably by colour, and with no cross-connection with or back-siphonage into the system carrying potable water (see also section 7.3.2).

4.3.13   Effluent and waste disposal

          Establishments should have an efficient effluent and waste disposal system which should at all times be maintained in good order and repair. All effluent lines (including sewer systems) should be large enough to carry peak loads and should be so constructed as to avoid contamination of potable water supplies.

4.3.14   Changing facilities and toilets

          Adequate, suitable and conveniently located changing facilities and toilets should be provided in all establishments. Toilets should be so designed as to ensure hygienic removal of waste matter. These areas should be well lit, ventilated and where appropriate heated and should not open directly on to food handling areas. Hand washing facilities with warm or hot and cold water, a suitable hand-cleaning preparation and with suitable hygienic means of drying hands, should be provided adjacent to toilets and in such a position that the employee must pass them when returning to the processing area. Where hot and cold water are available mixing taps should be provided. Where paper towels are used, a sufficient number of dispensers and receptacles should be provided near to each washing facility. Taps of a non-hand operable type are desirable. Notices should be posted directing personnel to wash their hands after using the toilet.

4.3.15   Hand washing facilities in processing areas

          Adequate and conveniently located facilities for hand washing and drying should be provided wherever the process demands. Where appropriate, facilities for hand disinfection should also be provided. Warm or hot and cold water and a suitable hand cleaning preparation should be provided. Where hot and cold water are available mixing taps should be provided. There should be suitable hygienic means of drying hands. Where paper towels are used, a sufficient number of dispensers and receptacles should be provided adjacent to each washing facility.

Taps of a non-hand operable type are desirable. The facilities should be furnished with properly trapped waste pipes leading to drains.

4.3.16   Disinfection facilities

Where appropriate adequate facilities for cleaning and disinfection of working implements and equipment should be provided. These facilities should be constructed of corrosion resistant materials, capable of being easily cleaned, and should be fitted with suitable means of supplying hot and cold water in sufficient quantities.

4.3.17   Lighting

Adequate natural or artificial lighting should be provided throughout the establishment. Where appropriate, the lighting should not alter colours and the intensity should not be less than:

540 lux (50 foot candles) at all inspection points
220 lux (20 foot candles) in work rooms
110 lux (10 foot candles) in other areas.

Light bulbs and fixtures suspended over food materials in any stage of production should be of a safety type and protected to prevent contamination of food in case of breakage.

4.3.18   Ventilation

Adequate ventilation should be provided to prevent excessive build up of heat, steam condensation and dust and to remove contaminated air. The direction of the air flow within the plant should never be from a dirty area to a clean area. Ventilation openings should be provided with a screen or other protecting enclosure of non-corrodible material. Screens should be easily removable for cleaning.

4.3.19   Facilities for storage of waste and inedible material

Facilities should be provided for the storage of waste and inedible material prior to removal from the establishment. These facilities should be designed to prevent access to waste or inedible material by pests and to avoid contamination of food, potable water, equipment, buildings or roadways on the premises.

4.4   Equipment and Utensils

4.4.1   Materials

All equipment and utensils used in food handling areas and which may contact food should be made of materials which does not transmit toxic substances, odour or taste, is non-absorbent, is resistant to corrosion and is capable of withstanding repeated cleaning and disinfection. Surfaces should be smooth and free from pits and crevices. The use of wood and other materials which cannot be adequately cleaned and disinfected should be avoided except when their use would clearly not be a source of contamination. The use of different materials in such a way that contact corrosion can occur should be avoided.

4.4.2   Sanitary design, construction and installation

4.4.2.1   <u>All equipment and utensils</u> should be so designed and constructed as to prevent hygienic hazards and permit easy and thorough cleaning and disinfection and, where practicable, be visible for inspection. Stationery equipment should be installed in such a manner as to permit easy access and thorough cleaning.

4.4.2.2   <u>Containers for inedible materials and waste</u> should be leak-proof, constructed of metal or other suitable impervious material which should be easy to clean or disposable and able to be closed securely.

4.4.2.3   <u>All refrigerated spaces</u> should be equipped with temperature measurement or recording devices.

4.4.3   Equipment identification

          Equipment and utensils used for inedible materials or waste should be so identified and should not be used for edible products.

SECTION V - ESTABLISHMENT: HYGIENE REQUIREMENTS

5.1   <u>Maintenance</u>

          The buildings, equipment, utensils and all other physical facilities of the establishment, including drains, should be maintained in good repair and in an orderly condition. As far as practicable, rooms should be kept free from steam, vapour and surplus water.

5.2   <u>Cleaning and Disinfection</u>

5.2.1   Cleaning and disinfection should meet the requirements of this Code. For further information on cleaning and disinfection procedures see Appendix I of this Code.

5.2.2   To prevent contamination of food, all equipment and utensils should be cleaned as frequently as necessary and disinfected whenever circumstances demand.

5.2.3   Adequate precautions should be taken to prevent food from being contaminated during cleaning or disinfection of rooms, equipment or utensils by water and detergents or by disinfectants and their solutions. Detergents and disinfectants should be suitable for the purpose intended and should be acceptable to the official agency having jurisdiction. Any residues of these agents on a surface which may come in contact with food should be removed by thorough rinsing with water, in compliance with section 7.3 of this Code, before the area or equipment is again used for handling food.

5.2.4   Either immediately after cessation of work for the day or at such other times as may be appropriate, floors, including drains, auxiliary structures and walls of food handling areas should be thoroughly cleaned.

5.2.5   Changing facilities and toilets should be kept clean at all times.

5.2.6   Roadways and yards in the immediate vicinity of and serving the premises should be kept clean.

5.3   Hygiene Control Programme

A permanent cleaning and disinfection schedule should be drawn up for each establishment to ensure that all areas are appropriately cleaned and that critical areas, equipment and material are designated for special attention. A single individual who should preferably be a permanent member of the staff of the establishment and whose duties should be independent of production, should be appointed to be responsible for the cleanliness of the establishment. He should have a thorough understanding of the significance of contamination and the hazards involved. All cleaning personnel should be well-trained in cleaning techniques.

5.4   By-Products

By-products should be stored in such a manner as to avoid contamination of food. They should be removed from the working areas as often as necessary and at least daily.

5.5   Storage and Disposal of Waste

Waste material should be handled in such a manner as to avoid contamination of food or potable water. Care should be taken to prevent access to waste by pests. Waste should be removed from the food handling and other working areas as often as necessary and at least daily. Immediately after disposal of the waste, receptacles used for storage and any equipment which has come into contact with the waste should be cleaned and disinfected. The waste storage area should also be cleaned and disinfected.

5.6   Exclusion of Domestic Animals

Animals that are uncontrolled or that could be a hazard to health should be excluded from establishments.

5.7   Pest Control

5.7.1   There should be an effective and continuous programme for the control of pests. Establishments and surrounding areas should be regularly examined for evidence of infestation.

5.7.2   Should pests gain entrance to the establishment eradication measures should be instituted. Control measures involving treatment with chemical, physical or biological agents should only be undertaken by or under direct supervision of personnel who have a thorough understanding of the potential hazards which may arise from residues retained in the product. Such measures should only be carried out in accordance with the recommendations of the official agency having jurisdiction.

5.8   Storage of Hazardous Substances

5.8.1   Pesticide or other substances which may represent a hazard to health should be suitably labelled with a warning about their toxicity and use. They should be stored in locked rooms or cabinets used only for that purpose and handled only by authorized and properly trained persons or by persons under strict supervision of trained personnel. Extreme care should be taken to avoid contaminating foods.

5.8.2   Except when necessary for hygienic or processing purposes, no substance which could contaminate food should be used or stored in food handling areas.

5.9   Personal Effects and Clothing

Personal effects and clothing should not be deposited in food handling areas.

SECTION VI - PERSONNEL HYGIENE AND HEALTH REQUIREMENTS

6.1   Hygiene Training

Managers of establishments should arrange for adequate and continuing training of all food handlers in hygienic handling of food and in personal hygiene so that they understand the precautions necessary to prevent contamination of food. Instruction should include relevant parts of this Code.

6.2   Medical Examination

Persons who come in contact with food in the course of their work should have a medical examination prior to their employment if the official agency having jurisdiction, acting on medical advice, considers that this is necessary, whether because of epidemiological considerations, the nature of the food prepared in a particular establishment or the medical history of the prospective food handler. Medical examination of a food handler should be carried out at other times when clinically or epidemiologically indicated.

6.3   Communicable Diseases

The management should take care to ensure that no person, while known or suspected to be suffering from, or to be a carrier of a disease likely to be transmitted through food or while afflicted with infected wounds, skin infections, sores or with diarrhoea, is permitted to work in any food handling area in any capacity in which there is any likelihood of such a person directly or indirectly contaminating food with pathogenic micro-organisms. Any person so affected should immediately report to the management that he is ill.

6.4   Injuries

Any person who has a cut or wound should not continue to handle food or food contact surfaces until the injury is completely protected by a water proof covering which is firmly secured, and which is conspicuous in colour. Adequate first-aid facilities should be provided for this purpose.

6.5   Washing of Hands

Any person, while on duty in a food handling area, should wash his hands frequently and thoroughly with a suitable hand cleaning preparation under running warm water in compliance with section 7.3 of this Code. Hands should always be washed before commencing work, immediately after using the toilet, after handling contaminated material and whenever else necessary. After handling any material which might be capable of transmitting disease, hands should be washed and disinfected immediately. Notices requiring hand- washing should be displayed. There should be adequate supervision to ensure compliance with this requirement.

6.6   Personal Cleanliness

Every person engaged in a food handling area should maintain a high degree of personal cleanliness while on duty, and should at all times while so engaged wear suitable protective clothing including head covering and footwear, all of which articles should be cleanable unless designed to be disposed of and should be maintained in a clean condition consistent with the nature of the work in which the person is engaged. Aprons and similar items should not be washed on the floor. During periods where food is manipulated by hand, any jewellery that cannot be adequately disinfected should be removed from the hands. Personnel should not wear any insecure jewellery when engaged in food handling.

6.7   Personal Behaviour

Any behaviour which could result in contamination of food, such as eating, use of tobacco, chewing (e.g. gum, sticks, betel nuts, etc.) or unhygienic practices, such as spitting, should be prohibited in food handling areas.

6.8   Gloves

Gloves, if used in the handling of food products, should be maintained in a sound, clean and sanitary condition. The wearing of gloves does not exempt the operator from having thoroughly washed hands.

6.9   Visitors

Precautions should be taken to prevent visitors to food handling areas from contaminating food. These may include the use of protective clothing. Visitors should observe the provisions recommended in sections 5.9, 6.3, 6.4 and 6.7 of this Code.

6.10   Supervision

Responsibility for ensuring compliance by all personnel with all requirements of sections 6.1 to 6.9, inclusive should be specifically allocated to competent supervisory personnel.

SECTION VII - ESTABLISHMENT: HYGIENIC PROCESSING REQUIREMENTS

7.1   Raw Material Requirements

7.1.1   No raw material or ingredient should be accepted by the establishment if known to contain parasites, micro-organisms or toxic, decomposed or extraneous substances which will not be reduced to acceptable levels by normal plant procedures of sorting and/or preparation or processing.

7.1.2   Raw materials or ingredients should be inspected and sorted prior to being moved into the processing line and where necessary laboratory tests should be made. Only clean sound raw materials or ingredients should be used in further processing.

7.1.3   Raw materials and ingredients stored on the premises of the establishment should be maintained under conditions that will prevent spoilage, protect against contamination and minimize damage. Stocks of raw materials and ingredients should be properly rotated.

7.2   Prevention of Cross-Contamination

7.2.1   Effective measures should be taken to prevent contamination of food material by direct or indirect contact with material at an earlier stage of the process.

7.2.2   Persons handling raw materials or semi-processed products capable of contaminating the end-product should not come into contact with any end- product unless and until they discard all protective clothing worn by them during the handling of raw material or semi-processed products which have come into direct contact with or have been soiled by raw material or semi-processed products and they have changed into clean protective clothing.

7.2.3   If there is a likelihood of contamination, hands should be washed thoroughly between handling product at different stages of processing.

7.2.4   All equipment which has been in contact with raw materials or contaminated material should be thoroughly cleaned and disinfected prior to being used for contact with end-products.

7.3   Use of Water

7.3.1   As a general principle only potable water, as defined in the latest edition of "International Standards of Drinking Water" (WHO), should be used in food handling.

7.3.2   Non-potable water may be used with the acceptance of the official agency having jurisdiction for steam production, refrigeration, fire control and other similar purposes not connected with food. However, non-potable water may, with specific acceptance by the official agency having jurisdiction, be used in certain food handling areas provided this does not constitute a hazard to health.

7.3.3   Water re-circulated for re-use within an establishment should be treated and maintained in a condition so that no health hazard can result from its use. The treatment process should be kept under constant surveillance. Alternatively, re-circulated water which has received no further treatment may be used in conditions where its use would not constitute a health hazard and will not contaminate either the raw material or the end-product. Re-circulated water should have a separate distribution system which can be readily identified. The acceptance of the official agency having jurisdiction should be required for any treatment process and for the use of re-circulated water in any food process.

7.4   Processing

7.4.1   Processing should be supervised by technically competent personnel.

7.4.2   All steps in the production process, including packaging, should be performed without unnecessary delay and under conditions which will prevent the possibility of contamination, deterioration, or the development of pathogenic and spoilage microorganisms.

7.4.3   Rough treatment of containers should be avoided to prevent the possibility of contamination of the processed product.

7.4.4   Methods of preservation and necessary controls should be such as to protect against contamination or development of a public health hazard and against deterioration within the limits of good commercial practice.

7.5   Packaging

7.5.1   All packaging material should be stored in a clean and sanitary manner.
The material should be appropriate for the product to be packed and for the
expected conditions of storage and should not transmit to the product objectionable
substances beyond the limits acceptable to the official agency having jurisdiction.
The packaging material should be sound and should provide appropriate protection
from contamination.

7.5.2   Product containers should not have been used for any purpose which may
lead to contamination of the product. Where practicable containers should be
inspected immediately before use to ensure that they are in a satisfactory
condition and where necessary cleaned and/or disinfected; when washed they should
be well drained before filling. Only packaging material required for immediate use
should be kept in the packing or filling area.

7.5.3   Packing should be done under conditions that preclude the introduction
of contamination into the product.

7.5.4   Lot Identification

           Each container shall be embossed or otherwise permanently marked in
code or in clear to identify the producing factory and the lot. A lot means a
definitive quantity of a commodity produced under essentially the same conditions.

7.5.5   Processing and production records

           Permanent, legible and dated records and pertinent processing and
production details should be kept concerning each lot. These records should be
retained for a period that exceeds the shelf life of the product, but unless a
specific need exists they need not be kept for more than two years. Records should
also be kept of the initial distribution by lot.

7.6   Storage and Transport of the End-Product

           The end-product should be stored and transported under such conditions
as will preclude the contamination with and/or proliferation of micro-organisms and
protect against deterioration of the product or damage to the container. During
storage, periodic inspection of the end-product should take place to ensure that
only food which is fit for human consumption is despatched and that end-product
specifications are complied with when they exist. The product should be despatched
in the sequence of the numbers.

7.7   Sampling and Laboratory Control Procedures

7.7.1   It is desirable that each establishment should have access to
laboratory control of the products processed. The amount and type of such control
will vary with the food product as well as the needs of management. Such control
should reject all food that is unfit for human consumption.

7.7.2   Where appropriate, representative samples of the production should be
taken to assess the safety and quality of the product.

7.7.3   Laboratory procedures used should preferably follow recognized or
standard methods in order that the results may be readily interpreted.

7.7.4   Laboratories checking for pathogenic micro-organisms should be well
separated from food processing areas.

SECTION VIII - END-PRODUCT SPECIFICATIONS

8.   Specifications such as microbiological, chemical or physical may be
required depending on the nature of the food. Such specifications should include
sampling procedures, analytical methodology and limits for acceptance.

CLEANING AND DISINFECTION

1.   **GENERAL PRINCIPLES**

1.1   Good hygiene demands effective and regular cleaning of establishments, equipment and vehicles to remove food residues and dirt which may contain food poisoning and spoilage micro-organisms and act as a source of food contamination. This cleaning process may where necessary be followed by, or associated with, disinfection to reduce the number of any micro-organisms remaining after cleaning to a level which will not cause harmful contamination of food. Sometimes the cleaning and disinfection stages are combined by the use of a detergent-disinfectant mixture, although it is generally considered that this is less efficient than a two-stage cleaning and disinfection process.

1.2   The methods of cleaning and disinfection should be considered satisfactory by the official agency having jurisdiction.

1.3   Cleaning and disinfection procedures should be properly established by a hygiene specialist after consultation with production management, plant engineers and detergent and disinfectant manufacturers. The cleaning and disinfection procedures should be designed to meet the particular needs of the process and product concerned, and should be set down in written schedules which should be made available for the guidance of employees and management. Procedures should be established not only for cleaning and disinfecting the establishment, equipment and vehicles but also for cleaning and disinfection of the equipment which is itself used for cleaning, e.g. mops, swabs, buckets, etc. There must be adequate supervision by management to ensure that the procedures set down are carried out in an effective manner at the specified intervals of time.

1.4   A single individual, who should preferably be a permanent member of the staff of the establishment and whose duties preferably should be independent of production, should be appointed to be responsible for cleaning and disinfection procedures and for supervision.

1.5   Industrial detergents and disinfectants require careful handling. Alkaline and acidic products must not be mixed. Hypochlorite solutions must not be mixed with acidic products as chlorine gas will be released. Operators handling strongly alkaline or acid products must wear protective clothing and goggles and must be thoroughly instructed in handling techniques. Containers in which such substances are kept should be clearly marked and stored separately from food and packaging materials. Manufacturers instructions should be carefully observed.

2.   **CLEANING**

2.1   Cleaning Procedures

2.1.1   Cleaning procedures will require:

2.1.1.1   The removal of gross debris from surfaces by brushing, vacuuming and scraping of deposits or other methods where necessary followed by the application of water in compliance with section 7.3 of the Recommended International Code of Practice - General Principles of Food Hygiene (Ref. No. CAC/RCP 1-1969, Rev. 2

(1985)). The temperature of the water used will depend upon the type of soil to be removed.

2.1.1.2   The application of detergent solution to loosen soil and bacterial film and hold them in solution or suspension.

2.1.1.3   Rinsing with water in compliance with section 7.3 of the General Principles of Food Hygiene to remove loosened soil and residues of detergent.

2.1.1.4   Care should be taken that the use of abrasive material does not alter the character of the food contact surface and that fragments from brushes, scrapers and other cleaning materials do not contaminate the food.

2.1.2   When these requirements have been met they may be followed by a disinfection process (see Section 3: Disinfection).

2.2   Cleaning Methods

2.2.1   Cleaning is carried out by the separate or combined use of physical methods, e.g. scrubbing or turbulent flow, and chemical methods, e.g. the use of detergent, alkalis or acids. Heat is an important adjunct to the use of physical and chemical methods. Care must be employed in the selection of the temperatures depending on the detergents and the nature of the soil and working surfaces. Some synthetic organic materials can absorb constituents of food, such as milk fat and the amount absorbed rises with the temperature.

2.2.2   One or more of the following methods is used according to the circumstances:

2.2.2.1   Manual: involving removal of soil by scrubbing in the presence of a detergent solution. For removable parts of machinery and for small items of equipment, soaking in a detergent solution in a separate receptacle may be necessary to loosen the soil prior to the scrubbing process.

2.2.2.2   In place cleaning: The cleaning of equipment including pipe runs, with water and detergent solution, without dismantling the equipment or pipe runs. The equipment must be properly designed for this cleaning method. A minimum fluid velocity of 1.5 metres per second (5 feet per second) with turbulent flow is required for effective cleaning of pipe runs. As far as possible parts of equipment which cannot be satisfactorily cleaned by this method should be identified and eliminated. If this cannot be done satisfactorily, the parts should be dismantled for cleaning to prevent build up of contamination (General Principles of Food Hygiene section 4.5.2).

2.2.2.3   Low pressure high volume spray: The application of a water or detergent solution in large volumes at pressures up to approximately 6.8 bar (100 psi).

2.2.2.4   High pressure low volume spray: The application of water or detergent solution in low volume at a high pressure, i.e. up to 68 bar (1,000 psi).

2.2.2.5   Foam cleaning: The application of a detergent in the form of a foam which is allowed to remain for 15 to 20 minutes and is then rinsed off with a water spray.

2.2.2.6   Washing machines: Some containers and equipment used in food processing can be washed by machines. These machines carry out the cleaning procedures set out above with the addition of disinfection by hot water rinse at the completion of the cleaning cycle. Good results can be obtained with such machines provided that the effectiveness and efficiency of the machine is maintained by adequate and regular servicing.

2.3   Detergents

Detergents must have a good wetting capacity and the ability to remove soil from surfaces and to hold the soil in suspension. They must also have good rinsing properties so that residues of soil and detergent can be easily removed from equipment. There are many types of detergent and advice should be sought to ensure that the detergent used in any particular circumstances is suitable to remove the type of soil resulting from a particular food process and is used at the correct concentration and temperature. The detergent used should be non-corrosive and compatible with other materials including disinfectants used in the sanitation programme. Whilst cold solutions of detergent may be effective in some circumstances, removal of residues of fat requires the use of heat. The deposition of mineral salts on equipment may form a hard scale ("stone") especially in the presence of fats or proteins; the use of an acid or alkaline detergent or both sequentially may be necessary to remove such deposits. The "stone" can be a major source of bacterial contamination. It can be easily detected by its fluorescence under ultraviolet light which will detect deposits usually missed by ordinary visual inspection.

2.4   Drying after Cleaning

2.4.1   If equipment is left wet after cleaning micro-organisms may grow in the water film. It is important to ensure that equipment is left dry as soon as possible after cleaning and where possible to allow equipment to air-dry naturally. Single use tissue or absorbent materials may be used for drying but they should be used once and discarded.

2.4.2   Adequate drainage points should be provided in equipment that cannot be dismantled and drying racks provided for small pieces of equipment that are dismantled for the purpose of cleaning.

2.4.3   Any equipment that unavoidably remains wet for a period during which significant microbial growth might occur should be disinfected immediately before use.

3.   **DISINFECTION**

3.1   General Considerations

While disinfection results in the reduction of numbers of living micro-organisms, it does not usually kill bacterial spores. Effective disinfection does not necessarily kill all micro-organisms present but reduces their numbers to a level at which they can be reasonably assumed to present no risk to health. No disinfection procedure can exert its full effect unless its use is preceded by thorough cleaning. Disinfectants should be chosen according to the micro-organisms to be killed, the type of food being processed and the material making up the food contact surfaces and where appropriate the criteria mentioned in section 3.4. Selection is also affected by the character of the water available and the method of cleaning used. The continued use of certain chemical disinfectants may lead to the selection of resistant micro-organisms. Chemical disinfectants should be used where use of heat would not be practicable. The methods used for cleaning under section 2.2 could also be used for the application of disinfectants.

3.2   Disinfection by Heat

3.2.1   The application of moist heat to raise the surface temperature to at least 70°C (160°F) is one of the commonest and most useful forms of disinfection. High temperatures, however, will denature protein residues and bake them on the surface of food equipment. It is therefore essential that all material such as residual food is removed by thorough cleaning before the application of heat for disinfection.

3.2.1.1   Hot water disinfection

This is the method of choice and is commonly used throughout the food industry. Removable parts of machinery and smaller items of equipment can be submerged in a sink or tank containing water at disinfection temperature for a suitable time, e.g. at 80°C (176°F) for two minutes. The disinfectant rinse in mechanical washing machines should reach this disinfection temperature and the period of immersion should be sufficient to allow the equipment surfaces to reach this temperature. Water at disinfection temperature will scald bare hands so basket racks or some other type of receptacle will have to be used where the process is manual.

3.2.1.2   Steam disinfection

Where steam is used the surface to be disinfected must be raised to a disinfecting temperature for a suitable time. It may not be practicable to have steam available for disinfection throughout the premises. Lances producing steam jets are useful to disinfect surfaces of machinery and other surfaces which are difficult to reach or which must be disinfected in situ on the factory floor. The heating of surfaces during the application of high temperature steam promotes their subsequent drying. The use of steam can present problems by creating condensation on other equipment and other parts of the structure. High pressure steam can strip paint from painted surfaces and lubricants from the working parts of machinery. Moreover, some types of materials, such as plastics, are unsuitable for treatment with live steam. Steam jets should only be used by trained personnel as they can be dangerous in unskilled hands.

3.3   Chemical Disinfection

3.3.1   The following factors after the performance of chemical disinfectants:

3.3.1.1   Inactivation by dirty conditions

The effectiveness of all chemical disinfectants is reduced by the presence of dirt and other soiling matter. Disinfectants will not act at all where there is gross soiling. Disinfection with chemicals, must therefore, always follow or be combined with a cleaning process.

3.3.1.2   Temperature of solution

In general, the higher the temperature the more effective will be the disinfection. A warm or hot solution is therefore preferable to a cold solution of disinfectant. There are, however, limitations to the temperature that may be used, and the manufacturer's guidance should be followed. Iodophors release iodine at temperatures above 43°C (110°F) which can result in staining of materials. The corrosive action of chlorine is increased when hot hypochlorite solutions are used.

3.3.1.3   Time

All chemical disinfectants need a minimum contact time to be effective. This minimum contact time will vary according to the activity of the disinfectant.

3.3.1.4   Concentration

The concentration of the chemical solution which is required will vary according to the conditions of use and must be suitable for the particular purpose and environment in which it is to be used. The solutions should therefore be made up strictly according to the manufacturer's instructions.

3.3.1.5   Stability

All disinfectant solutions should be freshly made in clean utensils. Topping up existing solutions or prolonged keeping of ready-to-use dilute solutions may render the disinfectant solution ineffective or may allow it to become a reservoir of resistant organisms. Disinfectants may be inactivated if mixed with detergents or other disinfectants. The strength of disinfectants should be checked regularly, particularly when diluted for use. Easy-to-use inexpensive test kits are available for this purpose.

3.4   Chemicals Suitable for Disinfection in Food Premises

3.4.1   Chemical disinfectants that are liable to taint the food such as phenolics should not be used in food premises or vehicles. Care should be taken that chemical disinfectants do not cause harm to personnel and when used in places where animals are kept or transported, such as lairages and vehicles, do not cause distress to the animals. Amongst the disinfectants more commonly used in the food industry are those listed below.

3.4.1.1   Chlorine and chlorine based products including hypochlorite compounds

Properly used, these substances are among the most suitable for food plants and vehicles. They can be obtained as liquid hypochlorite solutions containing 100,000 to 120,000 milligrammes of available chlorine per litre, or they can be combined with a detergent in a chlorinated crystal form. These disinfectants act rapidly against a wide range of micro-organisms and are relatively cheap. They are the most suitable for general purpose disinfection in food premises. These disinfectants should be used at concentrations of 100 to 250 milligrammes of available chlorine per litre. This group of disinfectants is corrosive to metals and they also have a bleaching action. Surfaces disinfected with them should therefore be subjected to a final rinsing as soon as possible after an adequate contact time. Chlorine disinfectants with the exception of chlorine dioxide are readily inactivated by the presence of organic soil.

3.4.1.2   Iodophors

These substances are always blended with a detergent in an acid medium and they are, therefore, particularly suitable in those circumstances where an acid cleaner is required. They have a rapid action and a wide range of antimicrobial activity. A solution of about 25-50 milligrammes per litre of available iodine at pH<4 is usually required for disinfection of clean surfaces. They are readily inactivated by organic matter. Iodophers give a visual indication of their effectiveness since they lose their colour when the residual iodine has dropped to ineffective levels. They are not toxic when used in normal concentrations but may add to the total dietary iodine load. They have little taste or smell, but may combine with substances in the food to cause taint. Iodophors may have a corrosive action on metals depending on the particular formulation of the iodophor and the nature of the surface to which the iodophor is being applied. For these reasons special care should be taken to rinse them away after use.

3.4.1.3   Quaternary ammonium compounds

All these compounds also have good detergent characteristics. They are colourless and are relatively non-corrosive to metal and non-toxic but may have a bitter taste. They are not as effective against Gram-negative bacteria as are chlorine, chlorine-based disinfectants and iodophors. The solutions tend to adhere to surfaces and thorough rinsing is necessary. They should be used at a concentration of approximately 200-1200 milligrammes per litre. The higher concentrations are necessary when used with hard water. They are not compatible with soaps or anionic detergents.

3.4.1.4   Amphoteric surfactants

This comparatively recent type of disinfectant consists of active agents with detergent as well as bactericidal properties. They are of low toxicity, relatively non-corrosive, tasteless and odourless and are efficient disinfectants when used according to the manufacturer's recommendations. They are inactivated by organic matter.

3.4.1.5   Strong acids and alkalies

In addition to their detergent properties strong acids and alkalies have considerable antimicrobial activity. Particular care should be taken that they do not contaminate food.

After an adequate contact time all surfaces which have been disinfected should be subjected to a final rinse with water which complies with section 7.3 of the General Principles of Food Hygiene referred to in section 2.1.1.1 of this Appendix.

4.   <u>CHECKS ON EFFECTIVENESS OF PROCEDURES</u>

4.1   The effectiveness of cleaning and disinfection procedures should be verified by microbiological monitoring of the product and food contact surfaces. Similar regular microbiological monitoring of the product at all stages of production will also give information on the effectiveness of cleaning and disinfection procedures.

4.2   When sampling for microbiological monitoring of equipment and food contact surfaces the use of a quenching (neutralizing) agent is required to eliminate any residual disinfectant.

SECTION 7.1

RECOMMENDED INTERNATIONAL CODE OF HYGIENIC
PRACTICE FOR LOW-ACID AND ACIDIFIED LOW-ACID CANNED FOODS

CAC/RCP 23-1979, Rev. 1 (1989)

INTRODUCTION

The Code of Practice for Low-Acid and Acidified Low-Acid Canned Food was adopted by the Codex Alimentarius Commission at its 13th Session in 1979 and subsequently revised in 1989 by the 18th Session. Additional information contained in Appendices IV and V was adopted by the 19th Session of the Commission in 1991. The Code has been sent to all Member Nations and Associate Members of FAO and WHO as an advisory text, and it is for individual governments to decide what use they wish to make of it. The Commission has expressed the view that codes of practice might provide useful checklists of requirements for national food control or enforcement authorities.

Its application requires knowledge and experience of canning technology. It is not intended to be used as a complete operating manual. It primarily addresses hygienic critical control points. It should be used in conjunction with appropriate texts and manuals on the subject.

RECOMMENDED INTERNATIONAL CODE OF HYGIENIC PRACTICE FOR LOW AND ACIDIFIED LOW ACID CANNED FOODS CAC/RCP 23-1979, Rev. 1 (1989)

CONTENTS

PAGE

RECOMMENDED INTERNATIONAL CODE OF HYGIENIC PRACTICE
FOR LOW-ACID AND ACIDIFIED LOW-ACID CANNED FOODS

CAC/RCP 23-1979, Rev. 1 (1989)

1.   SECTION I - SCOPE

          This Code of practice is concerned with the canning and heat processing of low-acid and acidified low-acid foods packed in hermetically sealed containers. It does not apply to foods in hermetically sealed containers which require refrigeration. Annex I applies specifically to acidified low-acid foods.

2.   SECTION II - DEFINITIONS

          For the purposes of this Code:

2.1   "Acid food" means a food that has a natural pH of 4.6 or below.

2.2   "Acidified low-acid food" means a food which has been treated so as to attain an equilibrium pH of 4.6 or lower after heat processing.

2.3   "Aseptic processing and packaging" means the filling of a commercially sterile product into sterilized containers followed by hermetical sealing with a sterilized closure in an atmosphere free from microorganisms.

2.4   "Bleeders" (Bleeds) means small orifices through which steam and other gases escape from the retort throughout the entire heat process.

2.5   "Canned food" means commercially sterile food in hermetically sealed containers.

2.6   "Cleaning" means the removal of food residues, dirt, grease or other objectionable material.

2.7   "Code lot" means all product produced during a period of time identified by a specific container code mark.

2.8   "Coming-up-time" means the time, including venting time, which elapses between the introduction of the heating medium into the closed retort and the time when the temperature in the retort reaches the required sterilization temperatures.

2.9   "Commercial sterility of thermally processed food" means the condition achieved by application of heat, sufficient, alone or in combination with other appropriate treatments, to render the food free from microorganisms capable of growing in the food at normal non-refrigerated conditions at which the food is likely to be held during distribution and storage.

2.10   "Commercial sterility of equipment and containers used for aseptic processing and packaging of food" means the condition achieved and maintained by application of heat, or other appropriate treatment, which renders such equipment and containers free from microorganisms capable of growing in the food at temperatures at which the food is likely to be held during distribution and storage.

2.11   "Disinfection" means the reduction, without adversely affecting the food, by means of hygienically satisfactory chemical agents and/or physical methods, of the number of microorganisms to a level that will not lead to harmful contamination of food.

2.12   "Equilibrium pH" is the pH of the macerated heat processed food product.

2.13   "Flame sterilizer" means an apparatus in which hermetically sealed containers of foods are agitated at atmospheric pressure, by either continuous, discontinuous or reciprocating movement, over gas flames to achieve commercial sterility of foods.

2.14   "Heating curve" means a graphical representation of the rate of temperature change in the food throughout the heat process; this is usually plotted on semi-log graph paper so that the temperature on an inverted log scale is plotted against time on a linear scale.

2.14.1   "Broken heating curve" means a heating curve which shows a distinct change in the rate of heat transfer such that the curve may be represented by two or more distinct straight lines.

2.14.2   "Simple heating curve" means a heating curve which approximates a straight line.

2.15   "Headspace" means the volume in a container not occupied by the food.

2.16   "Holding time", see sterilization time.

2.17   "Incubation tests" means tests in which the heat processed product is kept at a specific temperature for a specified period of time in order to determine if outgrowth of microorganisms occurs under these conditions.

2.18   "Initial temperature" means the temperature of the contents of the coldest container to be processed at the time the sterilizing cycle begins, as specified in the scheduled process.

2.19   "Low-acid food" means any food, other than alcoholic beverages, where any component has a pH value greater than 4.6 after heat processing.

2.20   "Potable water" means water fit for human consumption. Standards of potability should be no less strict than those contained in the latest edition of the "International Standards for Drinking Water", World Health Organization.

2.21   "Product container" means a container designed to be filled with food and hermetically sealed.

2.21.1   "Hermetically sealed containers" are containers which are sealed to protect the contents against the entry of microorganisms during and after heat processing.

2.21.2   "Rigid container" means that the shape or contours of the filled and sealed container are neither affected by the enclosed product nor deformed by an external mechanical pressure of up to 0.7 kg/cm^2 (10 psig), (i.e., normal firm finger pressure).

2.21.3   "Semi-rigid container" means that the shape or contours of the filled, sealed container are not affected by the enclosed product under normal atmospheric temperature and pressure but can be deformed by an external mechanical pressure of less than 0.7 kg/cm² (10 psig), (i.e., normal firm finger pressure).

2.21.4   "Flexible container" means that the shape or contours of the filled, sealed container are affected by the enclosed product.

2.22   "Retort" means a pressure vessel designed for thermal processing of food packed in hermetically sealed containers.

2.23   "Scheduled process" means the thermal process chosen by the processor for a given product and container size to achieve at least commercial sterility.

2.24   "Seals" of a semi-rigid container and lid or flexible container, means those parts which are fused together in order to close the container.

2.25   "Sterilization temperature" means the temperature maintained throughout the thermal process as specified in the scheduled process.

2.26   "Sterilization time" means the time between the moment sterilization temperature is achieved and the moment cooling started.

2.27   "Thermal process" means the heat treatment to achieve commercial sterility and is quantified in terms of time and temperature.

2.28   "Venting" means thorough removal of the air from steam retorts by steam prior to a scheduled process.

2.29   "Water Activity (a_w)" is the ratio of the water vapour pressure of the product to the vapour pressure of pure water at the same temperature.

3.   SECTION III - HYGIENE REQUIREMENTS IN PRODUCTION/HARVESTING AREA

3.1   Environmental Hygiene and Areas from which Raw Materials are derived

3.1.1   Unsuitable growing or harvesting areas

Food should not be grown or harvested where the presence of potentially harmful substances would lead to an unacceptable level of such substances in the food.

3.1.2   Protection from contamination by wastes

3.1.2.1   Raw food materials should be protected from contamination by human, animal, domestic, industrial and agricultural wastes which may be present at levels likely to be a hazard to health. Adequate precautions should be taken to ensure that these wastes are not used and are not disposed of in a manner which may constitute a health hazard through the food.

3.1.2.2   Arrangements for the disposal of domestic and industrial wastes in areas from which raw materials are derived should be acceptable to the official agency having jurisdiction.

3.1.3   Irrigation control

Food should not be grown or produced in areas where the water used for irrigation might constitute a health hazard to the consumer through the food.

3.1.4   Pest and disease control

Control measures involving treatment with chemical, physical or biological agents should only be undertaken by or under direct supervision of personnel who have a thorough understanding of the potential hazards to health, particularly those which may arise from residues in the food. Such measures should only be carried out in accordance with the recommendations of the official agency having jurisdiction.

3.2   Harvesting and Production

3.2.1   Techniques

Methods and procedures associated with harvesting and production should be hygienic and such as not to constitute a potential health hazard or result in contamination of the product.

3.2.2   Equipment and containers

Equipment and containers used for harvesting and production should be so constructed and maintained as not to constitute a hazard to health. Containers which are re-used should be of such material and construction as will permit easy and thorough cleaning. They should be cleaned and maintained clean and, where necessary, disinfected. Containers previously used for toxic materials should not subsequently be used for holding foods or food ingredients.

3.2.3   Removal of obviously unfit raw materials

Raw materials which are obviously unfit for human consumption should be segregated during harvesting and production. Those which cannot be made fit by further processing should be disposed of in such a place and in such a manner as to avoid contamination of the food and/or water supplies or other food materials.

3.2.4   Protection against contamination and damage

Suitable precautions should be taken to protect the raw materials from being contaminated by pests or by chemical, physical or microbiological contaminants or other objectionable substances. Precautions should be taken to avoid damage.

3.3   Storage at the Place of Production/Harvesting

Raw materials should be stored under conditions which provide protection against contamination and minimize damage and deterioration.

3.4   Transportation

3.4.1   Conveyances

Conveyances for transporting the harvested crop or raw materials from the production area or place of harvest or storage should be adequate for the purpose intended and should be of such material and construction as will permit easy and thorough cleaning. They should be cleaned and maintained clean, and where necessary disinfected and disinfested.

3.4.2   Handling procedures

All handling procedures should be such as will prevent raw materials from being contaminated. Care should be taken to prevent spoilage, to protect against contamination and to minimize damage. Special equipment - such as refrigeration equipment - should be used if the nature of the product or distances involved so indicate. If ice is used in contact with the product it should be of the quality required in Sub-Section 4.4.1.2 of this Code.

4.   SECTION IV - ESTABLISHMENT: DESIGN AND FACILITIES

4.1   Location

Establishments should be located in areas which are free from objectionable odours, smoke, dust or other contaminants and are not subject to flooding.

4.2   Roadways and Areas used by Wheeled Traffic

Such roadways and areas serving the establishment which are within its boundaries or in its immediate vicinity should have a hard paved surface suitable for wheeled traffic. There should be adequate drainage and provision should be made to allow for cleaning.

4.3   Buildings and Facilities

4.3.1   Buildings and facilities should be of sound construction and maintained in good repair.

4.3.2   Adequate working space should be provided to allow for satisfactory performance of all operations.

4.3.3   The design should be such as to permit easy and adequate cleaning and to facilitate proper supervision of food hygiene.

4.3.4   The buildings and facilities should be designed to prevent the entrance and harbouring of pests and the entry of environmental contaminants such as smoke, dust, etc.

4.3.5   Buildings and facilities should be designed to provide separation, by partition, location or other effective means, between those operations which may cause cross-contamination.

4.3.6   Buildings and facilities should be designed to facilitate hygienic operations by means of a regulated flow in the process from the arrival of the raw material at the premises to the finished product, and should provide for appropriate temperature conditions for the process and the product.

4.3.7   In food handling areas:

-      Floors, where appropriate, should be of water-proof, non-absorbent, washable, non-slip materials, without crevices, and should be easy to clean and disinfect. Where appropriate, floors should slope sufficiently for liquids to drain to trapped outlets.

- Walls, where appropriate, should be of water-proof, non-absorbent, washable materials, sealed and free of insects, and should be light coloured. Up to a height appropriate for the operation they should be smooth and without crevices, and should be easy to clean and disinfect. Where appropriate, angles between walls, between walls and floors and between walls and ceilings should be sealed and coved to facilitate cleaning.

- Ceilings should be so designed, constructed and finished as to prevent the accumulation of dirt and minimize condensation, mould development and flaking, and should be easy to clean.

- Windows and other openings should be so constructed as to avoid accumulation of dirt and those which open should be fitted with insect proof screens. Screens should be easily movable for cleaning and kept in good repair. Internal window sills, if present, should be sloped to prevent use as shelves.

- Doors should have smooth, non-absorbent surfaces and, where appropriate, be self-closing and close fitting.

- Stairs, lift cages and auxiliary structures such as platforms, ladders, chutes, should be so situated and constructed as not to cause contamination to food. Chutes should be constructed with inspection and cleaning hatches.

4.3.8   In food handling areas all overhead structures and fittings should be installed in such a manner as to avoid contamination directly or indirectly of food and raw materials by condensation and drip, and should not hamper cleaning operations. They should be insulated where appropriate and be so designed and finished as to prevent the accumulation of dirt and to minimize condensation, mould development and flaking. They should be easy to clean.

4.3.9   Living quarters, toilets and areas where animals are kept should be completely separated from and should not open directly on to food handling areas.

4.3.10   Where appropriate, establishments should be so designed that access can be controlled.

4.3.11   The use of materials which cannot be adequately cleaned and disinfected, such as wood, should be avoided unless its use would clearly not be a source of contamination.

4.4   Sanitary Facilities

4.4.1   Water supply

4.4.1.1   An ample supply of water, in compliance with Sub-Section 7.3 of the Recommended International Code of Practice - General Principles of Food Hygiene (Ref. No. CAC/RCP 1-1969, Rev. 2(1985)), under adequate pressure and of suitable temperature should be available with adequate facilities for its storage, where necessary, and distribution, and with adequate protection against contamination.

4.4.1.2   Ice should be made from water, in compliance with Sub-Section 7.3 of the General Principles referred to in Sub-Section 4.4.1.1, and should be manufactured, handled and stored so as to protect it from contamination.

4.4.1.3   <u>Steam</u> used in direct contact with food or food contact surfaces should contain no substances which may be hazardous to health or may contaminate the food.

4.4.1.4   <u>Non-potable water</u> used for steam production, refrigeration, fire control and other similar purposes not connected with food should be carried in completely separate lines, identifiable preferably by colour, and with no cross-connection with or back-siphonage into the system carrying potable water (see also Sub-Section 7.3.2).

4.4.2   <u>Effluent and waste disposal</u>

Establishments should have an efficient effluent and waste disposal system which should at all times be maintained in good order and repair. All effluent lines (including sewer systems) should be large enough to carry peak loads and should be so constructed as to avoid contamination of potable water supplies.

4.4.3   <u>Changing facilities and toilets</u>

Adequate, suitable and conveniently located changing facilities and toilets should be provided in all establishments. Toilets should be so designed as to ensure hygienic removal of waste matter. These areas should be well lit, ventilated and where appropriate heated and should not open directly on to food handling areas. Hand washing facilities with warm or hot and cold water, a suitable hand-cleaning preparation, and with suitable hygienic means of drying hands, should be provided adjacent to toilets and in such a position that the employee must pass them when returning to the processing area. Where hot and cold water are available mixing taps should be provided. Where paper towels are used, a sufficient number of dispensers and receptacles should be provided near to each washing facility. Taps of a non-hand operable type are desirable. Notices should be posted directing personnel to wash their hands after using the toilet.

4.4.4   <u>Hand washing facilities in processing areas</u>

Adequate and conveniently located facilities for hand washing and drying should be provided wherever the process demands. Where appropriate, facilities for hand disinfection should also be provided. Warm or hot and cold water and a suitable hand-cleaning preparation should be provided. Where hot and cold water are available mixing taps should be provided. There should be suitable hygienic means of drying hands. Where paper towels are used, a sufficient number of dispensers and receptacles should be provided adjacent to each washing facility. Taps of a non-hand operable type are desirable. The facilities should be furnished with properly trapped waste pipes leading to drains.

4.4.5   <u>Disinfection facilities</u>

Where appropriate, adequate facilities for cleaning and disinfection of working implements and equipment should be provided. These facilities should be constructed of corrosion-resistant materials, capable of being easily cleaned, and should be fitted with suitable means of supplying hot and cold water in sufficient quantities.

4.4.6   <u>Lighting</u>

Adequate natural or artificial lighting should be provided throughout the establishment. Where appropriate, the lighting should not alter colours and the intensity should not be less than:

540 lux (50 foot candles) at all inspection points
220 lux (20 foot candles) in work rooms
110 lux (10 foot candles) in other areas

Light bulbs and fixtures suspended over food materials in any stage of production
should be of a safety type and protected to prevent contamination of food in case
of breakage.

4.4.7   Ventilation

Adequate ventilation should be provided to prevent excessive heat,
steam condensation and dust and to remove contaminated air. The direction of that
air flow should never be from a dirty area to a clean area. Ventilation openings
should be provided with a screen or other protecting enclosure of non-corrodible
material. Screens should be easily removable for cleaning.

4.4.8   Facilities for storage of waste and inedible material

Facilities should be provided for the storage of waste and inedible
material prior to removal from the establishment. These facilities should be
designed to prevent access to waste or inedible material by pests and to avoid
contamination of food, potable water, equipment, buildings or roadways on the
premises.

4.5   Equipment and Utensils

4.5.1   Materials

All equipment and utensils used in food handling areas and which may
contact food should be made of material which does not transmit toxic substances,
odour or taste, is non-absorbent, resistant to corrosion and capable of
withstanding repeated cleaning and disinfection. Surfaces should be smooth and
free from pits and crevices. The use of wood and other materials which cannot be
adequately cleaned and disinfected should be avoided except when their use would
clearly not be a source of contamination. The use of different materials in such
a way that contact corrosion can occur should be avoided.

4.5.2   Sanitary design, construction and installation

4.5.2.1   All equipment and utensils should be so designed and constructed as to
prevent hygienic hazards and permit easy and thorough cleaning and disinfection
and, where practicable, be visible for inspection. Stationary equipment should be
installed in such a manner as to permit easy access and thorough cleaning.
Canneries should have suitable conveyor systems to transport empty product
containers to the filling stations. Their design, structure and installation
should ensure that such containers do not become contaminated or unacceptable
because of damage.

4.5.2.2   Containers for inedible material and waste should be leak-proof,
constructed of metal or other suitable impervious material which should be easy to
clean or disposable and able to be closed securely.

4.5.2.3   All refrigerated spaces should be equipped with temperature measurement
or recording devices.

4.5.2.4   Retorts must be designed, installed, operated and maintained in
accordance with the safety standards for pressure vessels of the agency having

jurisdiction. Over-pressure facilities required (e.g., for flexible containers) may mean that the safe working pressure rating of the retort may have to be considerably increased.

4.5.3   Equipment identification

Equipment and utensils used for inedible materials or waste should be so identified and should not be used for edible products.

4.6   Steam Supply

Steam supply to the thermal processing system should be adequate to the extent needed to ensure that sufficient steam pressure is maintained during thermal processing, regardless of other demands for steam by the plant.

5.   SECTION V - ESTABLISHMENT: HYGIENE REQUIREMENTS

5.1   Maintenance

The buildings, equipment, utensils and all other physical facilities of the establishment, including drains, should be maintained in good repair and in an orderly condition. As far as practicable, rooms should be kept free from steam, vapour and surplus water.

5.2   Cleaning and Disinfection

5.2.1   Cleaning and disinfection should meet the requirements of this Code. For further information on cleaning and disinfection procedures see Appendix I of the General Principles of Food Hygiene referred to in Sub-Section 4.4.1.1 of this Code.

5.2.2   To prevent contamination of food, all equipment and utensils should be cleaned as frequently as necessary and disinfected whenever circumstances demand.

5.2.3   Adequate precautions should be taken to prevent food from being contaminated during cleaning or disinfection of rooms, equipment or utensils by water and detergents or by disinfectants and their solutions. Detergents and disinfectants should be suitable for the purpose intended and should be acceptable to the official agency having jurisdiction. Any residues of these agents on a surface which may come into contact with food should be removed by thorough rinsing with water, in compliance with Sub-Section 7.3 of the General Principles of Food Hygiene referred to in Sub-Section 4.4.1.1, before the area or equipment is again used for handling of food.

5.2.4   Either immediately after cessation of work for the day or at such other times as may be appropriate, floors, including drains, auxiliary structures and walls of food handling areas should be thoroughly cleaned.

5.2.5   Changing facilities and toilets should be kept clean at all times.

5.2.6   Roadways and yards in the immediate vicinity of and serving the premises should be kept clean.

5.3   Hygiene Control Programme

A permanent cleaning and disinfection schedule should be drawn up for each establishment to ensure that all areas are appropriately cleaned and that critical areas, equipment and material are designated for special attention. A single individual who should preferably be a permanent member of the staff of the establishment and whose duties should be independent of production, should be appointed to be responsible for the cleanliness of the establishment. He should have a thorough understanding of the significance of contamination and the hazards involved. All cleaning personnel should be well-trained in cleaning techniques.

5.4   By-Products

By-products should be stored in such a manner as to avoid contamination of food. They should be removed from the working areas as often as necessary and at least daily.

5.5   Storage and Disposal of Waste

Waste material should be handled in such a manner as to avoid contamination of food or potable water. Care should be taken to prevent access to waste by pests. Waste should be removed from the food handling and other working areas as often as necessary and at least daily. Immediately after disposal of the waste, receptacles used for storage and any equipment which has come into contact with the waste should be cleaned and disinfected. The waste storage area should also be cleaned and disinfected.

5.6   Exclusion of Domestic Animals

Animals that are uncontrolled or that could be a hazard to health should be excluded from establishments.

5.7   Pest Control

5.7.1   There should be an effective and continuous programme for the control of pests. Establishments and surrounding areas should be regularly examined for evidence of infestation.

5.7.2   Should pests gain entrance to the establishment, eradication measures should be instituted. Control measures involving treatment with chemical, physical or biological agents should only be undertaken by or under direct supervision of personnel who have a thorough understanding of the potential hazards to health resulting from the use of these agents, including those hazards which may arise from residues retained in the product. Such measures should only be carried out in accordance with the recommendations of the official agency having jurisdiction.

5.7.3   Pesticides should only be used if other precautionary measures cannot be used effectively. Before pesticides are applied, care should be taken to safeguard all food, equipment and utensils from contamination. After application, contaminated equipment and utensils should be thoroughly cleaned to remove residues prior to being used again.

5.8   Storage of Hazardous Substances

5.8.1   Pesticides or other substances which may represent a hazard to health should be suitably labelled with a warning about their toxicity and use. They should be stored in locked rooms or cabinets used only for that purpose and dispensed and handled only by authorized and properly trained personnel or by persons under strict supervision of trained personnel. Extreme care should be taken to avoid contaminating food.

5.8.2   Except when necessary for hygienic or processing purposes, no substance which could contaminate food should be used or stored in food handling areas.

5.9   Personal Effects and Clothing

Personal effects and clothing should not be deposited in food handling areas.

6.   SECTION VI - PERSONAL HYGIENE AND HEALTH REQUIREMENTS

6.1   Hygiene Training

Managers of establishments should arrange for adequate and continuing training of all food handlers in hygienic handling of food and in personal hygiene so that they understand the precautions necessary to prevent contamination of food. Instruction should include relevant parts of this Code.

6.2   Medical Examination

Persons who come into contact with food in the course of their work should have a medical examination prior to their employment if the official agency having jurisdiction, acting on medical advice, considers that this is necessary, whether because of epidemiological considerations, the nature of the food prepared in a particular establishment or the medical history of the prospective food handler. Medical examination of a food handler should be carried out at other times when clinically or epidemiologically indicated.

6.3   Communicable Diseases

The management should take care to ensure that no person, while known or suspected to be suffering from, or to be a carrier of a disease likely to be transmitted through food or while afflicted with infected wounds, skin infections, sores or with diarrhoea, is permitted to work in any food handling area in any capacity in which there is any likelihood of such a person directly or indirectly contaminating food with pathogenic microorganisms. Any person so affected should immediately report to the management that he is ill.

6.4   Injuries

Any person who has a cut or wound should not continue to handle food or food contact surfaces until the injury is completely protected by a water-proofing covering which is firmly secured, and which is conspicuous in colour. Adequate first-aid facilities should be provided for this purpose.

6.5   Washing of Hands

Every person, while on duty in a food handling area should wash his hands frequently and thoroughly with a suitable hand cleaning preparation under running warm water in compliance with Sub-Section 7.3 of the General Principles of Food Hygiene referred to in Sub-Section 4.4.1.1 of this Code. Hands should always be washed before commencing work, immediately after using the toilet, after handling contaminated material and whenever else necessary. After handling any material which might be capable of transmitting disease, hands should be washed and disinfected immediately. Notices requiring hand-washing should be displayed. There should be adequate supervision to ensure compliance with this requirement.

6.6   Personal Cleanliness

Every person, while on duty in a food handling area should maintain a high degree of personal cleanliness, and should at all times while so engaged wear suitable protective clothing including head covering and footwear, all of which articles should be cleanable unless designed to be disposed of and should be maintained in a clean condition consistent with the nature of the work in which the person is engaged. Aprons and similar items should not be washed on the floor. During periods where food is manipulated by hand, any jewellery that cannot be adequately disinfected should be removed from the hands. Personnel should not wear any insecure jewellery when engaged in food handling.

6.7   Personal Behaviour

Any behaviour which could result in contamination of food, such as eating, use of tobacco, chewing (e.g., gum, sticks, betel nuts, etc.) or unhygienic practices such as spitting, should be prohibited in food handling areas.

6.8   Gloves

Gloves, if used in the handling of food products, should be maintained in a sound, clean and sanitary condition. The wearing of gloves does not exempt the operator from having thoroughly washed hands.

6.9   Visitors

Precautions should be taken to prevent visitors to food handling areas from contaminating food. These may include the use of protective clothing. Visitors should observe the provisions recommended in Sub-Sections 5.9, 6.3, 6.4 and 6.7 of this Code.

6.10   Supervision

Responsibility for ensuring compliance by all personnel with all requirements of Sub-Sections 6.1 - 6.9 inclusive should be specifically allocated to competent supervisory personnel.

7.   SECTION VII - ESTABLISHMENT: HYGIENIC PROCESSING REQUIREMENTS

7.1   Raw Material Requirements

7.1.1   No raw material or ingredient should be accepted by the establishment if known to contain parasites, microorganisms or toxic, decomposed or extraneous substances which will not be reduced to acceptable levels by normal plant procedures of sorting and/or preparation of processing.

7.1.2   Raw materials or ingredients should be inspected and sorted prior to being moved in to the processing line and where necessary laboratory tests should be made. Only clean sound raw materials or ingredients should be used in further processing.

7.1.3   Raw materials and ingredients stored on the premises of the establishment should be maintained under conditions that will prevent spoilage, protect against contamination and minimize damage. Stocks of raw materials and ingredients should be properly rotated.

7.1.4   Blanching by heat, when required in the preparation of food for canning, should be followed by either rapidly cooling the food or subsequent processing without delay. Thermophilic growth and contamination in blanchers should be minimized by good design, the use of adequate operating temperatures and by routine cleaning.

7.1.5   All steps in the production process, including filling, closing, heat processing and cooling should be performed as rapidly as possible and under conditions which will prevent contamination, and deterioration, and minimize the growth of microorganisms in the food.

7.2   Prevention of Cross-Contamination

7.2.1   Effective measures should be taken to prevent contamination of food material by direct or indirect contact with material at an earlier stage of the process.

7.2.2   Persons handling raw materials or semi-processed products capable of contaminating the end-product should not come into contact with any end-product unless and until they discard all protective clothing worn by them during the handling of raw materials or semi-processed products which have come into direct contact with or have been soiled by raw materials or semi-processed products and they have changed into clean protective clothing.

7.2.3   If there is a likelihood of contamination, hands should be washed thoroughly between handling products at different stages of processing.

7.2.4   All equipment which has been in contact with raw materials or contaminated material should be thoroughly cleaned and disinfected prior to being used for contact with end-products.

7.3   Use of Water

7.3.1   As a general principle only potable water, as defined in the latest edition of "International Standards of Drinking Water" (WHO), should be used in food handling.

7.3.2   With the acceptance of the official agency having jurisdiction non-potable water may be used for steam production, refrigeration, fire control and other similar purposes not connected with food. However, non-potable water may, with specific acceptance by the official agency having jurisdiction, be used in certain food handling areas provided this does not constitute a hazard to health.

7.3.3   Water re-circulated for re-use within an establishment should be treated and maintained in a condition so that no health hazard can result from its use. The treatment process should be kept under constant surveillance. Alternatively, re-circulated water which has received no further treatment may be used in conditions where its use would not constitute a health hazard and will not contaminate either the raw material or the end-product. Re-circulated water should have a separate distribution system which can be readily identified. The acceptance of the official agency having jurisdiction should be required for any treatment process and for the use of re-circulated water in any food process.

7.4   Packaging

7.4.1   Storage and characteristics of containers

        All packaging material should be stored in a clean and sanitary manner. The material should be appropriate for the product to be packed and for the expected conditions of storage and should not transmit to the product objectionable substances beyond the limits acceptable to the official agency having jurisdiction. The packaging material should be sound and should provide appropriate protection from contamination.   The product containers should be sufficiently durable to withstand the mechanical, chemical and thermal stresses encountered during normal distribution. **An overwrap may be necessary for flexible and semi-rigid containers.** With laminates particular attention should be paid to ensure that the combination of processing requirements and product characteristics does not cause delamination as this may result in loss of integrity.   The sealant material chosen must be compatible with the product as well as the container and closure systems.   The closures for glass containers are particularly susceptible to mechanical damage which may result in a temporary or permanent loss of hermetic seal.   The closures of sealed jars should therefore be contained within the glass body diameter to avoid closure to closure contact of the sealed jars.

7.4.2   Inspection of empty product containers

7.4.2.1   Appropriate sampling and inspection schemes should be used by both container manufacturer and canner to ensure that containers and closures are in compliance with jointly agreed specifications and any requirements of the agency having jurisdiction that may apply.   As a minimum these should include those inspections and measurements given in Sub-Section 7.4.8 of this Code.   **Empty containers are particularly subject to damage by fault operation of depalletizers and by badly designed or controlled conveyors to filling and seaming machines.**

7.4.2.2   Dirty containers should not be filled.   Immediately prior to filling, rigid containers should be cleaned mechanically in an inverted position by suitable air or water jet appliances.   Glass containers may also be cleaned by suction (vacuum).   Containers intended for use on aseptic filling lines should not be cleaned with water unless they are thoroughly dried prior to sterilization. Inspection is particularly important in the case of glass containers which might possibly contain fragments of glass and glass defects which are difficult to see.

7.4.2.3   Faulty containers should not be filled.   Faulty rigid containers and covers include those that have punctures or severe dents, defective side or bottom seams, deformed body flanges or cover curls, abnormal levels of scratches or flaws in the plating or enamel (lacquer) and covers with defective sealing compound or gaskets.   Care should be taken to avoid damage to empty containers, closures and container materials which can result from faulty handling prior to closure.   If **these are filled, material will be wasted and there is always a danger of damaged containers jamming a filling or sealing machine and necessitating a shutdown. Faulty containers may leak during or after thermal processing and storage.**

7.4.2.4   The canner should ensure that the container and closure specifications are such that the container is capable of withstanding the processing and subsequent handling strains to which the containers are normally subjected.   Since such specifications may vary depending upon the canning operation and subsequent handling, they should be established in consultation with the container or closure manufacturer.

7.4.3   Proper use of product containers

Product containers must never be used within the cannery for any purpose other than packing food. **They should never be used as ash trays, small waste containers, receptacles for small machine parts or for other purposes. This should be avoided because there is a considerable risk that such containers may accidentally find their way back onto the production line and result in the packing of food in the same container with very objectionable or possible dangerous material.**

7.4.4   Protection of empty product containers during plant cleaning

Empty containers should be removed from the packing room and from the conveyors which lead to the filling machines before production lines are washed down. If not practicable the containers may be shielded or located so they will not become contaminated or obstruct clean-up operations.

7.4.5   Filling of product containers

7.4.5.1   During filling of containers, contamination of seal or seam areas with product should be avoided and seam or seal areas should be kept as clean and dry as necessary to obtain a satisfactory closure. **Overfilling can lead to contamination of seam or seals and adversely affect container integrity.**

7.4.5.2   The filling of containers, either mechanically or by hand, should be controlled so as to meet the filling and headspace requirements as specified in the scheduled process. It is important to achieve a constancy of filling, not only for economic reasons, but also because both the heat penetration and the container integrity may be affected by excessive fill variation. In rotationally processed containers the headspace should be accurately controlled and sufficient to ensure consistent and adequate agitation of the contents. When flexible packaging is used, variations in product particle size, fill-weight and/or headspace may lead to variations in the filled pouch dimensions (thickness) which may adversely affect the heat penetration.

7.4.5.3   Air content of filled flexible and semi-rigid containers should be kept to within specified limits to prevent excessive stressing of the seals during thermal processing.

7.4.6   Exhausting of containers

The exhausting of containers for the removal of air should be controlled so as to meet the conditions for which the scheduled process was designed.

7.4.7   Closing operations

7.4.7.1   Particular attention should be given to the operation, maintenance, routine checking and adjustment of closing equipment. Sealing and closing machines should be fitted and adjusted for each type of container and cover used. Seams and other closures should be tight and secure and meet the requirements of the container manufacturer, the canner and those of the agency having jurisdiction.

The equipment manufacturer's or supplier's instructions should be followed meticulously.

7.4.7.2   For heat sealing, seal jaws should be plane-parallel to each other with one or both jaws being heated. The temperature of the jaws should be maintained at the specified temperature over the whole seal area. Pressure build-up on the jaws should be fast enough and final pressure high enough to allow product to be squeezed away from the seals before bonding commences. Flexible pouches are normally sealed in the vertical position. The requirements for the control and operation of sealing equipment are similar to those for semi-rigid containers. The sea area should be free from product contamination.

7.4.8   Inspection of closures

7.4.8.1   Inspection for external defects

During production runs, regular observations should be made for external container defects. At intervals of sufficient frequency to ensure proper closure, the operator, closure supervisor, or other person competent to inspect container closures should visually examine either the top seam of a can randomly selected from each seaming head, or the closure of any other type of container being used, and should make a record of the observations. Additional visual closure inspections should be made immediately following a jam in a closure machine, after adjustment of closure machines, or after starting up of machines following a prolonged shutdown. Side seams should be visually examined for defects or product leakage.

All pertinent observations should be recorded. Where irregularities are found, corrective action should be taken and recorded.

7.4.8.1.1 Inspection of glass container closures

Glass containers consist of two pieces, viz., a glass container and lid (closure) usually metal, which can be twisted or pried off according to the closure design. Appropriate detailed inspections and tests should be conducted by competent personnel at intervals of sufficient frequency to ensure consistently reliable hermetic sealing. Many different designs of closures exist for glass jars, so that it is impossible to give definitive recommendations for such closures. The recommendations of the manufacturer should be carefully followed. Records of such tests and corrective actions should be maintained.

7.4.8.1.2 Inspection and tear-down of double seams

In addition to regular observations for external container defects by visual inspections, tear-down inspections should be performed by a competent individual and the results recorded at intervals of sufficient frequency at each seaming station to ensure maintenance of seam integrity. In the case of reformed cans, both double seams should be observed and inspected. When abnormalities are found, the corrective actions taken should be recorded. Both the measurements and their trends are important in the assessment of seam quality for control purposes. (Note: References to standard texts or manuals dealing with methods for the tearing down of double seams can be found in Appendix III.)

Either of the two following systems should be used to evaluate can seams:

Micrometer measurement:

        The following measurements should be made to the nearest 0.1 mm (0.001 in) using a suitable micrometer. The dimension of each measurement is indicated in figure 1.

        Prior to tearing down the double seam, measure and record the following:

    a)   countersink depth (A)
    b)   double seam width (length or height) (W)
    c)   double seam thickness (S)

        The following measurements and evaluations should be made on the torn down seam:

    a)   body hook length (BH)
    b)   cover hook length (CH)
    c)   end plate thickness (Te)
    d)   body plate thickness (Tb)
    e)   overlap (OL)
    f)   tightness rating
    g)   juncture rating
    h)   pressure ridge (chuck impression)

        The overlap can be calculated by either of the following two equations:

    i)   Overlap = 0 = (CH + BH + Te) - W

    ii)   Percent Overlap = % 0 = $\dfrac{(BH + CH + Te - W)}{(W - (2Te + Tb))}$ x 100

        For evaluation of the tightness, juncture (internal droop) and pressure ridge the references given above should be consulted. For round cans the above measurements should be made at a minimum of three points approximately 120° apart around the double seam, (excluding the point of juncture with the side seam).

        The free space and body hook butting are also measurements useful in the evaluation of double seam quality. These may be calculated by the following formulae:

Free Space = S - (2Tb + 3Te)

Percent Body Hook Butting = $\dfrac{(BH - 1.1\ Tb)}{(W - 1.1\ (2\ Te + Tb))}$ x 100   or

    = b/c x 100 (fig. 2)

        Optical measurements: overlap, body and coverhook lengths are directly visible in a cross-section of the double seam. Dimensions which cannot be optically measured should be measured by the micrometer. (See 7.4.8.1.2). **Wrinkling and other visual attributes can only be observed by stripping of the coverhook.** The segments of the double seam to be examined should, for example, be taken at two or more places on the same double seam of round cans.

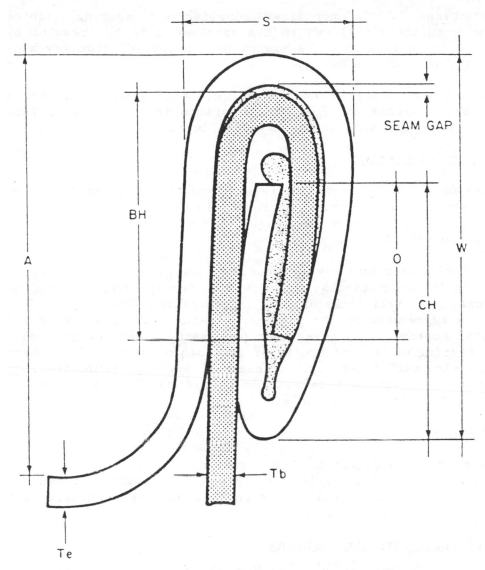

FIGURE 1

DOUBLE SEAM DIMENSIONAL TERMINOLOGY

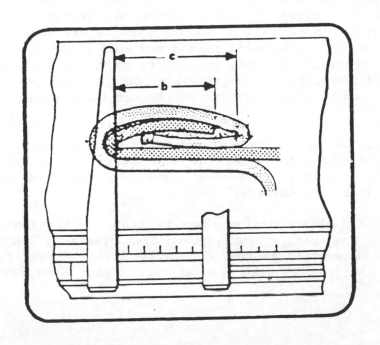

FIGURE 2

The instructions of the container supplier and seaming machine manufacturer should be accurately followed in the assessment of the results by either system and any additional tests. The agency having jurisdiction may have additional requirements which must be met.

Non-round cans require special consideration. Container manufacturer's specifications should be consulted and followed to ensure that the appropriate measurements and observations are made at the critical locations.

7.4.8.1.3   Inspection of heat seals

Appropriate visual inspections and tests should be conducted daily by competent, trained and experienced personnel at intervals of sufficient frequency to ensure consistent reliable hermetic sealing. Records of such tests and corrective action required should be maintained.

The strength of a heat seal may be reduced at the elevated temperatures used in retorts, hence it is important that such seals uniformly have the required strength prior to retorting. Small leaks or seal imperfections which may lead to loss of integrity can be aggravated by the physical strains induced by retorting and can permit microbial contamination after heat processing. Inspection should include some physical testing of the uniformity of strength of heat seals. There are several ways of checking seal integrity, for example, burst-pressure testing, seal thickness measurements. Appropriate methods should be obtained from the manufacturers of these containers or materials.

7.4.8.1.4   Closure defects

If a seam or closure defect is found upon routine inspection, which would result in a loss of hermetic integrity, all products produced between the discovery of the fault and the last satisfactory check should be identified and assessed.

7.4.9   Handling of containers after closure

7.4.9.1   At all times containers should be handled in a manner that protects container and closures from damage which may cause defects and subsequent microbial contamination. Design, operation and maintenance or container handling methods should be appropriate for the types of containers used. Poorly designed or incorrectly operated container conveying and loading systems are known to cause damage. For example, cans which are scramble packed may suffer damage, even when water cushioned, when the level of the cans in a crate or the crateless retort reduces the effectiveness of the cushion. Additionally, damage which may adversely affect integrity may be caused by poor alignment of the can feed mechanism, or by the presence of floaters.

Care should also be taken with semi and fully automatic crate loading systems as well as in-feed conveyor systems to continuous sterilizers. The accumulation of stationary containers on moving conveyors should be kept to a minimum, as this may also damage containers.

7.4.9.2   Semi-rigid and flexible containers may be prone to certain types of damage, (for example, snagging, tearing, cutting and flex cracking). Containers having sharp edges should be avoided as they may cause damage. Semi-rigid and flexible containers should be handled with special care. (See also Sub-Section 7.7.)

7.4.10   Coding

7.4.10.1   Each container should be marked with an identifying alphanumeric code which is permanent, legible and does not adversely affect the container integrity. Where the container does not permit the code to be embossed or inked, the label should be legibly perforated or otherwise marked, and securely affixed to the product container.

7.4.10.2   The code mark should identify the establishment where the product was packed, the product, the year and the day of the year and preferably the period of the day when the product was packed.

        The code mark permits the identification and isolation of code lots during production, distribution and sale. Canneries may find it useful to have a coding system from which the particular processing line and/or sealing machine can be identified. Such a system, supported by adequate cannery records, can be very helpful in any investigation.

        The identification of code lots on cases and trays is desirable.

7.4.11   Washing

7.4.11.1   Where necessary, filled and sealed containers should be thoroughly washed before sterilization to remove grease, dirt and product from the outside of the container.

7.4.11.2   Washing containers after sterilization should be avoided as it increases the risk of post-processing contamination and also it may be more difficult to remove food debris from the container external surface as it will adhere rather firmly after heating.

7.5   Thermal Processing

7.5.1   General considerations

7.5.1.1   Prior to use, after installation of a thermal processing system or following any modification to or in the use of a system, temperature distribution studies should be carried out to determine the uniformity of temperature within the thermal processing system. Appropriate records should be maintained.

7.5.1.2   Scheduled processes for low-acid canned foods must be established only by competent persons having expert knowledge of thermal processing and having adequate facilities for making such determinations. It is absolutely necessary to establish the required heat process with accepted scientific methods.

        The heat process required to make low-acid canned foods commercially sterile depends on the microbial load, storage temperature, the presence of various preservatives, water activity, composition of the products and container size and type. Low-acid foods with pH values above 4.6 may be able to support the growth of many kinds of microorganisms including the heat resistant sporeforming pathogens such as Clostridium botulinum. It should be emphasized that the thermal processing of low-acid canned foods is a very critical operation, involving public health risks and appreciable losses of finished product if under-sterilization occurs.

7.5.2   Establishing scheduled processes

7.5.2.1   The procedure to establish the required heat treatment for a product can be divided into two steps.   First the required heat process to achieve commercial sterility should be established on the basis of factors such as:

Microbial flora including *Clostridium botulinum* and spoilage microorganisms;

Container size and type;
pH of the product;
Product composition or formulation;
Levels and types of preservatives;
Water activity; and
Likely storage temperature of the product.

Due to the nature of the packaging materials used, flexible, and to some extent semi-rigid, containers will change dimensions when exposed to applied physical stress.   It is extremely important that the package dimensions, particularly the depth or thickness, shall be as specified in the scheduled process.

7.5.2.2   The second step is to determine the scheduled process taking into account the sterilizing facilities available and the desired product quality by carrying out heat penetration tests.   The heat penetration into the product must be determined under the most adverse conditions that are likely to be met in production.   For this purpose the temperature in the slowest heating point in the container contents should be monitored during a heat process.   It is essential to carry out an adequate number of heat penetration tests to determine the variations which should be taken into account in the scheduled process.   The scheduled process can be determined from the time temperature graph obtained.

7.5.2.3   Because of the nature of the packaging materials used in flexible and semi-rigid containers, the container alone cannot generally be used to fix the heat sensing element at the "cold point" in the container contents, which is vital to the proper interpretation of the results.   Therefore, other means may be required to ensure that the temperature sensing device is maintained at the pre-determined point in the container contents without altering the heat penetration characteristics.   During such testing the container dimensions, specially the thickness, must be controlled.

7.5.2.4   If the heat penetration tests have been made using laboratory simulators, the results should be verified in the production retort under conditions of commercial operation because there may be unexpected deviations in product heating and cooling characteristics.

7.5.2.5   If accurate heat penetration data cannot be obtained, alternative methods acceptable to the agency having jurisdiction should be used.

7.5.2.6   For products showing a simple heating curve only, where size of the container, sterilization temperature, initial temperature or process time are changed from an existing scheduled process the original heat penetration tests can be used to calculate the scheduled process for the new conditions.   The results should be verified by further heat penetration tests when the size of the container is substantially changed.

7.5.2.7   With products showing a broken heating curve, changes in the scheduled processes should be determined using further heat penetration tests or other methods acceptable to the agency having jurisdiction.

7.5.2.8   The result of these heat process determinations together with established critical factors should be incorporated into the scheduled process. For conventionally sterilized canned products such a scheduled process should include as a minimum the following data:

-    Products and filling specification, including any restrictions on ingredient changes;

-    Container size (dimensions) and type;

-    Container orientation and spacing in retort where appropriate;

-    Ingoing weight of product(s) including liquor where appropriate;

-    Headspace, where applicable;

-    Minimum initial product temperature;

-    Venting procedures, and come-up procedures for certain retort systems, where applicable, should be determined on fully loaded retorts;

-    Type and characteristics of heat processing system;

-    Sterilization temperature;

-    Sterilization time;

-    Overpressure, where applicable;

-    Cooling method.

        Any changes in the product specifications should be evaluated as to their effect on the adequacy of the process. If the scheduled process is found to be inadequate it must be re-established.

        Product and filling specifications should contain at least the following where applicable: full recipe and preparation procedures, filling weights, headspace, drained weight, temperature of product at filling, consistency. Small deviations from the product and filling specifications which may seem negligible can cause serious deviations in the heat penetration properties of the product. For rotational sterilization, viscosity (rather than consistency) can be an important factor, and this should be specified.

7.5.2.9   Air content of filled flexible and semi-rigid containers should be kept to a minimum to prevent excessive stressing of the seals during thermal processing.

7.5.2.10   For aseptically processed packs a similar list should be made which also should include equipment and container sterilization requirements.

7.5.2.11   Complete records concerning all aspects of the establishment of the scheduled process, including any associated incubation tests, should be permanently retained and available.

7.5.3   Heat processing room operations

7.5.3.1   Scheduled processes and venting procedures to be used for products and container sizes being packed should be posted in a conspicuous place near the processing equipment. Such information should be readily available to the retort or processing system operator and to the agency having jurisdiction. It is essential that all heat processing equipment should be properly designed, correctly installed and carefully maintained. Only properly determined scheduled processes must be used.

7.5.3.2   Heat processing and associated processing operations should be performed and supervised only by properly trained personnel. It is extremely important that the heat processing is carried out by operators under the supervision of personnel who understand the principles of heat processing and who realize the need to follow instructions closely.

7.5.3.3   Heat processing should be commenced as soon as possible after closing to avoid microbial growth or changes in heat transfer characteristics of the products. If during breakdowns the production rate is low, the product should be processed in partly filled retorts. Where necessary, a separate scheduled process should be established for partly filled retorts.

7.5.3.4   In batch operations the sterilization status of the containers should be indicated. All retort baskets, trucks, cars or crates containing unretorted food product or at least one of the containers on the top of each basket, etc., should be plainly and conspicuously marked with a heat sensitive indicator, or by other effective means, which will visually indicate whether or not each such unit has been retorted. Heat sensitive indicators attached to baskets, trucks, cars or crates must be removed before they are refilled with containers.

7.5.3.5   The initial temperature of the contents of the coldest containers to be processed should be determined and recorded with sufficient frequency to ensure that the temperature of the product is no lower than the minimum initial temperature specified in the scheduled process.

7.5.3.6   An accurate, clearly visible clock or other suitable timing device should be installed in the heat processing room and times should be read from this instrument and not from wristwatches, etc. Where two or more clocks or other timing devices are used in a heat processing room they should be synchronized.

7.5.3.7   Generally temperature/time recording devices are not satisfactory for measuring the sterilization or thermal process times.

7.5.4   Critical factors and the application of the scheduled process

In addition to the minimum product initial temperature, sterilization time and temperature together with overpressure, where applicable, as specified in the scheduled process, other critical factors specified should be measured, controlled and recorded at intervals of sufficient frequency to ensure that these factors remain within the limits specified in the scheduled process. Some examples of critical factors are:

(i)   Maximum fill-in or drained weight.

(ii)   Minimum headspace of product containers.

(iii) Product consistency or viscosity as determined by objective measurement on product taken before processing.

(iv) Product and/or container type which may result in layering or stratification of the product, or in changes in the container dimensions hence requiring specific orientation and spacing of the containers in the retort.

(v) Percent solids.

(vi) Minimum net weight.

(vii) Minimum closing vacuum (in vacuum packed products).

7.6   Equipment and Procedures for Heat Processing Systems

7.6.1   Instruments and controls common to different heat processing systems

7.6.1.1   Indicating thermometer

Each retort and/or product sterilizer should be equipped with at least one indicating thermometer. The mercury-in-glass thermometer is recognized as the most reliable temperature indicating instrument at the present time. An alternative instrument having equal or better accuracy and reliability may be used subject to the approval of the official agency having jurisdiction. The mercury-in-glass thermometer should have divisions that are easily readable to 0.5°C (1°F) and whose scale contains not more than 4.0°C per cm (17°F per inch) of graduated scale. Thermometers should be tested for accuracy against a known accurate standard thermometer. This should be done in steam or water as appropriate and in a similar position of aspect to that which it is installed in the retort. Such tests should be performed just prior to installation, and at least once a year thereafter or more frequently as may be necessary to ensure their accuracy. A dated record of such tests should be kept. A thermometer that deviates more than 0.5°C (1°F) from the standard should be replaced. A daily inspection of mercury-in-glass thermometers should be made to detect and replace, if found, thermometers with divided mercury column or other defects.

7.6.1.2   Where other types of thermometer are used, routine tests should be made which ensure at least equivalent performance to that described for mercury-in-glass thermometers. Thermometers which do not meet these requirements should be replaced or repaired immediately.

7.6.1.3   Temperature/time recording devices

Each retort and/or product sterilizer should be equipped with at least one temperature/time recording device. This recorder may be combined with the steam controller and may be a recording-controlling instrument. It is important that the correct chart is used for each device. Each chart should have a working scale of not more than 12°C per cm (55°F per in.) within a range of 10°C (20°F) of the sterilizing temperature. The recording accuracy should be equal to or better than ± 0.5°C (1°F) at the sterilizing temperature. The recorder should agree as closely as possible (preferably within 0.5°C (1°F)) and should not be higher than the indicating thermometer at the sterilizing temperature. A means of preventing unauthorized changes in the adjustment should be provided. It is important that the chart should also be used to provide a permanent record of the sterilization temperature in relation to time. The chart timing device should be accurate and checked as often as necessary to maintain accuracy.

7.6.1.4   <u>Pressure gauges</u>

Each retort should be equipped with a pressure gauge. The gauge should be checked for accuracy at least once a year. The gauge should have a range from zero such that the safe working pressure of the retort is about two-thirds of the full scale and be graduated in divisions not greater than 0.14 kg/cm² (2 p.s.i.). The gauge dial should not be less than 102 mm (4.0 in.) in diameter. The instrument may be connected to the retort by means of a gauge cock and syphon.

7.6.1.5   <u>Steam controller</u>

Each retort should be equipped with a steam controller to maintain the retort temperature. This may be a recording-controlling instrument when combined with a recording thermometer.

7.6.1.6   <u>Pressure relief valve</u>

An adjustable pressure relief valve of a capacity sufficient to prevent undesired increase in retort pressure and approved by the agency having jurisdiction should be fitted.

7.6.1.7   <u>Timing devices</u>

These should be checked as often as necessary to ensure accuracy.

7.6.2   <u>Pressure processing in steam</u>

7.6.2.1   <u>Batch (Still retorts)</u>

7.6.2.1.1   <u>Indicating thermometers and temperature/time recording devices</u> (see Sub-Sections 7.6.1.1, 7.6.1.2 and 7.6.1.3)

Bulb sheaths of indicating thermometers and probes of temperature recording devices should be installed either within the retort shell or in external wells attached to the retort. External wells should be equipped with an adequate bleeder opening so located as to provide a constant flow of steam past the length of the thermometer bulb or probe. The bleeder for external wells should emit steam continuously during the entire heat processing period. Thermometers should be installed where they can be accurately and easily read.

7.6.2.1.2   <u>Pressure gauges</u> (see Sub-Section 7.6.1.4)

7.6.2.1.3   <u>Steam controllers</u> (see Sub-Section 7.6.1.5)

7.6.2.1.4   <u>Pressure relief valve</u> (see Sub-Section 7.6.1.6)

7.6.2.1.5   <u>Steam inlet</u>

The steam inlet to each retort should be large enough to provide sufficient steam for proper operation of the retort, and should enter at a suitable point to facilitate air removal during venting.

7.6.2.1.6   <u>Crate supports</u>

A bottom crate support should be employed in vertical still retorts so as not to substantially affect venting and steam distribution. Baffle plates should not be used in the bottom of retorts. Centering guides should be installed in vertical retorts to ensure adequate clearance between the retort crate and the retort wall.

7.6.2.1.7 Steam spreaders

Perforated steam spreaders, if used, should be checked regularly to ensure they are not blocked or otherwise inoperative. Horizontal still retorts should be equipped with perforated steam spreaders that extend for the full length of the retort. In vertical still retorts the perforated steam spreaders, if used, should be in the form of a cross or coil. The number of perforations in spreaders for both horizontal and vertical still retorts should be such that the total cross-sectional area of the perforations is equal to 1 1/2 to 2 times the cross-sectional area of the smallest part of the steam inlet line.

7.6.2.1.8 Bleeders and condensate removal

Bleeders should be of suitable size, (e.g., 3 mm (1/8 in.)), and location and should be fully open during the entire process, including the coming-up-time. In retorts having top steam inlet and bottom venting, a suitable device should be installed in the bottom of the retort to remove condensate and a bleeder fitted to indicate condensate removal. All bleeders should be arranged in such a way that the operator can observe that they are functioning properly. Bleeders are not part of the venting system.

7.6.2.1.9 Stacking equipment

Crates, trays, gondolas, dividers, etc., for holding product containers should be so constructed that steam can adequately be circulated around the containers during the venting, coming-up and sterilization times.

7.6.2.1.10 Vents

Vents should be located in that portion of the retort opposite the steam inlet and should be designed, installed and operated in such a way that air is removed from the retort before timing of the thermal process is started. Vents should be fully opened to permit rapid removal of air from retorts during the venting period. Vents should not be connected directly to a closed drain system without an atmospheric break in the line. Where a retort manifold connects several pipes from a single still retort, it should be controlled by a single suitable valve. The manifold should be of a size such that the cross-sectional area of the manifold is larger than the total cross-subsection area of all connecting vents. The discharge should not be directly connected to a closed drain without an atmospheric break in the line. A manifold header connecting vents or manifolds from several still retorts should lead to the atmosphere. The manifold header should not be controlled by a valve and should be of a size such that the cross-subsectional area is at least equal to the total cross-sectional area of all connecting retort manifold pipes from all retorts venting simultaneously. Other vent piping arrangements and operating procedures which differ from the above specifications may be used, provided that there is evidence that they accomplish adequate venting.

7.6.2.1.11 Air inlets

Retorts using air for pressure cooling should be equipped with an adequate tight closing valve and piping arrangement on the air line to prevent air leakage into the retort during processing.

7.6.2.1.12 Critical factors (see Sub-Section 7.5.4)

7.6.2.2   Batch agitating retorts

7.6.2.2.1   Indicating thermometers and temperature/time recording devices (see Sub-Sections 7.6.1.1, 7.6.1.2 and 7.6.1.3)

7.6.2.2.2   Pressure gauges (see Sub-Section 7.6.1.4)

7.6.2.2.3   Steam controller (see Sub-Section 7.6.1.5)

7.6.2.2.4   Pressure relief valve (see Sub-Section 7.6.1.6)

7.6.2.2.5   Steam inlet (see Sub-Section 7.6.2.1.5)

7.6.2.2.6   Steam spreaders (see Sub-Section 7.6.2.1.7)

7.6.2.2.7   Bleeders and condensate removal (see Sub-Section 7.6.2.1.8)

        At the time the steam is turned on, the drain should be opened for a time sufficient to remove steam condensate from the retort and provision should be made for continuing drainage of condensate during the retort operation. The bleeders in the bottom of the shell serve as an indicator of continuous condensate removal. The retort operator should observe and periodically record how this bleeder is functioning.

7.6.2.2.8   Stacking equipment (see Sub-Section 7.6.2.1.9)

7.6.2.2.9   Vents (see Sub-Section 7.6.2.1.10)

7.6.2.2.10 Air inlets (see Sub-Section 7.6.2.1.11)

7.6.2.2.11 Retort or reel speed timing

        The rotational speed of the retort or reel is critical and should be specified in the scheduled process. The speed should be adjusted and recorded when the retort is started, and at intervals of sufficient frequency to insure that the retort speed is maintained as specified in the scheduled process. If a change of speed inadvertently occurs such should be recorded together with corrective action taken. Additionally, a recording tachometer may be used to provide a continuous record of the speed. The speed should be checked against a stop watch at least once per shift. A means of preventing unauthorized speed changes on retorts should be provided.

7.6.2.2.12 Critical factors (see Sub-Section 7.5.4)

7.6.2.3   Continuous agitating retorts

7.6.2.3.1   Indicating thermometers and temperature/time recording devices (see Sub-Sections 7.6.1.1, 7.6.1.2 and 7.6.1.3)

7.6.2.3.2   Pressure gauges (see Sub-Section 7.6.1.4)

7.6.2.3.3   Steam controllers (see Sub-Section 7.6.1.5)

7.6.2.3.4   Pressure relief valve (see Sub-Section 7.6.1.6)

7.6.2.3.5   Steam inlet (see Sub-Section 7.6.2.1.5)

7.6.2.3.6   Steam spreaders (see Sub-Section 7.6.2.1.7)

7.6.2.3.7   Bleeders and condensate removal (see Sub-Section 7.6.2.2.7)

7.6.2.3.8   Vents (see Sub-Section 7.6.2.1.10)

7.6.2.3.9   Retort and reel speed timing (see Sub-Section 7.6.2.2.11)

7.6.2.3.10   Critical factors (see Sub-Section 7.5.4)

7.6.2.4   Hydrostatic retorts

7.6.2.4.1   Indicating thermometers (see Sub-Section 7.6.1.1)

        Thermometers should be located in the steam dome near the steam-water
interface and preferably also at the tope of the dome. Where the scheduled process
specifies maintenance of particular temperatures of water in the hydrostatic water
legs, at least one indicating thermometer should be located in each hydrostatic
water leg so that it can accurately measure water temperature and be easily read.

7.6.2.4.2   Temperature/time recording device (see Sub-Section 7.6.1.3)

        The temperature recorder probe should be installed either within the
steam dome or in a well attached to the dome. Additional temperature recorder
probes should be installed in the hydrostatic water legs if the scheduled process
specifies maintenance of particular temperatures in these hydrostatic water legs.

7.6.2.4.3   Pressure gauges (see Sub-Section 7.6.1.4)

7.6.2.4.4   Steam controllers (see Sub-Section 7.6.1.5)

7.6.2.4.5   Steam inlet (see Sub-Section 7.6.2.1.5)

7.6.2.4.6   Bleeders

        Bleeders should be of suitable size, (e.g., 3 mm (1/8 in.)) and
location and should be fully open during the entire process, including the
come-up-time and should be suitable located in the steam chamber or chambers to
remove air which may enter with the steam.

7.6.2.4.7   Venting

        Before the start of processing operations, the retort steam chamber or
chambers should be vented to ensure removal of air.

7.6.2.4.8   Conveyor speed

        The speed of the container conveyor should be specified in the
scheduled process and should be determined with an accurate stop watch, and
recorded at the start of processing and at intervals of sufficient frequency to
insure that the conveyor speed is maintained as specified. An automatic device
should be used to stop the conveyor and provide warning when the temperature drops
below that specified in the scheduled process. A means of preventing unauthorized
speed changes should be provided. Additionally a recording device may be used to
provide a continuous record of the speed.

7.6.2.4.9   <u>Critical factors</u> (see Sub-Section 7.5.4)

7.6.3   <u>Pressure processing in water</u>

7.6.3.1   <u>Batch</u> (Still retorts)

7.6.3.1.1   <u>Indicating thermometer</u> (see Sub-Section 7.6.1.1)

        Bulbs of indicating thermometers should be located in such a position
that they are beneath the surface of the water throughout the process. On
horizontal retorts this should be in the side at the centre, and the thermometer
bulbs should be inserted directly into the retort shell. In both vertical and
horizontal retorts, the thermometer bulbs should extend directly in to the water
for a minimum of at least 5 cm (2 in.).

7.6.3.1.2   <u>Temperature/time recording device</u> (see Sub-Section 7.6.1.3)

        When the retort is equipped with a temperature recording device, the
recording thermometer bulb should be at a location adjacent to the indicating
thermometer or at a location which adequately represents the lowest temperature in
the retort. In any case, care should be taken that the steam does not strike the
controller bulb directly.

7.6.3.1.3   <u>Pressure gauge</u> (see Sub-Section 7.6.1.4)

7.6.3.1.4   <u>Pressure relief valve</u> (see Sub-Section 7.6.1.6)

7.6.3.1.5   <u>Pressure control valve</u>

        In addition to the pressure relief valve an adjustable pressure control
valve of a capacity sufficient to prevent undesired increases in retort pressure,
even when the water valve is wide open, should be installed in the overflow line.
This valve also controls the maximum water level in the retort. The valve should
be suitable screened to prevent blockage by floating containers or debris.

7.6.3.1.6   <u>Pressure recorder</u>

        A pressure recorder device is needed and may be combined with a
pressure controller.

7.6.3.1.7   <u>Steam controller</u> (see Sub-Section 7.6.1.5)

7.6.3.1.8   <u>Steam inlet</u>

        The steam inlet should be large enough to provide sufficient steam for
proper operation of the retort.

7.6.3.1.9   <u>Steam distribution</u> (see Sub-Section 7.6.2.1.7)

        Steam should be distributed from the bottom of the retort in a manner
to provide uniform heat distribution throughout the retort.

7.6.3.1.10   <u>Crate supports</u> (see Sub-Section 7.6.2.1.6)

7.6.3.1.11   Stacking equipment

Crates, trays, gondolas, etc. and divider plates when used for holding product containers, should be so constructed that the heating water can adequately circulate around the containers during the coming-up and sterilization times. Special equipment will be required to ensure that the thickness of filled flexible containers will not exceed that specified in the scheduled process and that they will not become displaced and overlap one another during the thermal process.

7.6.3.1.12   Drain valve

A screened, non-clogging, water-tight valve should be used.

7.6.3.1.13   Water level

There should be a means of determining the water level in the retort during operation (e.g. by using a water gauge glass or petcock(s)). Water should adequately cover the top layer of containers during the entire coming-up, sterilizing and cooling periods. This water level should be at least 15 cm (6 in.) over the top layer of product containers in the retort.

7.6.3.1.14   Air supply and controls

In both horizontal and vertical still retorts for pressure processing in water, a means should be provided for introducing compressed air at the proper pressure and rate. The retort pressure should be controlled by an automatic pressure control unit. A non-return valve should be provided in the air supply line to prevent water from entering the system. Air or water circulation should be maintained continuously during the coming-up-time, processing and cooling periods. Air is usually introduced with steam to prevent "steam hammer". If air is used to promote circulation it should be introduced into the steam line at a point between the retort and the steam control valve at the bottom of the retort.

7.6.3.1.15   Cooling water entry

In retorts processing glass jars the cooling water should be introduced in a manner which avoids direct impingement on the jars, in order to prevent breakage by thermal shock.

7.6.3.1.16   Retort headspace

The air pressure in the headspace of the retort should be controlled throughout the process.

7.6.3.1.17   Water circulation

All water circulation systems, whether by pumps or air, used for heat distribution should be installed in such a manner that an even temperature distribution throughout the retort is maintained. Checks for correct operation should be made during each processing cycle, for example, alarm systems to indicate malfunction of water circulation.

7.6.3.1.18   Critical factors in the application of the scheduled process (see Sub-Section 7.5.4)

7.6.3.2   Batch agitating retorts

7.6.3.2.1   <u>Indicating thermometer</u> (see Sub-Section 7.6.3.1.1)

7.6.3.2.2   <u>Temperature/time recording device</u> (see Sub-Section 7.6.1.2)

        The recording thermometer probe should be located adjacent to the bulb of the indicating thermometer.

7.6.3.2.3   <u>Pressure gauges</u> (see Sub-Section 7.6.1.3)

7.6.3.2.4   <u>Pressure relief valve</u> (see Sub-Section 7.6.1.5)

7.6.3.2.5   <u>Pressure control valve</u> (see Sub-Section 7.6.3.1.5)

7.6.3.2.6   <u>Pressure recorder</u> (see Sub-Section 7.6.3.1.6)

7.6.3.2.7   <u>Steam controller</u> (see Sub-Section 7.6.1.4)

7.6.3.2.8   <u>Steam inlet</u> (see Sub-Section 7.6.2.1.5)

7.6.3.2.9   <u>Steam spreader</u> (see Sub-Section 7.6.2.1.7)

7.6.3.2.10   <u>Drain valve</u> (see Sub-Section 7.6.3.1.12)

7.6.3.2.11   <u>Water level indicator</u> (see Sub-Section 7.6.3.1.13)

7.6.3.2.12   <u>Air supply and controls</u> (see Sub-Section 7.6.3.1.14)

7.6.3.2.13   <u>Cooling water entry</u> (see Sub-Section 7.6.3.1.15)

7.6.3.2.14   <u>Water circulation</u> (see Sub-Section 7.6.3.1.17)

7.6.3.2.15   <u>Retort speed timing</u> (see Sub-Section 7.6.2.2.11)

7.6.3.2.16   <u>Critical factors in the application of the scheduled process</u> (see Sub-Section 7.5.4)

7.6.4   <u>Pressure processing in steam-air mixtures</u>

        Both the temperature distribution and the rates of heat transfer are critically important in the operation of steam-air retorts. There should be a means of circulating the steam-air mixtures to prevent formation of low temperature pockets. The circulating system used should provide acceptable heat distribution as established by adequate tests. The operation of the processing system should be the same as that required by the scheduled process. A recording pressure controller should control the air inlet and the steam-air mixture outlet. Because of the variety of existing designs, reference should be made to the equipment manufacturer and to the agency having jurisdiction for details of installation, operation and control. **Some items of equipment may be common to those already in this code and those standards given may be relevant.**

7.6.5   <u>Aseptic processing and packaging systems</u>

7.6.5.1   <u>Product sterilization equipment and operation</u>

7.6.5.1.1   Temperature indicating device (see Sub-Section 7.6.1.3)

The device should be installed in the product holding section outlet in such a way that it does not interfere with product flow.

7.6.5.1.2   Temperature recording device (see Sub-Section 7.6.1.3)

The temperature sensor should be located in the sterilized product at the holding section outlet in such a way that it does not interfere with the product flow.

7.6.5.1.3   Temperature recorder-controller

An accurate temperature recorder-controller should be located in the product sterilizer at the final heater outlet in such a way as not to interfere with product flow. It should be capable of ensuring that the desired product sterilization temperature is maintained.

7.6.5.1.4   Product-to-product regenerators

Where a product-to-product regenerator is used to heat the cold unsterilized product entering the sterilizer by means of a heat exchange system, it should be designed, operated and controlled so that the pressure of the sterilized product in the regenerator is greater than the pressure of any unsterilized product.

This ensures that any leakage in the regenerator will be from the sterilized product into the unsterilized product.

7.6.5.1.5   Differential pressure recorder-controller

Where a product-to-product regenerator is used, there should be an accurate differential pressure recorder-controller installed on the regenerator. The scale divisions should be easily readable and should not exceed 0.14 kg per cm^2 (2 lbs per square in.) on a working scale of not more than 1.4 $kg/cm^2/cm$ (20 lbs per square inch per inch). The controller should be tested for accuracy against a known accurate standard pressure indicator, upon installation and at least once every three months of operation thereafter or more frequently as may be necessary to ensure its accuracy. One pressure sensor should be installed at the sterilized product regenerator outlet, and the other pressure sensor should be installed at the unsterilized product regenerator inlet.

7.6.5.1.6   Metering pump

A metering pump should be located upstream from the holding section and should be operated consistently to maintain the required rate of product flow. A means of preventing unauthorized speed changes should be provided. The product flow rate, which is the critical factor controlling the sterilization holding time, should be checked with sufficient frequency to ensure that it is as specified in the scheduled process.

7.6.5.1.7   Product-holding section

The product sterilizer holding section should be designed to give continuous holding of the product, including particulates, for at least the minimum holding time specified in the scheduled process. It should be sloped upward at

least 2.0 cm/m (0.25 in. per foot). The holding section should be designed so that
no portion between the product inlet and the product outlet can be heated.

7.6.5.1.8   Startup

Prior to the start of aseptic processing operations, the product
sterilizer should be brought to a condition of commercial sterility.

7.6.5.1.9   Temperature drop in product holding section

When product temperature in the holding section drops below the
temperature specified in the scheduled process, the product in the holding section
and any downstream portions affected should be diverted to recirculation or waste
and the system returned to a condition of commercial sterility before flow is
resumed to the filter.

7.6.5.1.10   Loss of proper pressures in the regenerator

Where a regenerator is used the product may lose sterility whenever the
pressure of sterilized product in the regenerator is less than 0.07 kg/cm^2 (1 lb
per square in.) greater than the pressure of unsterilized product. Product flow
should be directed either to waste or recirculated until the cause of the improper
pressure relationship has been corrected and the affected system(s) has been
returned to a condition of commercial sterility.

7.6.5.2   Product container sterilization, filling and closing operations

7.6.5.2.1   Recording device

The systems for container and closure sterilization, as well as filling
and closing should be instrumented to show that the scheduled conditions are
achieved and maintained. During pre-sterilization as well as production, automatic
recording devices should be used to record, where applicable, the sterilization
media flow rates and/or temperatures. Where a batch system is used for container
sterilization, the sterilization conditions should be recorded.

7.6.5.2.2   Timing method(s)

A method(s) should be used either to give the retention time of
containers, and closure if applicable, as specified in the scheduled process, or
to control the sterilization cycle at the rate as specified in the scheduled
process. A means of preventing unauthorized speed changes should be provided.

7.6.5.2.3   Startup

Prior to the start of filling, both the container and closure
sterilizing system and the product filling and closing system should be brought to
a condition of commercial sterility.

7.6.5.2.4   Loss of sterility

In the event of loss of sterility, the system(s) should be returned to
a condition of commercial sterility before resuming operations.

7.6.6   Flame sterilizers, equipment and procedures

The container conveyor speed should be specified in the scheduled process. The container conveyor speed should be measured and recorded at the start of operations and at intervals of sufficient frequency to ensure that the conveyor speed is as specified in the scheduled process. Alternatively, a recording tachometer may be used to provide a continuous record of the speed. Speed should be checked against a stop watch at least once per shift. A means of preventing unauthorized speed changes on the conveyor should be provided. The surface temperature of at least one container from each conveyor channel should be measured and recorded at the end of the pre-heat section and at the end of the holding period at intervals of sufficient frequency to ensure that the temperatures specified in the scheduled process are maintained.

7.6.7   Other systems

Systems for the thermal processing of low-acid foods in hermetically sealed containers should conform to the applicable requirements of this Code and should ensure that the methods and control used for the manufacture, processing and/or packing of such foods are operated and administered in a manner adequate to achieve commercial sterility.

7.6.8   Cooling

To avoid thermophilic spoilage and/or organoleptic deterioration of the product, the containers should be cooled as rapidly as possible to an internal temperature of 40°C (104°F). In practice, water cooling is usually used for this purpose. Further cooling is done in air to evaporate the adhering water film. This aids in preventing both microbiological contamination and corrosion. Air cooling alone may also be used for products in which thermophilic spoilage is not a problem, provided that the product and the containers are suitable for air cooling. Unless otherwise indicated, extra pressure should be applied during cooling to compensate for the internal pressure inside the container at the beginning of cooling to prevent the deformation or leakage of containers. This can be minimized by equating the over pressure with the internal pressure.

When the integrity of the container is not adversely affected, water or air under atmospheric pressure may be used for cooling. Extra pressure is commonly achieved by introducing water or compressed air into the retort under pressure.

To reduce thermal shock to glass containers the temperature of the cooling medium in the retort should be reduced slowly during the initial cooling phase.

In all instances the container and closure manufacturers' instructions should be followed.

7.6.8.1   Cooling water quality

Cooling water should consistently be of low microbial content, for example, with an aerobic mesophile count of less tan 100 c.f.u./ml. Records should be kept of cooling water treatment and of its microbiological quality. Although containers may normally be considered hermetically sealed, a small number of containers may allow intake of water during the cooling period mainly due to mechanical stress and pressure differential.

7.6.8.2   To ensure effective disinfection, chlorine or an alternative disinfectant must be thoroughly mixed with the water to a level which will minimize the risk of contamination of the can contents during cooling: for chlorination a 20 minute minimum contact time at suitable pH and temperature is normally considered adequate.

The adequacy of a suitable chlorination treatment may be established by:

a)   the presence of a measurable residual free chlorine in the water at the end of the contact time; and

b)   detectable amounts of residual free chlorine in the water after it has been used for cooling containers. (Residual free chlorine content of 0.5 to 2 p.p.m. is usually considered adequate. Chlorine levels in excess of this may accelerate corrosion of certain metallic containers.)

c)   a low microbial content of the water at the point of use. The temperature and pH of the water should be measured and recorded for reference.

Once a suitable system has been established, the adequacy of treatment is indicated by measuring and recording the free residual chlorine according to b) above. In addition water temperature and pH should be measured and recorded since marked changes from the reference values previously established may adversely affect the disinfecting action of the added chlorine.

The amount of chlorine required for adequate disinfection will depend upon the chlorine demand of the water, its pH and temperature. Where water with a high level of organic impurity, (e.g. surface water) is used as a source of supply, it will usually be necessary to provide suitable treatment for separation of impurities, prior to disinfection by chlorine thereby reducing excessive chlorine demand. Recirculated cooling water may gradually increase in organic load and it may be necessary to reduce this by separation or other means. If the pH of cooling water is greater than 7.0 or its temperature is above 30°C it may be necessary to increase the minimum contact time or concentration of chlorine to achieve adequate disinfection. Similar actions may be necessary with water disinfected by means other than addition of chlorine.

It is essential that cooling water storage tanks be constructed of impervious materials and protected by close-fitting covers thus preventing contamination of the water by seepage, entry of surface waters or other sources of contamination. These tanks should also be fitted with baffles or other means of ensuring thorough mixing of water and chlorine or other disinfectant. They should be of sufficient capacity to ensure that the minimum residence time is achieved under maximum throughput conditions. Particular attention should be paid to positioning of inlet and outlet pipes to ensure all water follows a pre-determined flow pattern within the tank. Cooling tanks and systems should be drained, cleaned and refilled periodically to prevent excessive organic and microbial buildup. Records should be kept of such procedures.

Measurements of microbial content and chlorine or alternative disinfectant levels should be made with sufficient frequency to enable adequate control of cooling water quality. Records should be kept of cooling water treatment and of its microbiological quality.

7.6.8.3   Where contaminated water with a high level of organic impurity, such as river water, is used as a source of supply it will be necessary to provide a suitable treatment system to cope with suspended impurities followed by chlorination or other suitable disinfection treatment.

7.7   Post Process Container Handling

A small proportion of correctly made and closed cans may be subject to temporary leaks (microleakage) during the later stages of cooling and for as long as the cans and their seams remain externally wet. The risk of microleakage may be increased if poor seam quality and inadequately designed container conveyor, handling, labelling and packaging equipment result in increased can abuse. When such leakage occurs, water on the can provides a source and a transport medium for microbial contamination from conveyor and equipment surfaces to areas on or near the can seams. To control leaker infection it is necessary to ensure that:

1)   cans are dried as soon as possible after processing;

2)   conveying systems and equipment are designed to minimize abuse of the containers; and

3)   conveyor and equipment surfaces are effectively cleaned and disinfected.

Glass jars may be similarly affected.

The post-process area should be effectively separated from raw food to avoid cross contamination. Precautions should also be taken to ensure personnel from the raw food areas do not have uncontrolled access to the post-process area.

Temporary leaks are not a problem with correctly formed heat seals on semi-rigid and flexible containers. However, leakage may occur through defective seals and perforations in the container bodies. Therefore the requirements for drying containers, minimizing abuse and ensuring effective cleaning and disinfection of conveyor systems are equally applicable to these types of containers.

7.7.1   Retort crate unloading

To minimize leaker infection especially by pathogenic microorganisms, processed containers should not be manually handled while still wet.

Before unloading retort crates, water should be drained from container surfaces. In many instances this can be accomplished by tilting the retort crates as far as possible and allowing sufficient time for the water to drain. The containers should remain in the crates until dry before manual unloading. Manual unloading of wet containers presents a risk of contamination from pathogenic microorganisms which may be transferred from the hands onto the container.

7.7.2   Container drying precautions

Where used, dryers should be shown not to cause damage to or contaminate containers and should be readily accessible for routine cleaning and disinfection. Not all driers meet these requirements. The drying unit should be employed in the line as soon as practicable after cooling.

Driers do not remove all cooling water residues from container external surfaces but they reduce significantly the time containers are wet. This reduces the length of post-drier conveying equipment that becomes wet during production periods and which requires extra cleaning and disinfection measures.

The drying of batch processed containers may be accelerated by dipping the filled retort crates in a tank of a suitable surfactant solution. After immersion (15 sec) the crates should be tipped and allowed to drain.

It is essential that any dipping solution be kept at not less than 80°C to avoid microbial growth and be changed at the end of each shift. Technically appropriate anti-corrosion agents may also be incorporated in dipping solutions.

7.7.3   Container abuse

Mechanical shock or abuse is mainly caused by either containers knocking into each other, (for example, on gravity runways), or by pressing against each other, for example, when the backup of containers on cable runways results in the development of excessive pressure and possible seam damage due to cable burn. Abuse may also be caused by containers hitting protruding sections on conveying systems. Such mechanical shocks may cause temporary or permanent leaks and result in infection if the containers are wet.

Careful attention to the design, layout, operation and maintenance of conveying systems is necessary if abuse is to be reduced to a minimum. One of the commonest design faults is unnecessary changes in the height of different sections of the conveying system. For lines speeds above 300 cpm, (containers per minute), multi-lane conveying systems coupled with container accumulation tables are recommended. Sensors should be installed to allow the conveyor to be stopped if excessive buildup of containers occur. Poor seam quality in combination with inadequately designed, adjusted or maintained unscrambling, labelling and packaging equipment increases the risk of microleakage. Special care should be taken to prevent abuse to glass containers and their closures, as well as to semi-rigid and flexible containers.

Abuse of semi-rigid and flexible containers may lead to perforation of the container or to flexcracking in the case of pouches. Therefore these types of containers should not be allowed to fall or slide from one section to another of the conveying system.

7.7.4   Post process cleaning and disinfection

Any container conveyor or equipment surface that is wet during production periods will permit rapid growth of infecting microorganisms unless it is effectively cleaned at least once every 24 hours and, in addition,l regularly disinfected during production periods. The chlorine in the cooling water deposited on these surfaces from cooled cans is not an adequate disinfectant. Any cleaning and disinfection program that is instituted should be carefully evaluated before being adopted as a routine procedure. For example, properly treated surfaces should have a mesophilic aerobic bacterial level of less than 500 c.f.u. per $25/cm^2$ ($4/in^2$). The assessment of the continuing effectiveness of post process cleaning and disinfection programs can only be made by bacteriological monitoring.

Conveying systems and equipment should be critically examined with the view to replacing unsuitable materials. Porous materials should not be used and surfaces which become porous, heavily corroded or damaged should be repaired or replaced.

All personnel should be made fully aware of the importance of personal hygiene and good habits in relation to the avoidance of post process container recontamination through handling of containers.

Post-cooling areas of continuous cookers, including hydrostatic cookers, may constitute continuing sources of high bacterial concentrations unless stringent measures are taken to clean and disinfect them regularly to avoid microbial buildup.

7.7.5   Containers should be overwrapped if such is required to protect container integrity. If they are overwrapped containers should be dry.

7.8   Evaluation of Deviation in Heat Processing

7.8.1   Whenever the in-process monitoring records, processor check or other means disclose that a low-acid food or container system has received a thermal or sterilization treatment less than that stipulated in the scheduled process, the processor should:

a)   identify, isolate and then reprocess to commercial sterility that part of the code lot or lots involved. Complete reprocessing records should be retained; or

b)   isolate and retain that part of the code lot or lots involved to permit further detailed evaluation of the heat processing records. Such evaluation should be made by competent processing experts in accordance with procedures recognized as being adequate to detect any hazard to public health. If this evaluation of the processing records demonstrates that the product has not been given a safe thermal treatment, the product isolated and retained shall be either fully reprocessed to render it commercially sterile or suitably disposed of under adequate and proper supervision to assure the protection of the public health. A record should be made of the evaluation procedures used, the results obtained and the actions taken on the product involved.

7.8.2   In the case of continuous agitating retorts emergency scheduled processes may be established to permit compensation for temperature deviations, not to exceed 5°C (10°F). Such scheduled processes must be established in accordance with Sub-Sections 7.5.1 and 7.5.2 of this Code.

8.   SECTION VIII - QUALITY ASSURANCE

It is important that scheduled processes be properly established, correctly applied, sufficiently supervised and documented to provide positive assurance that the requirements have been met. these assurances apply also to the seaming and sealing operations. for practical and statistical reasons, an end-product analysis by itself is not sufficient to monitor the adequacy of the scheduled process.

8.1   <u>Processing and Production Records</u>

Permanent and legible dated records of time, temperature, code mark and other pertinent details should be kept concerning each load. Such records are essential as a check on processing operations and will be invaluable if some question arises as to whether a particular lot had received adequate heat processing. These records should be made by the retort or processing system operator or other designated person, on a form which should include: product name and style, the code lot number, the retort or processing system and recorder chart identification, the container size and types, the approximate number of containers per code lot interval, the minimum initial temperature, the scheduled and actual processing time and temperature, the indicator and recorder thermometer reading, and other appropriate processing data. Closing vacuum (in vacuum-packed products), fill-in weights, filled flexible pouch thickness, and/or other critical factors specified in the scheduled process should also be recorded. Records of water quality and plant hygiene should be kept. When deviations occur in the application of the scheduled process refer to Sub-Section 7.8 of this Code. In addition, the following records should be maintained.

8.1.1   <u>Processing in steam</u>

8.1.1.1   <u>Batch still retorts</u>

Time steam on, venting time and temperature, time sterilization temperature reached, time steam off.

8.1.1.2   <u>Batch agitating retorts</u>

As for still retorts (Sub-Section 8.1.1.1) with additions of functioning of condensate bleeder as well as retort and/or reel speed. Where specified in the scheduled process it is important to also record containers headspace and critical factors such as in-going product consistency and/or viscosity, maximum drained weight, minimum net weight and percent solid (Sub-Section 7.5.4).

8.1.1.3   <u>Continuous agitating retorts</u> (see Sub-Section 8.1.1.2)

8.1.1.4   <u>Hydrostatic retorts</u>

The temperature in the steam chamber at just above the steam-water interface, at the top of the dome, if applicable, speed of the container conveyor, and, where the scheduled process specifies, measurements of particular temperatures and water levels in the hydrostatic water legs.

In addition, for agitating hydrostatic retorts, rotative chain speed, and other critical factors such as the headspace and in-going product consistency.

8.1.2   <u>Processing in water</u>

8.1.2.1   <u>Batch still retorts</u>

Time steam on, coming-up time, time sterilization starts, sterilization temperature, water level, water circulation and pressure maintained, time steam off.

8.1.2.2   Batch agitating retorts

As for still retorts (Sub-Section 8.1.2.1) with the addition of retort and reel speed. where specified in the scheduled process it is important to record container headspace and critical factors such as in-going product consistency, maximum drained weight, minimum net weight and percent solids (Sub-Section 7.5.4).

8.1.3   Processing in steam/air mixtures

8.1.3.1   Batch still retorts

Time steam on, coming-up-time, time sterilization starts, maintenance of circulation of steam/air mixture, pressure, sterilization temperature, time steam off.

8.1.4   Aseptic processing and packaging

Detailed automatic and manual record requirements depend on the type of aseptic processing and packaging system, but they must provide complete and accurate documentation of the pre-sterilization and running conditions actually used.

8.1.4.1   Product container sterilization conditions

Sterilization media flow rate and/or temperature, where applicable, retention time in the sterilizing equipment of containers and closures. Where a batch system is used for container and/or closure sterilization, sterilization cycle times and temperatures.

8.1.4.2   Product line conditions

Pre-sterilization of the product line, "stand-by" and/or "change-to-product", as well as running conditions. Running condition records should include product temperature at the final heater outlet, product temperature at holding section outlet, differential pressures if a product-to-product regenerator is used, and the product flow rate.

8.1.4.3   Filling and closing conditions (see Sub-Section 8.1.4.1)

8.1.5   Flame sterilizers

Container conveyor speed, can surface temperature at the end of the process holding period, nature of container.

8.2   Record Review and Maintenance

8.2.1   Process Records

Recorder charts should be identified by date, code lot and other data as necessary, so they can be correlated with the written record of lot processed. Each entry of the record should be made by the retort or processing system operator, or other designated person, at the time the specific retort or processing system condition or operation occurs, and the retort of processing system operator or such designated person should sign or initial each record form. Prior to shipment or release for distribution, but not later than one working day after the actual process, a representative of plant management who is competent should review and ensure that all processing and production records are complete and that all

products received the scheduled process.   The records, including the recorder
thermometer chart, should be signed or initialled by the person conducting the
review.

8.2.2   Container closure records

          Written records of all container closure examinations should specify
the code lot, the date and time of container closure inspections, the measurements
obtained, and all corrective actions taken. Records should be signed or initialled
by the container closure inspector and should be reviewed by a representative of
plant management, who is competent, with sufficient frequency to ensure that the
records are complete and that the operation has been properly controlled.

8.2.3   Water quality records

          Records should be kept of tests showing that effective treatment was
maintained or that the microbiological quality was suitable.

8.2.4   Distribution of product

          Records should be maintained identifying initial distribution of the
finished product to facilitate, if necessary, the segregation of specific food lots
that may have been contaminated or otherwise unfit for their intended use.

8.3   Retention of records

          The records specified in Sub-Section 7.6.1.1, 8.1 and 8.2, should be
retained for not less than three years. They should be held in a manner which will
permit ready reference.

9.   SECTION IX - STORAGE AND TRANSPORT OF FINISHED PRODUCT

          Conditions of storage and transport should be such that the integrity
of the product container and the safety and quality of the product are not
adversely affected. Attention is drawn to common forms of damage such as that
caused by improper use of fork lift trucks.

9.1   Warm containers should not be stacked so as to form incubatory
conditions for the growth of thermophilic organisms.

9.2   If containers are kept at high humidities particularly for a long time
especially in the presence of mineral salts or substances which are even very
weakly alkaline or acidic they are likely to corrode.

9.3   Labels or label adhesives which are hygroscopic and therefore liable
to promote rusting of tinplate should be avoided as should pastes and adhesives
that contain acids or mineral salts.

          Cases and cartons should be thoroughly dry. If they are made of wood
it should be well seasoned.   They should be of the proper size so that the
containers fit snugly and are not subject to damage from movement within the case.
They should be strong enough to withstand normal transport.

          Metal containers should be kept dry during storage and transportation
to prevent their corrosion.

9.4   **The mechanical properties of outer cartons, etc. are adversely affected by moisture and the protection of the containers against transport damage may become insufficient.**

9.5   The storage conditions, including temperature, should be such as to prevent deterioration or contamination of the product. Rapid temperature changes during storage should be avoided as this may cause the condensation of moist air on the containers and thus lead to container corrosion.

9.6   Any of the above conditions may necessitate reference to the guidelines for the Salvage of Canned Foods Exposed to Adverse Conditions, (currently under preparation).

10.   <u>SECTION X - LABORATORY CONTROL PROCEDURES</u>

10.1   It is desirable that each establishment should have access to laboratory control of the processes used as well as the products packed. The amount and type of such control will vary with the food product as well as the needs of management. Such control should reject all food that is unfit for human consumption.

10.2   Where appropriate, representative samples of the production should be taken to assess the safety and quality of the product.

10.3   Laboratory procedures used should preferably follow recognized or standard methods in order that the results may be readily interpreted.

10.4   Laboratories checking for pathogenic microorganisms should be well separated from food processing areas.

11.   <u>SECTION XI - END-PRODUCT SPECIFICATIONS</u>

           Microbiological, chemical, physical or extraneous material specifications may be required depending on the nature of the food. Such specifications should include sampling procedures, analytical methodology and limits for acceptance.

11.1   To the extent possible in good manufacturing practice the products should be free from objectionable matter.

11.2   The products should be commercially sterile, and not contain any substances originating from microorganisms in amounts which may represent a hazard to health.

11.3   The products should be free from chemical pollutants in amounts which may represent a hazard to health.

11.4   The products should comply with the requirements set forth by the Codex Alimentarius Commission on pesticide residues and food additives as contained in permitted lists or Codex Commodity Standards, and should comply with the requirements on pesticide residues and food additives of the country in which the product will be sold.

ACIDIFIED LOW-ACID CANNED FOODS

1.   **SECTION I - SCOPE**

This Appendix applies to the manufacture and processing of low-acid canned foods which have been acidified, fermented and/or pickled prior to canning to have an equilibrium pH of 4.6 or less after heat processing. These foods include but are not limited to, artichokes, beans, cabbage, cauliflower, cucumber, fish, olives (other than ripe olives), peppers, puddings and tropical fruits, singly or in combination.

Excluded are acid beverages and foods, jams, jellies, preserves, salad dressings, vinegar, fermented dairy products, acid foods that contain small amounts of low-acid foods but having a resultant pH that does not significantly differ from that of the predominant acid food, and those foods where scientific evidence clearly shows that the product does not support the growth of *Clostridium botulinum*; for example, those tomato or tomato products where the pH does not exceed 4.7.

2.   **SECTION II - DEFINITIONS**

(See definitions, SECTION II of the principal document)

3.   **SECTION III - HYGIENE REQUIREMENTS IN PRODUCTION/HARVESTING AREA**

As stated in SECTION III of the principal document.

4.   **SECTION IV - ESTABLISHMENT: DESIGN AND FACILITIES**

4.1   Location

As stated in Sub-Section 4.1 in the principal document.

4.2   Roadways and Yards

As stated in Sub-Section 4.2 in the principal document.

4.3   Buildings and Facilities

As stated in Sub-Section 4.3 in the principal document.

4.4   Sanitary Facilities

As stated in Sub-Section 4.4 in the principal document.

4.5   Equipment and Utensils

As stated in Sub-Section 4.5 in the principal document, except that 4.5.2.4 is modified as follows:

4.5.2.4   Retorts and product sterilizers are pressure vessels and as such must be designed, installed, operated and maintained in accordance with the safety standards for pressure vessels of the agency having jurisdiction. Where open canal cookers, spray cookers and heat exchangers are used to achieve commercial sterility of acidified low-acid foods they must be designed, installed, operated and maintained in accordance with applicable safety standards of the agency having jurisdiction.

5.   **SECTION V - ESTABLISHMENT: HYGIENIC REQUIREMENTS**

All this section as stated in SECTION V of the principal document.

6.   **SECTION VI - PERSONNEL HYGIENE AND HEALTH REQUIREMENTS**

All this section as stated in SECTION VI of the principal document.

7.   **SECTION VII - ESTABLISHMENT: HYGIENIC PROCESSING REQUIREMENTS**

7.1   Raw Material Requirements and Preparation

7.1.1   As stated in Sub-Section 7.1.1 of the principal document.

7.1.2   As stated in Sub-Section 7.1.2 of the principal document.

7.1.3   As stated in Sub-Section 7.1.3 of the principal document.

7.1.4   Blanching by heat, when required in the preparation of food for canning, should be followed by either rapidly cooling the food or subsequent processing without delay.

7.1.5   All steps in the process, including canning, should be performed under conditions which will prevent contamination, deterioration, and/or the growth of microorganisms of public health significance in the food product.

7.2   Prevention of Cross-Contamination

As stated in Sub-Section 7.2 of the principal document.

7.3   Use of Water

As stated in Sub-Section 7.3 of the principal document.

7.4   Packaging

As stated in Sub-Section 7.4 of the principal document.

7.4.1   Storage of Containers

As stated in Sub-Section 7.4.1 of the principal document.

7.4.2   Inspection of Empty Product Containers

As stated in Sub-Section 7.4.2 of the principal document.

7.4.3   <u>Proper Use of Product Containers</u>

As stated in Sub-Section 7.4.3 of the principal document.

7.4.4   <u>Protection of Empty Product Containers During Plant Cleaning</u>

As stated in Sub-Section 7.4.4 of the principal document.

7.4.5   <u>Filling of Product Containers</u>

As stated in Sub-Section 7.4.5 of the principal document.

7.4.6   <u>Exhausting of Containers</u>

As stated in Sub-section 7.4.6 of the principal document.

7.4.7   <u>Closing Operations</u>

As stated in Sub-Section 7.4.7 of the principal document.

7.4.8   <u>Inspection of Closures</u>

7.4.8.1   Inspection for gross defects.

As stated in Sub-Section 7.4.8.1 of the principal document.

7.4.8.1.1   Inspection of glass container closures.

As stated in Sub-Section 7.4.8.1.1 of the principal document.

7.4.8.1.2   Inspection of can seams.

As stated in Sub-Section 7.4.8.1.2 of the principal document.

7.4.8.1.3   Inspection of seams for deep-drawn aluminum containers.

As stated in Sub-Section 7.4.8.1.3 of the principal document.

7.4.8.1.4   Inspection of seals of semi-rigid and flexible containers.

As stated in Sub-Section 7.4.8.1.4 of the principal document.

7.4.9   <u>Handling of Containers After Closure</u>

As stated in Sub-Section 7.4.9 of the principal document.

7.4.10   <u>Coding</u>

As stated in Sub-Section 7.4.10 of the principal document.

7.4.11   <u>Washing</u>

As stated in Sub-Section 7.4.11 of the principal document.

7.5   <u>Acidification and Heat Processing</u>

7.5.1   General Considerations

          Scheduled processes for acidified low-acid canned foods must be
established only by competent persons having expert knowledge of acidification and
thermal processing and having adequate facilities for making such determinations.
It is absolutely necessary to establish the required acidification and heat process
with accepted scientific methods.

          **The microbiological safety of acidified low-acid foods depends
primarily upon the care and accuracy by which the process has been carried out.**

          **The acidification and heat process required to make acidified low-acid
canned foods commercially sterile depends upon the microbial load, type and
procedure of acidification, storage temperature, the presence of various
preservatives and composition of the products.** Acidified low-acid foods with pH
values above 4.6 may be able to support the growth of many kinds of microorganisms
including the heat resistant spore-forming pathogens such as *Clostridium botulinum*.
It should be emphasized that acidification and heat processing of acidified
low-acid canned foods are very critical operations involving public health risks
and appreciable losses of finished product if inadequately processed.

          Instances have been known where improperly processed or sealed acidified
canned foods have supported mould and other microbial growth which raised the
product pH to above 4.6 and allowed the growth of *Clostridium botulinum*.

7.5.2   Establishing Scheduled Processes

7.5.2.1   A scheduled process shall be established by a qualified person who has
expert knowledge acquired through appropriate training and experience in the
acidification and heat processing of acidified, fermented and pickled foods.

7.5.2.2   The required acidification and heat process to achieve commercial
sterility should be established on the basis of factors such as:

-          pH of the product;

-          time to reach equilibrium pH;

-          product composition or formulation, including dimensional tolerances of solid
          ingredients;

-          levels and types of preservatives;

-          water and activity;

-          microbial flora including *Clostridium botulinum* and spoilage microorganisms;

-          container size and type; and

-          organoleptic quality.

7.5.2.3   The heat treatment necessary to achieve commercial sterility of an
acidified low-acid canned food is much less than that necessary for low-acid canned
foods.

7.5.2.4   Since the acidity of the final product will generally prevent bacterial spore outgrowth, the heat treatment may only be required to kill moulds, yeasts, vegetative cells of bacteria and to inactivate enzymes.

7.5.2.5   The results of these acidification and heat process determination together with established critical factors should be incorporated into the scheduled process. Such a scheduled process should include as the minimum the following data:

-    product code or recipe identification;-container size (dimensions) and type;

-    pertinent details of the acidification process;

-    in-going weight of product(s) including liquor where appropriate;

-    minimum initial temperature;

-    type and characteristics of heat processing system;

-    sterilization temperature;

-    sterilization time; and

-    cooling method.

7.5.2.6   For aseptically processed foods a similar list should be made which also should include equipment and container sterilization requirements.

7.5.2.7   The product code (identity) should correspond clearly to a complete and accurate product specification containing at least the following where applicable:

-    full receipt and preparation procedures;

-    pH;

-    in-going weight of product(s), including liquor where appropriate;

-    headspace;

-    drained weight;

-    maximum dimensions of product components;

-    temperature of product at filling; and

-    consistency.

7.5.2.8   Small deviations from the product specification which may seem negligible may seriously affect the adequacy of the process for that product. any changes in product specifications should be evaluated as to their effect on the adequacy of the process. If the scheduled process is found to be inadequate it must be re-established.

7.5.2.9   Complete records concerning all aspects of the establishment of the scheduled process, including any associated incubation tests, should be permanently retained by the processing plant or by the laboratory establishing the scheduled process.

7.5.3 Acidification and Heat Processing Operations

7.5.3.1 Processing operations for control of pH and other critical factors specified in the scheduled process should be performed and supervised only by properly trained personnel.

7.5.3.2 Acidified, fermented and pickled foods shall be so manufactured, processed and packaged that an equilibrium pH value of 4.6 or lower is achieved within the time designated in the scheduled process and maintained.

7.5.3.3 To accomplish this the processor should monitor, using pertinent tests, the acidification process at critical control points with sufficient frequency to assure the safety and quality of the product.

7.5.3.4 Commercial sterility must be accomplished using such equipment and instruments as are needed to ensure that the scheduled process is achieved and to provide proper records.

7.5.3.5 Both temperature distribution and rates of heat transfer are important; because of the variety of existing designs in equipment, reference should be made to the equipment manufacturers and to the agency having jurisdiction for details of installation, operation and control.

7.5.3.6 Only properly determined scheduled processes must be used. Scheduled processes to be used for products and container sizes and types being packed should be posted in a conspicuous place near the processing equipment. Such information should be readily available to the retort or processing system operator and to the agency having jurisdiction.

7.5.3.7. It is essential that all processing equipment should be properly designed, correctly installed and carefully maintained.

7.5.3.8 In batch operations the sterilization status of the containers should be indicated. All retort baskets, trucks, cars or crates containing food product not thermally processed, or at least one of the containers on the tope of each basket, etc., should be plainly and conspicuously marked with a heat sensitive indicator, or by other effective means which will visually indicate whether or not each unit has been thermally processed. Heat sensitive indicators attached to baskets, trucks, cars or crates must be removed before they are refilled with containers.

7.5.3.9 The initial temperature of the contents of the coldest containers to be processed should be determined and recorded with sufficient frequency to ensure that the temperature of the product is no lower than the minimum initial temperature specified in the scheduled process.

7.5.3.10 An accurate, clearly visible clock or other suitable timing device should be installed in the processing room and times should be read from this instrument and not from wristwatches, etc. When two or more clocks are used in a processing room they should be synchronized.

7.5.4   <u>Critical Factors and the Application of the Scheduled Process</u>

In addition to the maximum pH, minimum initial product temperature, sterilization time and temperature specified in the scheduled process, other critical factors specified should be measured, controlled and recorded at intervals of sufficient frequency to ensure that these factors remain within the limits specified in the scheduled process. Some examples of critical factors are:

i)   maximum fill-in or drained weight;

ii)   headspace of filled product containers;

iii)   product consistency as determined by objective measurement on product taken before processing;

iv)   product style and/or container type which results in layering or stratification of the product in the containers or alteration of the container dimensions (thickness) requiring specific orientation of the containers in the retort;

v)   percent solids;

vi)   net weight;

vii)   minimum closing vacuum (in vacuum packed product);

viii)   pH equilibrium time;

ix)   salt, sugar and/or preservative concentrations; and

x)   dimensional tolerance of solid ingredients.

7.6   <u>Equipment and Procedures for Acidification and Heat Processing Systems</u>

7.6.1   <u>Acidification Systems</u>

The manufacturer shall employ appropriate control procedures to ensure that the finished goods do not present a health hazard. Sufficient control, including frequent testing and recording of results, shall be exercised so that the equilibrium pH values for acidified, fermented and pickled foods are not higher than 4.6. Measurements of acidity of foods in-process may be made by potentiometric methods, titratable acidity, or in certain instances colorimetric methods. In-process measurements by titration or colorimetry should be related to the finished equilibrium pH. If the finished equilibrium pH is 4.0 or below, the acidity of the final product may be determined by any suitable method. If the finished equilibrium pH of the food is above 4.0 the measurement of the finished equilibrium pH shall be by a potentiometric method.

7.6.1.1   <u>Direct Acidification</u>

Procedures for acidification to attain acceptable pH levels in the final food include, but are not limited to the following:

i)   blanching of the food ingredients in acidified aqueous solutions;

ii) immersion of the blanched food in acid solutions. Although immersion of food in an acid solution is a satisfactory method for acidification, care should be taken to assure that the acid concentration is properly maintained;

iii) direct batch acidification. This can be achieved by adding a known amount of an acid solution to a specified amount of food during acidification;

iv) direct addition of a predetermined amount of acid to individual containers during production. Liquid acids are generally more effective than solid or pelleted acids. Care should be taken to ensure that the proper amount of acids is added to each container and distributed uniformly;

v)   addition of acid foods to low-acid foods in controlled proportions to conform to specific formulations; and

vi) the time for equilibrium and buffering effects should always be taken into account.

7.6.1.2   Acidification by Fermentation and Salt Curing

Temperature, salt concentration and acidity are important factors in controlling the fermentation and salt-curing in foods. The process and control of the fermentation should be monitored by appropriate tests. The concentration of salt in the brine should be determined by a chemical or physical test, at sufficient intervals to assure the control of the fermentation. The process of the fermentation should be monitored by pH measurements or acid/base titrations or both according to the methods set forth in Sub-Section 7.6.2 or by equivalent methods, at sufficient intervals to assure the control of the fermentation. The concentration of salt or acid in the brine in bulk tanks containing salt stock may become significantly diluted. Therefore it should be routinely checked and adjusted as necessary.

7.6.2   Instruments and Control Procedures for Acidification Processes (see Appendix II)

7.6.3   Instruments and Controls Common to Different Heat Processing Systems

7.6.3.1   Indicating Thermometer

Each sterilizer or cooker should be equipped with at least one indicating thermometer. the mercury-in-glass thermometer is recognized as the most reliable temperature indicating instrument at the present time. An alternative instrument having equal or better accuracy and reliability may be used subject to the approval of the official agency having jurisdiction. The mercury-in-glass thermometer should have divisions that are easily readable to 1C° (2F°) and whose scale contains not more than 4C°/cm (17F° per in.) of graduated scale.

Thermometers should be tested for accuracy, in steam or water as appropriate, in the operational aspect against a known accurate standard thermometer. This should be done upon installation, and at least once a year thereafter or more frequently as may be necessary to ensure their accuracy. A thermometer that deviates more than 0.5C° (1F°) from the standard should be replaced. A daily inspection of mercury-in-glass thermometers should be made to detect, and if found, replace thermometers with divided mercury columns or other defects.

7.6.3.2   Where other types of thermometer are used, routine tests should be made which ensure at least equivalent performance to that described for mercury-in-glass thermometers.   Thermometers which do not meet these requirements should be replaced.

7.6.3.3   Temperature/Time Recording Devices

Each sterilizer or cooker should be equipped with at least one temperature/time recording device. This recorder may be combined with the steam controller and may be a controlling recording instrument. It is important that the correct chart is used for each device. The recording accuracy should be equal to or better than ± 1C° (± 2F°) at the process temperature. The recorder should agree within 1C° (2F°) of the indicating thermometer at the process temperature. A means of preventing unauthorized changes in the adjustment should be provided. It is important that the chart should also be used to provide a permanent record of the sterilization time. The chart timing device should also be accurate.

7.6.3.4   Pressure Gauges

As stated in sub-Section 7.6.1.3 of the principal document with the addition of the following sentence:

If a retort is only used at atmospheric pressure, a pressure gauge may not be necessary.

7.6.3.5·   Steam Controller

When appropriate each sterilizer or cooker should be equipped with a steam controller to maintain temperature. This may be a recording-controlling instrument when combined with a recording thermometer.

7.6.3.6   Pressure Relief Valves

As stated in Sub-Section 7.6.1.5 of the principal document with the addition of the following sentence:

If a retort is only at atmospheric pressure, a pressure relief valve may not be necessary.

7.6.4   Commonly Used Heat Processing Systems

7.6.4.1   Processing at Atmospheric Pressure or by Hot-fill and Hold

Commercial sterility should be accomplished using suitable equipment and the necessary instrumentations as in Sub-Section 7.6.3 of this Appendix to ensure that the scheduled process is achieved and to provide proper records. Both temperature distribution and rates of heat transfer are important. Because of the variety of equipment available, reference should be made to the manufacturer and the agency having jurisdiction for details of installation, operation and control. Where a hot-fill and hold technique is used it is important that all inner surfaces of the container reach the scheduled container sterilization temperature.

7.6.4.2   Processing Under Pressure in Retorts

As stated in Sub-Sections 7.6.2, 7.6.3 and 7.6.4 in their entirety in the principal document.

7.6.5   Aseptic Processing and Packaging Systems

As stated in Sub-Section 7.6.5 in its entirety in the principal document.

7.6.6   Flame Sterilizers, Equipment and Procedures

As stated in Sub-Section 7.6.6 in its entirety in the principal document.

7.6.7   Other Systems

Systems for thermal processing of acidified low-acid foods in hermetically sealed containers should conform to the applicable requirements of this Code and should ensure that the methods and controls used for the manufacture, processing and/or packaging of such foods are operated and administered in a manner adequate to achieve commercial sterility.

7.6.8   Cooling

As stated in Sub-Section 7.6.8 of the principal document.

7.6.8.1   Cooling Water Quality

As stated in Sub-Section 7.6.8.1 of the principal document.

7.7   Post-Processing Contamination

As stated in Sub-Section 7.7 of the principal document.

7.8   Evaluation of Deviations in the Scheduled Process

Whenever any process operation deviates from the scheduled pressures for any acidified, fermented or pickled food, or whenever the equilibrium pH value of the finished product is higher than 4.6 as determined by appropriate analysis (see Appendix II of this Code as disclosed from records, or otherwise, the commercial processor) should either:

a)   fully reprocess that code lot of the food by a process established by a competent processing authority as adequate to assure a safe product; or

b)   set aside that portion of the food involved for further evaluation as to any potential public health significance. Such evaluation should be made by competent processing experts in accordance with procedures recognized as being adequate to detect any potential hazard to public health and should be acceptable to the agency having jurisdiction unless such evaluation demonstrates that the food code lot has undergone a process that has rendered it safe, the food set aside shall either be fully reprocessed to render it safe or destroyed. A record should be made of the procedures used in the evaluation, the results obtained, and the actions taken on the product involved. Either upon completion of full reworking and the attainment of a safe food or after the determination that no potential for public health hazard exists, that portion of the food involved may be shipped in normal distribution. Otherwise, the portion of the food involved shall be suitably disposed of under adequate and proper supervision to assure the protection of the public health.

8.   **SECTION VIII - QUALITY ASSURANCE**

As stated in Section 8 of the principal document.

8.1   Processing and Production Records

Records should be maintained of examination of raw materials, packaging materials and finished products, and of suppliers' guarantees or certifications that verify compliance with the requirements of this Code.

8.2   Record Review and Maintenance

Processing and production records showing adherence to scheduled processes, including records of pH measurements and other critical factors intended to ensure a safe product, should be maintained and should contain sufficient additional information such as product code, date, container size and product, to permit a public health hazard evaluation of the processes applied to each code lot, batch or other portion of production.

8.3   Deviations from Scheduled Processes

All departures from scheduled processes having a possible bearing on public health or the safety of the food shall be noted and the affected portion of the product identified. Such departures should be recorded and made the subject of a separate file, or a log identifying the appropriate data and delineating them, the action taken to rectify them, and the disposition of the portion of the product involved.

8.4   Distribution of Product

Records should be maintained identifying initial distribution of the finished product to facilitate, when necessary, the segregation of specific food lots that may have become contaminated or otherwise unfit for their intended use.

8.5   Retention of Records

Copies of all records provided for in Sub-Sections 8.2, 8.3 and 8.4 above should be retained at the processing plant or other reasonably accessible location for a period of three years.

9.   **SECTION IX - STORAGE AND TRANSPORT OF THE FINISHED PRODUCT**

As stated in SECTION IX of the principal document.

10.   **SECTION X - LABORATORY CONTROL PROCEDURES**

As stated in SECTION X of the principal document.

11.   **SECTION XI - END-PRODUCT SPECIFICATIONS**

As stated in SECTION XI in its entirety in the principal document, except that Sub-Section 11.3 will be altered to read, "Acidified low-acid foods should have received a processing treatment sufficient to provide commercial sterility".

APPENDIX II

1.   ANALYTICAL METHODOLOGY FOR pH MEASUREMENT[1]

Methods that may be used to determine pH or acidity for acidified, fermented and pickled food include, but are not limited to the following:

1.1   Potentiometric Method for the Determination of pH

1.1.1   Principles

The term "pH" is used to designate the intensity or degree of acidity. The value of pH, the logarithm of the reciprocal of the hydrogen ion concentration in solution, is determined by measuring the difference in potential between two electrodes immersed in a sample solution. A suitable system consists of a potentiometer, a glass electrode, and a reference electrode. A precise pH determination can be made by making an electromotive force (emf) measurement of a standard buffer solution whose pH is known, and then by comparing that measurement to an emf measurement of a sample of the solution to be tested.

1.1.2   Instruments

The primary instrument for use of pH determination is the pH meter or potentiometer. For most work, an instrument with a direct-reading pH scale is necessary. Battery and line-operated instruments are available commercially. If the line voltage may be unstable, line-operated instruments should be fitted with voltage regulators to eliminate drifting of meter-scale readings. Batteries should be checked frequently to assure proper operation of batter operated instruments. An instrument using an expanded unit scale or a digital readout system is preferred since it allows more precise measurements.

1.1.3   Electrodes

The typical pH meter is equipped with a glass membrane electrode. The most commonly used reference electrode is the calomel electrode, which incorporates a salt bridge filled with saturated potassium chloride solution.

   i)   Care and use of electrodes. Calomel electrodes should be kept filled with saturated potassium chloride solution, or other solution specified by the manufacturer because they may become damaged if they are allowed to dry out. For best results, electrodes should be soaked in buffer solution, distilled or deionized water or other liquid specified by the manufacturer for several hours before using and kept ready by storing with tips immersed in distilled water or in buffer solution used for standardization. Electrodes should be rinsed with water before immersing in the standard buffers and rinsed with water or the solution to be measured next between sample determinations. A lag in meter response may indicate aging effects or fouling of the electrodes, and cleaning and rejuvenation of the electrodes may be necessary. This may be accomplished by placing the electrodes in 0.1 molar sodium hydroxide solution for 1 minute and then transferring them to 0.1 molar hydrochloric acid solution for 1 minute. The cycle

---

   [1]   (If and when a suitable I.S.O. text becomes available it will be considered as a replacement for this Appendix)

should be repeated twice, ending with the electrodes in the acid solution. The electrodes should then be thoroughly rinsed with water and blotted with soft tissue before proceeding with the standardization.

ii) Temperature. To obtain accurate results, the same temperature should be used for the electrodes, the standard buffer solutions, the samples, for the standardization of the meter, and pH determinations. Tests should be made at a temperature between 20°C to 30°C (68°F to 86°F). When tests have to be made outside this temperature range appropriate correction factors should be established and applied. While thermal compensators are available, they should not be relied upon to give accurate results.

iii) Accuracy. The accuracy of most pH meters is stated to be approximately 0.1 pH unit, and reproducibility is usually ± 0.05 pH unit or less. Some meters permit the expansion of any pH unit range to cover the entire scale and have an accuracy of approximately ± 0.01 pH unit and reproducibility of ± 0.005 pH units.

1.1.4   General Procedure for Determining pH

When operating an instrument, the manufacturer's instructions should be used and the following techniques for pH determination observed:

i) switch the instrument on and allow the electronic components to warm up and stabilize before proceeding;

ii) standardize the instrument and electrodes with commercially-prepared standard 4.0 pH buffer or with freshly prepared 0.05 molar potassium acid phthalate buffer solution prepared as outlined in "Official Methods of Analysis of the Association of Official Analytical Chemists", 14th ed., 1984, section 50.007(c). Note the temperature of the buffer solution and set the temperature compensator control at the observed temperature;

iii) rinse the electrodes with water and blot but do not wipe with soft tissue;

iv) immerse the tips in the buffer solution and take the pH reading, allowing about 1 minute for the meter to stabilize. Adjust the standardization control so that the meter reading corresponds to the pH of the known buffer (for example, 4.0) for the temperature observed. Rinse the electrodes with water and blot with soft tissue. Repeat procedure with fresh portions of buffer solution until the instrument remains in balance on two successive trials. To check the operation of the pH meter, check the pH reading using another standard buffer such as one having a pH of 7.0 or check it with freshly prepared 0.025 molar phosphate solution prepared as outlined in "Official Methods of Analysis of the Association of Official Analytical Chemists", 14th ed., 1984, section 50.007(e). Expanded scale pH meters may be checked with pH 3.0 or pH 5.0 standard buffers. Buffers and instruments can be further checked by comparison with values obtained with a second properly standardized instrument;

v) indicating electrodes may be checked for proper operation by first using an acid buffer then a base buffer. First standardize the electrodes using a pH 4.0 buffer at or near 25°C. Standardization control should be adjusted so that the meter reads exactly 4.0. Electrodes should be rinsed with water, then blotted and immersed in a pH 9.18 borax buffer prepared as outlined in "Official Methods of Analysis of the Association of Official Analytical Chemists", 14th ed., 1984, section 50.007(f). The pH reading should be within ± 0.3 units of the 9.18 value; and

vi)   the pH meter can be tested for proper operation by shorting the glass and reference electrode inputs, thereby reducing the voltage to zero. In some meters this is done by switching the instrument to standby, and in other instruments by use of a shorting strap. With the instrument shorted out, standardization control should be turned from one extreme to another. This operation should produce a deflection greater than ± 1.5 pH unit from centre scale.

1.1.5   Determining pH on Samples

i)   adjust the temperature of the sample to room temperature (25°C), and set the temperature compensator control to the observed temperature. With some expanded scale instruments, the sample temperature must be the same as the temperature of the buffer solution used for the standardization;

ii)   rinse and blot the electrodes. Immerse the electrodes in the sample and take the pH reading, allowing 1 minute for the meter to stabilize. Rinse and blot the electrodes and repeat on a fresh portion of sample. Oil and grease from the samples may coat the electrodes, therefore, it is advisable to clean and standardize the instrument frequently. When oily samples cause fouling problems, it may become necessary to rinse the electrode with ethyl ether; and

iii) determine two pH values on the well-mixed sampled. These readings should be in agreement with one another to indicated that the sample is homogeneous. Report values to the nearest 0.05 pH unit.

1.1.6   Preparation of Samples

Some food products may consist of a mixture of liquid and solid components that differ in acidity. Other food products may be semi-solid in character. The following are examples of preparation procedures for pH testing for each of these categories.

i)   Liquid and solid component mixtures. Drain the contents of the container for 2 minutes on a U.S. standard No. 8 sieve (preferably stainless steel) or equivalent inclined at a 17 to 20° angle. Record weights of the liquid and solid portions and retain each portion separately.

a)   if the liquid contains sufficient oil to cause electrode fouling, separate the layer with a separatory funnel and retain the aqueous layer. The oil layer may be discarded. Adjust the temperature of the aqueous layer to 25°C and determine its pH;

b)   remove the drained solids from the sieve. Blend to a uniform paste, adjust the temperature of the paste to 25°C and determine its pH; and

c)   mix aliquots of solid and liquid fractions in the same ratio as found in the original container and blend to a uniform consistency. Adjust the temperature of the blend to 25°C and determine the equilibrated pH. Alternately, blend the entire contents of the container to a uniform paste, adjust the temperature of the paste to 25°C and determine the equilibrated pH.

ii) <u>Marinated oil products</u>. Separate the oil from the solid product. Blend the solid in a blender to a paste consistency; it may become necessary to add a small amount of distilled water to some samples to facilitate the blending. A small amount of added water will not alter the pH of most food products, but caution must be exercised concerning poorly buffered foods. No more than 20 milliliters of distilled water should be added to each 100 grams of product. Determine the pH by immersing electrodes in the prepared paste after adjusting the temperature to 25°C.

iii) <u>Semi-solid products</u>. Food products of semi-solid consistency such as puddings, potato salad, etc., may be blended to a paste consistency, and the pH may be determined on the prepared paste. Where more fluidity is required, 10 to 20 milliliters of distilled water may be added to 100 grams of product. Adjust the temperature of the prepared paste to 25°C and determine its pH.

iv) pour off the oil, blend the remaining product to a paste and determine the pH of the blended paste. Where more fluidity is required, add 10 to 20 milliliters of distilled water to each 100 grams of product and blend. Adjust the temperature of the prepared paste to 25°C and determine its pH.

v)   <u>Large solid components</u>. The internal pH should be checked with spear electrodes as near as possible to the geometric centre.

1.1.7   <u>Process pH Determination</u>

Standardize the meter against standard buffer solution having a pH as close as possible to that of the product. This should be done at the beginning and end of each series of product determination or not less than twice daily.

i)   for process liquids, adjust the temperature of the liquid to 25°C and determine the pH by immersing the electrodes in the liquid;

ii) drain solid materials on a sieve and blend to a workable paste. Adjust the temperature of the prepared paste to 25°C and determine its pH; and

iii) where enough solid materials are available to make a paste, blend representative aliquots of liquid and solid materials to a workable paste. Adjust the temperature of the prepared paste to 25°C and determine the equilibrated pH. Alternately, blend the entire contents of the container to a uniform paste, adjust the temperature of the paste to 25°C and determine the equilibrated pH.

1.2   <u>Colorimetric Method for the Determination of pH</u>

This method may be used in lieu of potentiometric method if the pH is 4.0 or lower.

1.2.1   <u>Principle</u>

The colorimetric method for pH involves the use of indicator dyes in solution that gradually change colour over limited pH ranges. An indicator that has the greatest colour change at approximately the pH of the sample being tested is selected. The pH is determined by the colour of the indicator when exposed to the sample under tests.

1.2.2   <u>Indicator Solutions</u>

Most indicator solutions are prepared as a 0.04 percent solution of the indicator dye in alcohol. In testing, a few drops of indicator solution are added to 10 millilitre portions of the sample solution. Colours should be compared using a bright background. Approximate determinations can be made on white porcelain spot plates, the test colours being compared thereon with a set of colour standards. More accurate colorimetric tests can be made using a comparator block fitted with sets of tubes of standard indicator solutions of known pH. Indicators should be verified regularly, at least once per day before use, against the standard buffer solution.

1.2.3   <u>Indicator Paper</u>

A paper tape treated with indicator dye is dipped into the sample solution. Depending upon the pH of the solution, the tape will change colour and an approximate pH can be determined by comparison with a standard colour chart.

1.3   <u>Titratable Acidity</u>

Acceptable methods for determining titratable acidity are described in "Official Methods of Analysis of the Association of Official Analytical Chemists", 14th ed., 1984, sections 22.060-22.061. The procedure for preparing of standardizing the sodium hydroxide solution is described in ibid, sections 50.032-50.035.

APPENDIX III

REFERENCES FOR THE TEAR-DOWN EVALUATION OF A DOUBLE SEAM

1.   Canned Food: Principles of Thermal Process Control, Acidification, and Container Closure Evaluation, Revised 4th edition, 1982, Chapter 9 (Container Closure Evaluation) (English). Item #FB 7500, the Food Processors Institute, 1401 New York Ave., N.W., Washington D.C. 20005, U.S.A.

        A Spanish version may be obtained from Jose R. Cruz, University of Puerto Rico, Mayagues Campus, College of Agricultural Sciences, Venezuela Contact Station, Rico Piedras, Puerto Rico.

2.   Can Seam Formation and Evaluation, Item #FA 0003 (English) - audio/visual presentation 16 mm film, 20 minutes. The Food Processors Institute, 1401 New York Ave., N.W., Washington, D.C. 20005, U.S.A.

3.   Evaluation of Double Seams, Parts 1 and 2 (English), audio/visual presentation, 138 slides and audio cassette with illustrated script/employees handbook. The Food Processors Institute, 1401 New York Ave., N.W., Washington, D.C. 20005, U.S.A.

4.   Draft Recommended Hold for Investigation Guidelines for Double Seam Measurements, Round Metal Containers for Low-Acid Foods, 1984 (English). NFPA/CMI Container Integrity Task Force, National Food Processors Association, 1401 New York Ave., N.W., Washington, D.C. 20005, U.S.A.

5.   Evaluating a Double Seam, 1971 (English, French and Spanish). Dewey and Almy Chemical Division of W.R. Grace & Co., Cambridge, Massachusetts, U.S.A.

6.   Double Seam Manual, (English) 1978, Metal Box Ltd., England.

7.   Top Double Seam Manual (English), Continental Can Company, Inc., 633 Third Avenue, New York, N.Y., 10017, U.S.A.

8.   Examination of Metal Container Integrity, Chapter XXII, U.S.F.D.A. Bacteriological Analytical Manual (BAM) 6th edition 1984 (English), Association of Official Analytical Chemists.

9.   Method for the Tear-Down Examination of Double Seams of Metal cans, MFHPB-25(f) (English & French), Bureau of Microbial Hazards, Health Protection Branch, Health and Welfare Canada, Ottawa, Ontario, K1A 0L2, Canada.

10.   Double Seams for Steel-Based Cans for Foods (English), 1984, Australian Standard 2730-1984, Standards Association of Australia, Standards House, 80 Arthur St., North Sydney, N.S.W., Australia.

11.   Défauts et Altérations des Conserves - Nature et Origine (French), 1982, 1ère édition, Edité par AFNOR Tour Europe, Cedex 7, 92080, Paris, la Défense.

12.   Le Sertissage - boîtes rondes (French) 1977, Carnaud s.a., 65 av. Edouard Vaillant, B.P. 405, 92103 Boulogne s/Seine, Cedex.

APPENDIX IV

GUIDELINES FOR THE SALVAGE OF CANNED FOODS
EXPOSED TO ADVERSE CONDITIONS

EXPLANATORY PREFACE

The purpose of this document is to provide guidelines for the salvage of canned foods manufactured in compliance with the International Code of Hygienic Practice for Low-acid and Acidified Low-Acid Canned Foods (CAC/RCP 23-1979 (Rev. 1, 1989)) which are suspected of having become contaminated or otherwise rendered unsuitable for human consumption as a result of being subjected to adverse conditions, for example, flood, fire or other accidents, during their storage, transportation and/or distribution. The guidelines are designed to permit the salvage of canned food unaffected by such conditions and thus reduce the loss of wholesome food whilst preventing the sale or distribution of canned foods which may have been rendered unfit for human consumption.

The salvage operations should only be carried out by trained personnel under the direct supervision of person(s) having expert knowledge of canning and container technology.

The Hazard Analysis Critical Control Point (HACCP) concept should be applied when salvaging canned foods and should include:

1.   An assessment of the hazards associated with the adverse conditions which led to the food being suspect and the various salvage operations to which it may be subjected.

2.   Identification of the critical control points for the salvage operations and the type or frequency of the control measures deemed necessary.

3.   Guidance for the monitoring of the critical control points including maintenance of adequate records.

1.   SCOPE

These guidelines concern the salvage of lots of canned foods which are suspected of having been contaminated as a result of exposure to adverse conditions, (fire, flood, freezing or other accident), during storage, transportation and distribution. It is not intended to cover canned foods which are suspect as a result of errors or omissions on the part of the processor (canner); however, it may be applied to product subjected to adverse conditions while under the direct control of the processor (canner). A flow chart showing the sequence of events in the salvage of canned foods exposed to adverse conditions is shown in Appendix 1.

2.   DEFINITIONS

2.1   Adverse conditions are those conditions which may result in physical damage to and/or contamination of a container or its contents rendering the food unsuitable for human consumption.

2.2   <u>Canned food</u> means commercially sterile food in hermetically sealed containers.

2.3   <u>Cleaning</u> means the removal of soil, food residues, dirt, grease or other objectionable matter from the external surface of the container and for the purposes of this code may be extended to the removal of rust and other products of corrosion.

2.4   <u>Code lot</u> means all products produced during a period of time identified by a specific container code mark.

2.5   <u>Commercial sterility of a thermally processed food</u> means the condition achieved by application of heat, sufficient, alone or in combination with other appropriate treatments, to render the food free from microorganisms capable of growing in the food under normal non-refrigerated conditions at which the food is likely to be held during distribution and storage.

2.6   <u>Contamination</u> means the presence of any objectionable material on the surface of a container, or in a food.

2.7   <u>Disinfection</u> of a container means the reduction, without adversely affecting the container or contents, of the number of microorganisms on the container surface to a level that will not lead to harmful contamination of the food.

2.8   <u>Disposal</u> means an action (e.g. incineration, burial, conversion to animal feed, etc.) which will prevent a contaminated product from being sold or distributed for human consumption.

2.9   <u>Hermetically sealed container</u> means containers which are designed and intended to protect the contents against the entry of microorganisms during and after processing.

2.10   <u>Potable water</u> means water fit for human consumption. Standards of potability should be no less strict than those contained in the latest edition of the "International Standards for Drinking Water", World Health Organization.

2.11   <u>Recanning</u> means the transfer and sealing of a product into a new hermetically sealable container followed by a scheduled process.

2.12   <u>Reconditioning</u> means the cleaning of sound containers and may include disinfection.

2.13   <u>Reprocessing</u> means the treatment of a canned food in its original container recovered in a salvage operation followed by a scheduled process.

2.14   <u>Salvage</u> means any appropriate process or procedure by which food is recovered from a suspect lot of canned food and by which its safety and fitness for consumption is ensured.

2.15   <u>Salvor</u> means the person responsible for carrying out the salvage operations including any or all of the on-site operations.

2.16   <u>Scheduled process</u> means the thermal process chosen by the processor for a given product and container size to achieve at least commercial sterility.

2.17   <u>Suspect Lot of Canned Food</u> means a group of containers which is suspected of being contaminated as a result of exposure to adverse conditions and may include a part of, the whole of, or a number of code lots.

3.   <u>**ON-SITE OPERATIONS**</u>

3.1   <u>Assessment of Adverse Conditions</u>

The nature and circumstances of the adverse conditions which gave rise to the canned foods being suspect should be assessed and recorded. Special attention should be given to the cause and likely consequences in terms of contamination of the container and/or its contents.

3.2   <u>Notification</u>

The salvor should, as soon as possible, supply the appropriate agency having jurisdiction with the results of the assessment of the adverse conditions as well as the types and quantities of food products involved.

3.3   <u>Product Inventory and Identification of Product Location</u>

Whenever possible prior to removal of any containers of canned food, (including the taking of samples, product segregation, disposal, etc.), a complete inventory of all product involved should be made. The inventory should record the location of all product exposed to the adverse conditions, the quantity of each product type identifying by trade name, container type and size, can and/or carton codes, etc. Before commencing with any salvage operations, the salvor should notify the owner or legal agency of all affected product and provide an inventory of the affected product to the appropriate agency having jurisdiction.

3.4   <u>Feasibility of Salvage</u>

All canned foods subjected to the adverse conditions should be assessed as to whether any salvage is feasible. If salvage operations are not feasible then all product should be disposed of as soon as possible in a manner described in Section 4.2.

3.5   <u>Preliminary Sorting</u>

When salvage is feasible, the product should, whenever possible, be segregated into the following categories: potentially salvageable, not salvageable and unaffected product. This is a general sorting, that is by cartons, cases, pallets, etc., and not by individual containers. Sorting by individual containers is dealt with in Section 4.1. A complete inventory of the not salvageable product should be recorded and the product disposed of in a manner described in Section 4.2. Product not subjected to the adverse conditions and hence unaffected should be separated from that which was involved and can be released for distribution and sale. Such unaffected product would not be subject to the coding requirement of Section 4.7.

3.6   <u>Removal from Site and Storage</u>

In situations when adverse conditions may continue to prevail, all product should be removed from the site as soon as possible.

The official agency having jurisdiction and the owner of the product should be informed as soon as possible by the salvor of the movement of a suspect lot of canned food.

All product involved in the salvage operation should be stored under conditions which protect against their unauthorized removal. Potentially salvageable product should also be stored under conditions which minimize damage, deterioration and contamination and prevent mixing with other products.

A complete record of any product removed from the site in which the quantities, manner of removal and place of subsequent storage are detailed should be made and retained.

4. **TREATMENT OF POTENTIALLY SALVAGEABLE CANNED FOODS**

4.1   Evaluation and Sorting

Each container of canned food deemed as potentially salvageable from the preliminary sorting (Section 3.5) should be thoroughly inspected. Containers showing visible evidence that their integrity has been lost and/or the contents have become contaminated should be set aside as not salvageable and disposed of in the manner given in Section 4.2.

The remaining salvageable canned food should, by visual inspection, be segregated into the following categories: (a) visually unaffected (appearing normal) containers which do not require reconditioning (4.4), and (b) those that require reconditioning (4.5). Where possible, labels should be removed to permit visual inspection of the entire container surface. The containers which require reconditioning should be further segregated into two groups, those which can be reconditioned (4.5.2) and those which are not reconditionable (4.5.1). The nature and extent of the adverse conditions will dictate which categories may be present in the suspect lot(s).

The inspection, sorting, sampling and evaluation should be conducted by persons trained and experienced in carrying out such procedures.

An inventory of the product in each of the above categories should be recorded. Records of the inventory, inspection, sorting, sampling and subsequent evaluation shall be made and kept for a period acceptable to the agency having jurisdiction.

4.2   Product Not Salvageable

Canned food which is not salvageable should be carefully disposed of under adequate supervision of the agency having jurisdiction to assure the protection of the public health. Records should be kept detailing the manner and location of disposal and be maintained for a period acceptable to the agency having jurisdiction.

4.3   Evaluation for Contamination

Whenever loss of container integrity and/or contamination of the contents in salvageable canned foods is suspected but, not visually indicated, samples of a size in keeping with the degree of safety required should be tested and evaluated. Microbiological evaluation of the contents should be carried out according to the procedures outlined in "Guideline Procedures to Establish Microbiological Causes of Spoilage in Canned Foods", or "Official Methods of

Analysis of the Association of Analytical Chemists", 14th ed., sections 46.063 - 46.070.

4.4   Visually Unaffected Containers Not Requiring Reconditioning

It should not be assumed that the contents of containers appearing normal (i.e., visually unaffected, and do not require reconditioning) are free of contamination. Unless there is evidence that the containers and/or their contents are free of contamination, such containers and their contents should be evaluated in accordance with Section 4.3 above. Where the results of such an evaluation indicate that there is virtually no possibility of the contents being contaminated, the remaining normal appearing containers can be released for distribution and sale. Where the results indicate that the product may be contaminated, the product should be classed as unsalvageable and disposed of as detailed in Section 4.2. In some instances potentially contaminated product may be salvaged by reprocessing (see Section 4.6).

4.5   Containers Requiring Reconditioning

4.5.1   Containers Not Reconditionable

Some containers by virtue of their type or condition are not capable of being reconditioned without adversely affecting their contents. The following list some examples of not reconditionable containers:

-        containers with any indication of swelling, with the exception of intentionally pressurized containers and some containers which by virtue of their shape, size or type of contents are prone to overfilling and appear slightly swollen.

-        glass jars with any indication of a raised lid, raised button or showing evidence of loosening of the closures.

-        containers with visible evidence of leakage.

-        containers with punctures, holes or fractures. (These conditions may be indicated by the accumulation of product on or around the puncture, hole or fracture in a can, under the lip of a glass jar, in the seal or on the body of a flexible pouch).

-        pull-top containers with fractures or dents on the score lines or in the rivet area.

-        corroded containers with severe pitting such that any cleaning and disinfection may result in perforation.

-        rigid containers crushed to the point where they cannot be stacked normally on shelves or opened with wheel-type can openers.

-        cans severely dented at or in the immediate vicinity of either an end or side seam.

-        cuts or fractures through at least one layer of metal on the doubleseam of cans.

-        containers with gross seam or seal defects.

Containers which are not reconditionable should be disposed of according to Section 4.2. Under certain circumstances further salvage operations may be undertaken to recover product in such containers. However, before any further action is taken, the contents should be evaluated for the possibility of contamination as stated in Section 4.3. If test results indicate that the contents may be contaminated then the containers should be classed as not salvageable and disposed of in accordance with Section 4.2. Where the test results indicate that the contents are not contaminated, the product may be recanned in accordance with Section 4.6. Since these containers do require reconditioning, special care should be taken to avoid contamination of the product during the process of recanning.

In some cases, for example, containers with external pitted corrosion only, the product may be expedited for immediate consumption as long as the contents have been shown to be free of contamination.

4.5.2   Reconditionable Containers

Prior to reconditioning, the contents of this group of containers should be evaluated for the possibility of contamination in accordance with Section 4.3. When the test results indicate that the contents may be contaminated then the containers should be disposed of in accordance with Section 4.2. However, depending upon the nature and extent of the contamination, the containers may be reconditioned followed by reprocessing (Section 4.6) and as long as that reprocessing will produce a product safe and suitable for human consumption.

All salvageable and reconditionable containers of food which have been in contact with not potable water or other deleterious substances as the result of flood, sewer backup or similar mishaps should be reconditioned by methods approved by the agency having jurisdiction. (Guidance for cleaning and disinfection is found in the "General Principles of Food Hygiene, Appendix 1, CAC/Vol. A-Ed. 1-1979"). Surface corrosion should be removed from reconditionable containers by cleaning. The containers should then be treated and stored in a manner to minimize further deterioration.

(Note: Certain types of containers which have been in contact with not potable water, foam, or other deleterious substances as a result of fire fighting efforts, flood, sewer backups or similar mishaps present special problems in reconditioning and require expert evaluation).

In those instances where salvage is confined to separation of normal appearing from mechanically damaged containers and where there is no possibility of contamination of the contents, the normal appearing containers should, if necessary, be reconditioned and then upon approval of the agency having jurisdiction be released for distribution and sale.

Where there is a possibility of contamination of the contents of normal appearing containers, appropriate testing in accordance with Section 4.3 should be carried out on both normal appearing and rejected containers. The sampling, analyses and evaluations should be carried out by persons trained and experienced in carrying out such procedures with canned foods.

In some circumstances recanning of the contents of the normal appearing containers may be necessary. In other circumstances reprocessing of the containers may be sufficient.

4.6   Recanning or Reprocessing

Recanning or reprocessing should be carried out in compliance with the "International Code of Hygienic Practice for Low-Acid and Acidified Low-Acid Canned Foods, CAC/RCP 23-1979 (Rev. 1, 1989)". The prior history of the product should be considered in the development of an appropriate scheduled process for recanning or reprocessing. For instance, the heating characteristics of the product may be changed as a result of the heat process originally applied.

4.7   Coding

Before a salvaged canned food is released for sale or distribution in its original container, each container shall be permanently marked with a legible, visible and specific code to permit its subsequent identification as a salvaged product.

5.   QUALITY ASSURANCE

It is important that all salvage operations be properly established, correctly applied, sufficiently supervised, monitored and documented.

Section 8 of the "International Code of Hygienic Practice for Low-Acid and Acidified Low-Acid Canned Foods, CAC/RCP 23-1979 (Rev. 1, 1989)", is applicable with the following substitution for 8.2.4.

Records should be kept identifying each lot of salvaged canned foods as well as the conditions under which the original food became suspect and the means by which it was salvaged.

6.   STORAGE AND TRANSPORT OF SALVAGED PRODUCT

As given in the "International Code of Hygienic Practice for Low-Acid and Acidified Low-Acid Canned foods, CAC/RCP 23-1979 (Rev. 1, 1989)", with the following addition:

Where such foods are released for export, the agency having jurisdiction in the importing country should be notified that the product has been salvaged.

7.   LABORATORY CONTROL PROCEDURES

As given in the "International Code of Hygienic Practice for Low-Acid and Acidified Low-Acid Canned Foods, CAC/RCP 23-1979 (Rev. 1, 1989)".

8.   END PRODUCT SPECIFICATIONS

As stated in the "International Code of Hygienic Practice for Low-Acid and Acidified Low-Acid Canned Foods, CAC/RCP 23-1979 (Rev. 1, 1989)".

APPENDIX 1

FLOW CHART SHOWING THE SEQUENCE OF EVENTS IN THE SALVAGE OF CANNED FOODS EXPOSED TO ADVERSE CONDITIONS (DETAILS PROVIDED IN TEXT OF MAIN DOCUMENT)

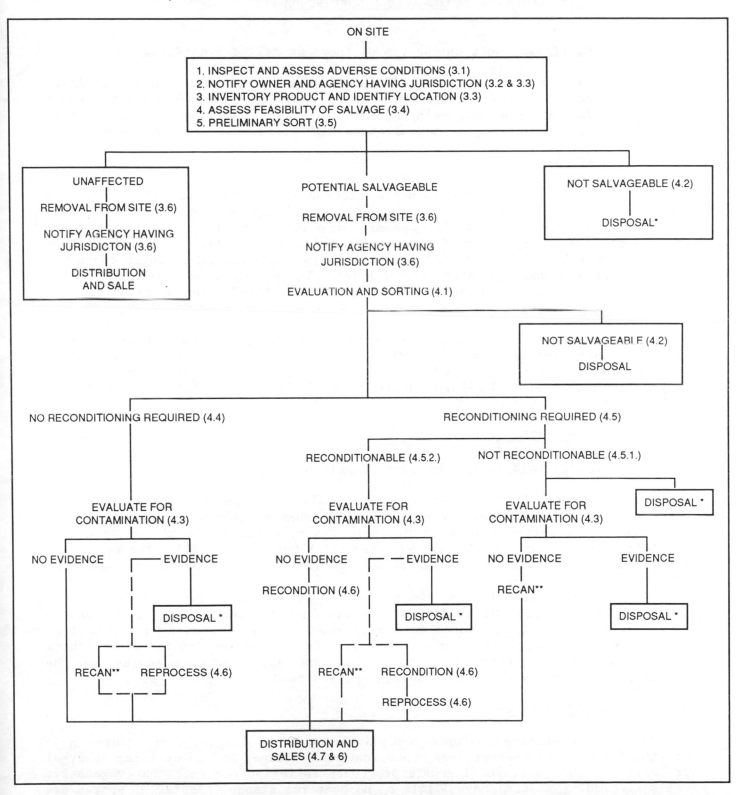

(The solid lines indicate the usual courses of action. The broken lines indicate alternate actions which may be undertaken under special circumstances and should always be carried out under the direct supervision of person(s) knowledgeable and experienced in the particular aspects of salvage as well as the methods of sampling and evaluating the possibility of contamination).

* Notify the agency having jurisdiction and product owner of removal from site and plan for disposal.
** Cleaning and/or disinfection of the containers prior to opening may be necessary.

GUIDELINE PROCEDURES TO ESTABLISH MICROBIOLOGICAL
CAUSES OF SPOILAGE IN LOW-ACID AND ACIDIFIED
LOW-ACID CANNED FOODS

Cautionary Note on the Use of these Guideline Procedures

The proper diagnosis of the causes of microbiological spoilage requires considerable training and experience. Anyone not experienced in spoilage diagnosis should use these guidelines and identified references only in consultation with canned food laboratory experts.

1.   SCOPE

These guidelines summarize procedures to establish the causes of microbiological spoilage in low-acid and acidified low-acid canned foods; references to appropriate techniques are supplied. It is intended that these procedures be used in the investigation of the causes of microbiological spoilage and not to establish the total absence of viable organisms in a single container or to determine commercial sterility of a lot. These methods may also be used for the initial identification of potential safety problems. They have no role in establishing commercial sterility.

Water activity controlled foods (e.g., canned bread, cheese spread, chorizo sausage and pasta in pouches), aseptically processed and packaged foods, and perishable cured meat products require special consideration and are not covered in this text. Spoilage diagnosis should be carried out in consultation with experts in that commodity.

2.   EXPLANATORY PREFACE

Microbiological End-Product Specifications

Canned foods should be commercially sterile and not contain any substances originating from microorganisms in amounts which may present a hazard to health (International Code of Hygienic Practice for Low-Acid and Acidified Low-Acid Canned Foods, CAC/RCP 23-1979 (Rev. 1, 1989), Section XI). The key is the term "commercial sterility", which is defined in the Code of Hygienic Practice.

Strict adherence to the procedures presented in the Code of Hygienic Practice for Low-Acid and Acidified Low-Acid Canned Foods will give reasonable assurance that a lot of canned food will meet this end-product specification. While sampling and analysis of the end-product is not recommended for establishing the commercial sterility of a lot, they are important procedures in the investigation of lots which may contain spoiled food.

3.   INTRODUCTION

The primary reasoning behind the spoilage diagnosis procedure is to distinguish between post-process contamination (leakage) and insufficient thermal processing. The spoilage diagnosis procedure relies on the fact that vegetative cells (including yeasts) have little or no heat resistance. Bacterial spores are heat resistant, so a pure culture of spore forming organisms usually means insufficient thermal processing. A mixed flora of different vegetative organisms

usually means leakage.   Therefore to distinguish between thermally resistant and
sensitive organisms, heat treatment of inocula for cultural examination is
necessary.   Heat treatment can be performed before or after cultural examination.
Interpretation of results from the heat treatment step should take into
consideration the possibility that all spores present may have germinated and would
thus be heat sensitive.   Figures 2 and 3 reflect only the heat treatment step
performed after culturing.   Since microbiological examination of canned foods is
an integral part of any investigation of the cause of spoilage, it is important
that reliable and reproducible procedures for the examination of both the container
as well as its contents be employed.   Such procedures can be used by a processor,
an independent laboratory or a regulatory agency.

It should be remembered that spoilage can also indicate a potential
hazard to the health of the consumer.   If there is evidence that a search for a
specific pathogen is necessary, appropriate procedures should be applied.   Methods
for the identification and enumeration of various pathogens associated with foods
can be found in a number of texts on the subject.   Various texts which have been
found generally useful are referenced at the end of the document.

As spoilage of canned foods may result from poor handling of
ingredients prior to processing, under-processing, or post-thermal processing
leaker contamination, procedures to establish the cause of spoilage ought not to
be limited solely to examination of the food contents for viable organisms. They
should also include the physical examination of the container and an evaluation of
its integrity, as well as, where possible, the examination of pertinent cannery
records of the can seam teardown, the processing and shipping history of the
product.   The results of these should be taken into account, together with the
microbiological results, in arriving at a final conclusion.

4.   **PROCEDURES FOR DETERMINING THE CAUSE OF SPOILAGE IN LOTS OF CANNED FOOD**

The identification of the lot, the compilation of its history including
can seam teardown and thermal processing records, together with knowledge of
distribution are needed, as well as the sampling, inspection and examination of
containers and contents.

4.1   Lot Identification and History

It is important to compile as much information as possible about the
suspect product lots.   This should not be restricted solely to the acquisition of
microbiological data.   It is also important that the information and data be
examined for the presence of trends or patterns before arriving at any conclusions.
A check list of the information required is helpful to ensure that essential data
are not missed. An example of information needed in such a check list is given in
Appendix 1.

A note should be made as to the source of the can (sample), e.g., from
an inspector, or from a domicile or establishment where there has been an outbreak
of food poisoning.

4.2   Laboratory Examination

An outline of procedures for examining a product and its container are
shown in the following flow diagram (figure 1).   Specific information relating to
each of the stages in this procedure is contained in the following sections of the
text.   While certain of the procedures relate mainly to the examination of rigid
metal cans, they can be adapted for all types of containers used for packaging
thermally processed foods.   There are sections in the report concerning the

interpretation of the results of these procedures and guidance on where hygiene problems may exist so that corrective action can be taken.

4.2.1   External inspection

4.2.1.1   Each container in the sample should be examined visually before and after removal of any labels.   All identifying marks and stains or signs of corrosion on the containers and labels should be carefully and accurately recorded. The label, after removal in one piece and inspection of both sides, should be identified with the same reference as the container and be retained.

4.2.1.2   The visual examination should be carried out under good illumination and preferably with the aid of a magnifying lens before opening or attempting any seam measurements. With respect to metal cans, particular attention should be paid to the examination of the seams for the defects, such as cutovers, dents (adjacent to or on the seam), droops, vees or spurs, pleats, knocked down flanges and for lap faults. Other less noticeable defects may occur, for example, faults in tin plate, score marks caused by supermarket case opening knives, small pin holes in welded side seams, rust holes, etc. Therefore, careful visual examination of the whole of the container is essential. A list of some of the visual external defects commonly found to occur in metal cans is given in Table 1.

4.2.1.3   During examination of the container an attempt should be made to establish whether the defects are the result of damage caused by mishandling during shipment or is a result of damage within the processing establishment. All observations should be recorded.

       The location of any defect on the can is important and should be marked on the can and recorded.

4.2.1.4   Non-destructive measurements of seals or seams should be carried out. For example, for cylindrical cans, measurements of double seam height and thickness, and countersink should be carried out at at least three locations approximately 120° apart around the double seam, exclusive of the juncture with the side seam. Blown, badly distorted or damaged containers are usually only suitable for visual examination since the seams are often too distorted for proper seam measurements to be made. However, they should not be discarded, for even badly distorted cans should be retained for detailed structural and possibly other, (e.g., chemical), examination and until the investigating authority and the manufacturer are quite satisfied that they need not be kept any longer. Tests or measurements, e.g., tap-test, countersink or centre depth can be used to give comparative measures of the internal vacuum with respect to a normal can.

4.2.1.5   Determination of Net Weight

       The gross weight of the container and contents should be measured and recorded at this stage. The determination of the net weight is delayed.

Figure 1

FLOW DIAGRAM OF THE PROCEDURES FOR THE EXAMINATION OF A THERMALLY PROCESSED FOOD IN A HERMETICALLY SEALED CONTAINER

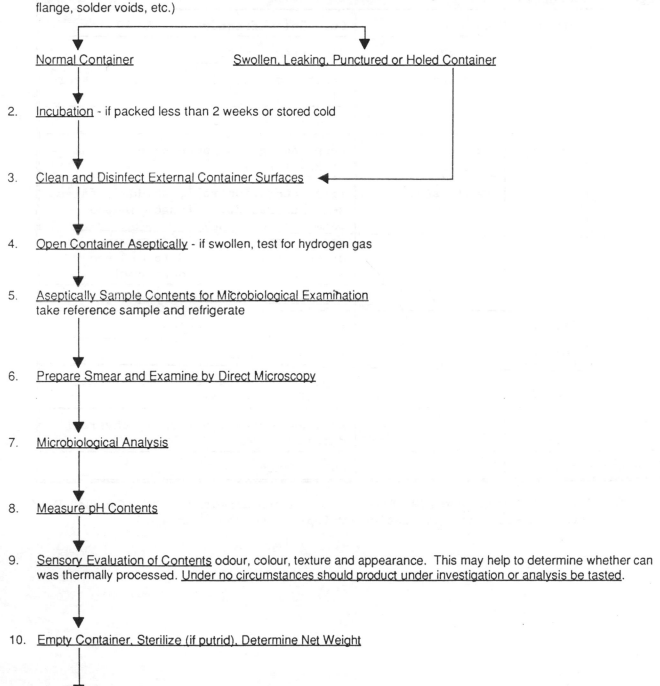

1. <u>External Visual Inspection and Physical Non-Destructive Measurements</u>
   (Inspect label, read code, then weigh can and contents. Mark can and label; remove label; inspect inside of label for location of stains and can for corrosion. Inspect seams for product leakage and visible defects such as knocked down flange, solder voids, etc.)

   <u>Normal Container</u>   <u>Swollen, Leaking, Punctured or Holed Container</u>

2. <u>Incubation</u> - if packed less than 2 weeks or stored cold

3. <u>Clean and Disinfect External Container Surfaces</u>

4. <u>Open Container Aseptically</u> - if swollen, test for hydrogen gas

5. <u>Aseptically Sample Contents for Microbiological Examination</u>
   take reference sample and refrigerate

6. <u>Prepare Smear and Examine by Direct Microscopy</u>

7. <u>Microbiological Analysis</u>

8. <u>Measure pH Contents</u>

9. <u>Sensory Evaluation of Contents</u> odour, colour, texture and appearance. This may help to determine whether can was thermally processed. <u>Under no circumstances should product under investigation or analysis be tasted</u>.

10. <u>Empty Container, Sterilize (if putrid), Determine Net Weight</u>

11. <u>Test Container for Leaks</u> (e.g. vacuum, dye testing, etc.)

12. <u>Assess Seams and/or Seals for Correct Formation</u>

TABLE 1

SOME VISUAL EXTERNAL DEFECTS FOUND IN METAL CANS*

Place where fault Probably occurred		Position on Can	Type of Defect
Can Manufacture		Can end/body	Cut, hole, fracture in tin plate
		Can Body	Side seam faults
		Easy open strip	Fractured score line, excessive score line
Cannery			
	Seamer	Can end	Deep coding, compound squeeze, damage to key fixing
		Double seam	First operation roll, skidder, false seam knocked down flange, jumped seam, broken chuck. Second operation roll, cutover, droop, split droop, deformed end seam, spur, knocked down curl
		Can body	Perforated, pierced, cut dents
	Filling		Peaked, flipper, springer
	Cooling		Peaked, Panelled
	Can runways		Cable burn, abrasions, dents under rim of double seam
Storage			External corrosion (rust), physical damage
Transit/Retail			Cuts, dents

*   Based on R.H. Thorpe and P.M. Baker, "Visual can defects", 1984, Campden Food Preservation Research Association, Chipping Campden, England

The net or drained weight, whichever is appropriate, should be determined for each container in the sample. (A close approximation of net weight can be obtained by subtracting the average weight, if known, of empty containers plus the second cover from the gross weight of the filled, sealed container.)

4.2.1.6   Over-filling

Over-filling reduces the headspace and may adversely affect the vacuum when the container is sealed. With solid products it may cause containers to have a zero internal vacuum and even result in bulging of the container ends giving the appearance of a swollen can. Over-filling may decrease the effectiveness of a thermal treatment. This is particularly true when agitating sterilization or flexible containers are used. It causes excessive strain on seals or seams during processing. Over-filling of a container may be indicated when the net weight exceeds a reasonable tolerance of the declared or target net weight or of the average net weight determined by examination of a significant number of containers of normal appearance.

4.2.1.7   Under-filling

Under-weights may indicate that either the container was underfilled or leakage has occurred. Other evidence that leakage may be the cause of under-weight should be sought, e.g., stains or product residues on the container surface, label or surrounding containers in the same carton. Panelled cans may indicate loss of liquid during thermal processing.

4.2.2   Incubation

Swollen, punctured, or holed containers must not be incubated.

Consideration should be given as to whether the container(s) should be incubated before opening for microbiological examination of the contents. The aim of incubation is to increase the likelihood of finding viable microorganisms in subsequent microbiological examinations. _Incubation results alone should not be used to decide the fate of the affected lot_.

Considering the length of time involved in international shipments of canned foods, incubation may not be necessary. Containers should be incubated at, for example, 30°C for 14 days and/or 37°C for 10 to 14 days. Note that a number of leakage spoilage organisms will not grow above 30°C. In addition, if the product is intended to be distributed in areas of the world with tropical climate or is to be maintained at elevated temperatures (vending machines for hot product), containers should also be incubated at higher temperatures, e.g., for 5 days at 55°C. Since thermophiles may die during such incubation period, it is desirable to examine containers periodically for the evidence of gas production before the end of incubation.

4.2.3   Cleaning, disinfection and opening of containers

4.2.3.1   Swollen containers

The external surfaces of containers should be cleaned with a suitable detergent and rinsed. Containers should be disinfected for at least 10 to 15 minutes in freshly prepared 100-300 ppm chlorinated water, buffered to approximately pH 6.8, or by flooding the end with an appropriate alcoholic iodine solution (e.g., 2.5% w/v iodine in ethanol) and leaving for 20 minutes. Alternatively the end can be decontaminated by flooding or spreading with a 2% solution of peracetic acid in an appropriate wetting agent (e.g., 0.1% polysorbitan

80) for 5 minutes.   Containers should be dried immediately after disinfection,
using clean sterile disposable paper tissues or towels.   Appropriate safety
precautions should be taken when using any of these chemical disinfectants.

All containers should be handled as if they contained botulinum toxin
or pathogens.   Horizontal laminar flow cabinets which blow air over the operator
should not be used.   A safety cabinet may be used when opening containers suspected
of not being commercially sterile.   Swollen containers should be opened within the
cabinet while inside a sterile bag or by using the sterile inverted funnel method
to contain any spraying of the contents.   When not sampling the contents, cover the
open end with a sterile cover (e.g., sterile half Petri dish or other suitable
sterile covers).

It is usual to open the non-coded end of the metal container.   For cans
containing liquid or semi-liquid components, a sterile stainless steel spike with
a shield can be used to pierce the container and the contents sampled using a
sterile pipette or equivalent apparatus.   For opening cans containing solid product
a sterile disc cutter should be used, or alternatively the side may be aseptically
pierced and the can opened by aseptically cutting round the body.   It is essential
that damage to the seams and seals be avoided when opening containers.   Open
plastic containers from the bottom or side to prevent damage to the seal area
and/or lid.   After disinfection lightly flame dry avoiding damage to the plastic
container and with a small heated sterile device such as a soldering iron equipped
with a sharp tip, cut a hole large enough for the aseptic removal of the samples.

If a safety cabinet is not used, it is recommended that a face shield
be worn and that the side seam point away from the person opening the container.
To test for hydrogen, gas may be collected in a test tube over the point of
puncture and the open end of the tube immediately exposed to a flame.   A loud "pop"
indicates the presence of hydrogen.   If the can to be used for gas analysis is also
to be used for cultural analysis, precautions should be taken to prevent external
contamination.

Describe and record any unusual odours from the contents which may be
noticed immediately after opening.   However direct sniffing must be avoided.

Unless a swollen can is suspected of containing gas-producing
thermophilic anaerobes, it may be stored at 4°C before opening to reduce the
internal pressure and reduce spraying of the contents.   However prolonged storage
at such temperatures should be avoided as it may effectively reduce the number of
viable organisms and hamper attempts to isolate the causative microorganisms.

4.2.3.2   Flat (not swollen) containers

With liquid foods, stratification or sedimentation of the
microorganisms may occur.   To ensure mixing of any contaminating microorganisms,
it is advisable to shake the container just before opening.

The end of the container which is to be opened for sampling should
first be decontaminated by the methods described in 4.2.3.1 and/or by flame
sterilizing the end.   Open with a sterile opening device.   Describe and record any
unusual odours from the contents which may be noticed immediately after opening,
and as for the swollen cans, direct sniffing must be avoided.

When not sampling the contents, cover the open end of the container
with a sterile cover (e.g., sterile half Petri dish or other suitable sterile
cover).

4.2.4   Microbiological Analysis

Appendix 2 and standard texts, e.g., Speck (1984), C.F.P.R.A. Technical Manual No. 18 (1987) and Buckle (1985) should also be consulted.

4.2.4.1   Reference sample

A reference sample of at least 20 g or ml should be aseptically removed from the contents and transferred to a sterile container, sealed and held at a temperature below 5°C until required. The reference sample may be required to permit confirmation of results at a later stage. Care should be taken to avoid freezing as this may kill a significant number of bacteria in the reference sample. If thermophilic contamination or spoilage is the concern the reference sample should not be refrigerated. The reference sample also provides material for non-microbiological tests or analyses, e.g., for analysis for tin, lead, toxins, etc., but if these are anticipated appropriate amounts must be taken. For solid, and in some instances semi-solid foods, the reference sample should be made up from samplings taken from various suspect points, e.g., the centre core, product surfaces in contact with the end or double seam (specially that in contact with the cross-over), product in contact with the side seam, (if there is one). Transfer all samplings to a sterile container and store as described above.

4.2.4.2   Analytical sample and inoculation of media

For the purpose of preparing analytical samples, canned products can be divided into two main groups, namely solid and liquid. Separate procedures may be required to prepare analytical samples of these products.

4.2.4.2.1   Liquid products

These products may be sampled using suitable sterile, plugged pipettes with wide-bore tips. (Pipetting by mouth suction should be avoided.) The sample should be inoculated into both liquid and solid media.

It is recommended that each tube of liquid medium be inoculated with at least 1 to 2 ml of the sample of the container contents. Each solid media plate should be streaked with at least one loopful (approximately 0.01 ml) of the sample of the container contents.

4.2.4.2.2   Solid and semi-solid products

For such products both core and surface samplings should be taken.

For taking a core sample, a suitable sterile device (e.g., a large bore glass tube or a cork borer) having an adequate diameter and length should be used.

In the case of spoilage resulting from underprocessing, the most likely location in which microorganisms may be expected to survive would be the geometric centre of the can contents. Thus the central portion of the core sample is of prime interest. Sufficient product should be aseptically excised from the central portion of the core to provide 1 to 2 g for each tube of liquid media to be inoculated and for the streaking of each plate of solid media. For multiple tubes and pour plates, the central portion can be chopped or blended with a suitable diluent.

Post-process contamination may give rise to localized surface contamination and growth in solid products. If this is suspected the surface should be sampled. Using a sterile scalpel, knife or other suitable device scrape product from the surface, paying particular attention to those areas which were in contact with the double or side seams and any easy opening feature. The scraped product should be put into a sterile container. As an alternative or additionally, it may be sufficient to swab those areas of the double and side seams plus any easy opening feature of the containers which had come into contact with the product. After swabbing, the swab should be placed into a suitable sterile diluent and shaken vigorously; portions should be used to inoculate the tubes and for streaking the plates.

The core sample and the surface samplings should be treated as separate analytical units.

Wherever possible identical microbiological analyses should also be done on at least one apparently normal can of the same code lot or batch for comparative purposes. Where cans from the same code lot or batch are not readily available, apparently normal cans from codes or batches as close as possible to the suspect lot or batch should be used.

A flow diagram of aerobic and anaerobic microbiological analysis of canned foods is found in figures 1 and 2, (see also Appendix 2). These may be useful in the interpretation of the microbiological examination.

4.2.4.3   Direct microscopic examination

This is a very useful test in the hands of an experienced worker.

Different techniques can be used for direct microscopic examination, e.g., stain with 1% aqueous crystal violet or 0.05% polychrome methylene blue, phase contrast technique, fluorescent stain procedure.

It may be necessary to defat some oily foodstuffs on the slide using a solvent, e.g., xylene.

There is an advantage in using both wet film and dry stain techniques. Remember when using a Gram stain that old cultures often give a variable Gram reaction. Therefore report morphology only.

A slide of the can contents should be prepared for examination. Control slides prepared from the contents of apparently normal cans of the same code lot or batch should also be prepared, particularly if the analyst is unfamiliar with the product or if numbers of cells per field are to be compared.

It is important to note the following:

It is easy to confuse particles of product with microbial cells, therefore it may be prudent to dilute the sample before preparing the smear.

Dead microbiological cells resulting from incipient (pre-process) spoilage or autosterilization may show up on smears at this stage and no growth will be evident in the inoculated culture media.

Do not assume that apparent absence of microbial cells in a single field means that none are present in the product.

The entire smear or wet mount should be carefully scanned to locate areas of microbiological interest from which at least five fields should be

examined in detail.   Record observations giving approximate numbers of each
morphological type observed in each field.

4.2.5   Measurement of pH of contents

        The pH of the contents should be measured in accordance with existing
methodology (see Appendix II, Recommended International Code of Hygienic Practice
for Low-Acid and Acidified Low-Acid Canned Foods, CAC/RCP 23-1979 (Rev. 1, 1989))
and compared to that of normal cans. A significant change in the pH of the contents
from that of normal product may indicate that there has been microbial growth.
However absence of such change does not always indicate that no growth has
occurred.

4.2.6   Sensory examination

        This is an important part of the examination of canned foods.   During
this procedure note should be taken of any evidence of product breakdown, off or
unusual colour, odour or in the case of liquid components (brine) cloudiness or
sedimentation. Under no circumstances should the product be tasted.

        Normal changes in texture of solid products can be perceived by feeling
or squeezing the product with a rubber or plastic gloved hand.   For proper
organoleptic evaluation, product temperature should not be less than 15°C and
preferably not more than 20°C.   Where possible, the results of the sensory
evaluation should be compared to the same evaluation of the contents from
apparently normal cans from the same or neighbouring code lots or batches.

4.2.7   Emptying and sterilization of the suspect container

        The remaining contents should be emptied out into a suitable waste
receptacle.   It is important that cans containing spoiled product be disinfected
or autoclaved prior to washing and further testing, e.g., leak testing, seam
teardown etc.   After washing, examine the internal surfaces for any evidence of
discolouration, corrosion or other defects.

        If required for the determination of the net or drained weight, the
empty container should then be dried and then weighed, (see 4.2.1.5).

        The empty container and any parts should be clearly identified and
retained as long as there is any chance that it may be required for further
examination or evidence.

4.2.8   Leak detection methods

        A number of methods may be used for determining leakage in containers.
The method chosen is often determined by the degree of accuracy required, the
number of suitable containers available for testing and the need to simulate
conditions thought to exist when the containers originally leaked. Often more than
one type of test is employed in combination with microbiological testing to
determine the type and cause of the spoilage being investigated.   Data obtained
from tests for container leaks are often used to corroborate microbiological test
results obtained on product from the same containers.   The information may be
useful for preventing problems from the same cause.

        Each leak testing method has its advantages and disadvantages.   For
example, air pressure testing, while usually rapid, may be criticized for not
testing the can in its natural vacuum state. Helium testing may be too sensitive
and indicate leakage when none actually occurred.   Also it does not indicate the

point of leakage. The hydrogen sulphide test is useful for determining the location and size of the leakage as well as provide a permanent record; some find the method too slow for testing a large number of cans. Preparing the cans for testing as well as the ability of the operator to conduct the test properly and interpret the results accurately are as important as choosing the appropriate test for leakage.

It is not always possible to recreate leakage in containers that may have leaked at some time during or after processing. Product often plugs the leakage path and it may not be possible to remove it when cleaning the can prior to testing.

In these instances, many more suspect cans than were tested microbiologically may have to be tested to establish leakage in a lot. It is sometimes helpful to leak test cans from the same lot which are not suspect when leakage cannot be recreated in cans with spoiled product.

Procedures and discussions of various methods of container leakage testing may be found in the following references: U.S. F.D.A. (1984), N.C.A. (1972), C.F.P.R.A. (1987), AFNOR-CNERNA (1982), H.W.C. (1983) and Buckle (1985).

4.2.9   Seam tear-down

The procedures for examining and assessing double seams of canned foods subject to investigation for cause of spoilage are the same as those given in Section 7.4.8.1.2 of the Recommended International Code of Hygienic Practice for Low-Acid and Acidified Low-Acid Canned Foods, CAC/RCP 23-1979 (Rev. 1, 1989).

However the interpretation of results from such seam examinations may be different for spoilage investigation than for process control. When microbiological results indicate recontamination spoilage, the presence of obvious seam abnormalities often confirms leakage. On the other hand, recontamination may occur in the absence of obvious seam defects. Examples of other sources of recontamination are: seam damage after closure, temporary leakage, sealing compound effects, and plate pinholes and fractures. In such instances the additional procedures given under leak testing as well as the microbiological results are necessary.

For these reasons, results from seam tear-down as part of spoilage investigation must be considered only in context with all other spoilage investigation efforts and require expert interpretation.

5.   <u>GUIDELINES FOR THE INTERPRETATION OF LABORATORY DATA</u>

The interpretation of the laboratory data in Tables 2 and 3 as well as figures 2 and 3 (Appendix 2) should be considered together with the overall pattern of the particular spoilage incident being investigated and the product history.

TABLE 2

INTERPRETATION OF LABORATORY DATA CONCERNING A LOW-ACID CANNED FOOD

Condition of Can	Odour	Appearance (3)	pH (1)	Smear	Key Points from Cultures (2)	Possible interpretations
Swell	Sour	Frothy, Possibly ropy brine	Below normal	Cocci and/or rods and/or yeasts	Positive aerobe and/or Anaerobe; growth at 30°C and/or 37°C	Post-process leakage
Swell	Slightly off (sometimes ammoniacal)	Normal to frothy	Slightly to definitely abnormal may be higher	Rods (spores sometimes seen)	Positive; aerobe and/or Anaerobe; growth at 30°C; often pellicle formation in aerobic broths	Post-process leakage or gross underprocessing
Swell	Sour	Frothy possibly ropy brine. Food firm and uncooked	Below normal	Mixed Population (often spores)	Positive; aerobe and/or anaerobe; growth at 30°C and 37°C and often at 55°C	No thermal process given
Swell	Normal to sour	Pale colour or distinct colour change, frothy	Slightly to definitely below normal	Medium to long rods, often granular, spores seldom seen	Positive anaerobic growth at 55°C. No growth 30°C, possibly growth at 37°C	Thermophilic anaerobe; inadequate cooling or storage at elevated temperatures
Swell	Normal to cheesy to putrid	Unusually frothy with disinte-gration of solid particles	Slightly to definitely below normal	Rods (spores may be seen)	Growth and gas in anaerobic culture at 37°C and/or 30°C but no growth in aerobic cultures	Under-processing, mesophilic anaerobic HIGH RISK consider survival of *Clostridium botulinum*
Swell	Normal to metallic	Normal to frothy	Normal to slightly elevated	Normal	Negative	Low filling temperature; insufficient exhausting of can before seaming; over-fill or hydrogen swell**
Swell or flat	Little or no gas on opening; fruity odour	Normal	Normal to below normal	Large numbers of evenly stained cocci and/or rods	Negative	Pre-process (incipient) spoilage

Condition of Can	Odour	Appearance (3)	pH (1)	Smear	Key Points from Cultures (2)	Possible interpretations
Swell	Sour to cheesy	Frothy	Often below Normal	Poorly stained cocci and/or rods	Negative	Leaker spoilage followed by auto-sterilization
Apparently sound	Sulphurous	Contents blackened	Normal to below normal	Rods	Anaerobic growth without gas at 55°C only	Thermophilic sulphur stinker; inadequate cooling
Apparently sound	Normal to sour	Normal to cloudy brine	Normal to below normal	Cocci and/or rods	Positive; aerobe and/or anaerobe; growth at 30°C, and usually at 37°C	Post-process leakage
Apparently sound	Normal to sour	Normal to cloudy	Below normal	Rods (often granular)	No growth below 37°C. Aerobic growth without gas at 55°C; may get no growth if samples old or incubated for long period	Thermophilic aerobes (flat sour) *Bacillus spp.*. Inadequate cooling or storage at elevated temperatures
Apparently sound	Normal to sour	Normal to cloudy	Below normal	Rods, (spores may be seen)	Positive; aerobic growth at 37°C and 30°C	Under-processing or leakage. Mesophilic aerobic spore-formers. (*Bacillus spp*)
Apparently sound	Normal to sour	Normal to cloudy brine	Below normal	Granular rods	Negative	Under-processing or auto-sterilization; thermophilic spores
Apparently sound	Normal to sour	Normal	Normal to below normal	Large numbers of evenly stained coci and/or rods per field	Negative	Pre-process spoilage
Apparently sound	Normal	Normal	Normal	Negative or occasional rods and/or cocci, i.e. normal	Negative	No microbiological problem

(1) The pH may rise particularly with microbial growth in meat or protein rich food.

(2) There may be difficulty in isolating *Flavobacterium spp* from milk or milk-based products at 25°C as they may not grow in aerobic broths

(3) These refer principally to brined product. For other products, abnormal colour, texture and appearance may also indicate defects but are product-related and therefore cannot be tabulated.

* Based upon M.L. Speck, Compendium of Methods for the Microbiological Examination of Foods, 1984, American Public Health Assoc.

** Nitrite detinning can result in swollen containers.

TABLE 3

INTERPRETATION OF LABORATORY DATA CONCERNING ACIDIFIED LOW-ACID CANNED FOOD

Condition of Can	Odour	Appearance*	Normal pH Group	Smear	Key Points from Cultures	Possible interpretations
Swell	Normal to metallic	Normal to frothy	4.6 and below	Normal	Negative	Hydrogen swell
Swell	Sour	Frothy Possibly ropy brine	4.6 and below	Rods and/or cocci and/or yeasts	Positive aerobic and/or anaerobic growth at 30°C	No process given or post-process leakage
Swell	Sour	Normal to frothy	4.6 and below	Rods	Growth and/or gas aerobically and/or anaerobically at 30°C	Lactobacilli; grossly insufficient processing or post-process leakage
Swell	Butyric	Normal to frothy	4.6 to 3.7	Rods (spores may be seen)	Growth and gas in anaerobic culture at 30°C	Under processing; mesophilic aerobe
Apparently sound	Sour	Normal to cloudy juice	4.6 to 3.7	Rods (often granular)	Aerobic Growth without gas at 37°C and/or 55°C	Thermophilic/mesophilic aerobe. Aciduric flat sour (B. coagulans)
Apparently sound	Normal to sour	Normal cloudy juice possibly mouldy	4.6 and below	Rods and/or cocci and/or moulds	Positive aerobe and/or anaerobe growth at 30°C	Leakage, under-processing
Apparently sound	Normal	Normal	4.6 and below	Normal	Negative	No microbiological problem

* These refer principally to brined products. For other products, abnormal colour, texture, and appearance may also indicate defects but are product-related and therefore cannot be tabulated.

6.   GUIDELINES TO ASSIST IN IDENTIFYING CAUSES OF SPOILAGE

It is important that all available data be used in identifying causes
of spoilage. It is essential that a complete assessment be made for each incident
of spoilage. Data must be gathered (see Appendix 1) from the processing plant and
the laboratory analyses and other sources by the appropriate expert(s). A careful
and comprehensive analysis of such data is imperative in the accurate
identification of the cause of spoilage. The following guidelines, though not all
inclusive, should assist this identification.

6.1   Number of spoiled
       containers   a)   Isolated container - usually a random leaker and
                                 containers rarely the result of under-processing.

                           b)   Several containers - mixed microflora, probably due
                                 to post-process contamination and leakage.

                                 Leaker spoilage may occur with or without defective
                                 seams or visible dents and may be related to
                                 over-cooling, inadequate chlorination, contaminated
                                 cooling water and/or dirty, wet post-processing
                                 equipment. Handling cans while warm and wet or
                                 excessive rough can handling practices may increase
                                 likelihood of leaker spoilage. If there is a high
                                 proportion of spoiled containers and only
                                 sporeformers are present, under-processing is
                                 usually indicated. However, leakage should not be
                                 ruled out.

6.2   Age of Product and
       Storage   a)   Excessive age and/or excessively high temperature
                                 may give rise to hydrogen swells. This is more
                                 likely to occur with canned vegetables e.g.,
                                 artichoke hearts, celery, pumpkin and cauliflower.

                           b)   Corrosion or damage causing perforations of
                                 container may lead to leaker spoilage and secondary
                                 damage to other cans.

                           c)   Thermophilic spoilage may result from storage at
                                 high temperatures, e.g., 37°C (99°F) and above.

6.3   Location
       of Spoilage   a)   Spoilage in centre of container stacks, or near
                                 ceiling, may indicate insufficient cooling resulting
                                 in thermophilic spoilage.

                           b)   Spoilage scattered throughout the stacks or cases
                                 may   indicate   post-processing   leakage   or
                                 under-processing.

6.4   Processing
       Records   a)   Records showing poor control of thermal processing
                                 may correlate with spoilage from under-processing.

b)   Adequate processing records may eliminate under-processing spoilage and indicate post-processing leaker contamination.

c)   Incorrect retort operation, i.e., leaking air or cooling water valves, broken thermometers and incorrect reel speed of rotary cookers may lead to under-processing.

d)   Delays coupled with unhygienic pre-process conditions may result in incipient or pre-process spoilage.

e)   High thermophilic counts in blanchers may correlate with thermophilic spoilage.

f)   Changes in product formulation without reevaluation of process parameters may lead to under-processing.

g)   Inadequate sanitation may lead to a build-up of microorganisms, which either result in pre-process spoilage or render the scheduled process inadequate. Post-process leaker contamination may also be caused by inadequate sanitation.

6.5 Laboratory data   a)   See Tables 2 and 3 and Figures 2 and 3 which correlate with the verification of positive tubes as discussed in Appendix 1.

7.   **CONCLUDING REMARKS**

The foregoing is concerned with the cause of spoilage in canned foods. Such determinations are, of necessity, different from those required to establish that commercial sterility has been achieved within a given code lot of product.

It is not within the scope of this procedure to give any guidance as to the disposal of lots which have been demonstrated to be not commercially sterile.

The reasons for spoilage are many and varied. Therefore, a decision as to the disposal of such lots needs to be made on a case-by-case basis, utilizing much of the information obtained in assessing the status of the lot from which the container was obtained. Whether or not a lot can be salvaged will depend, for example, on factors such as the reason for spoilage, the ability and reliability of physically separating satisfactory from unsatisfactory products, etc. These factors will of course, vary widely. Therefore, the general principles outlined in the "Guidelines for the Salvage of Canned Foods Exposed to Adverse Conditions" apply and in some cases may be used for lots in which spoilage has been identified.

Figure 2

FLOW SHEET FOR THE AEROBIC CULTURAL EXAMINATION OF
LOW-ACID CANNED FOODS FOR SPOILAGE AND DIAGNOSIS OF RESULTS

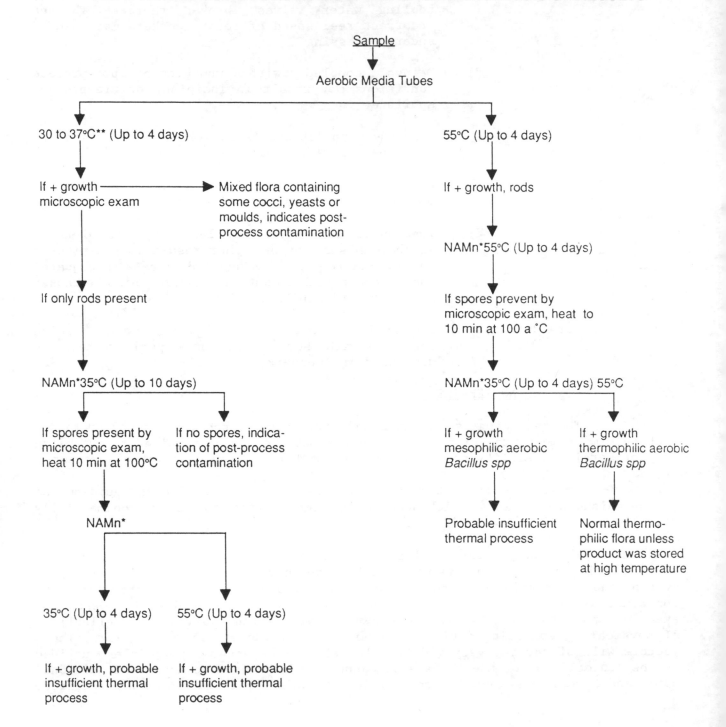

(* NAMn = Nutrient agar plus manganese)

(** Conditions for microbial growth are optimal at 30 to 35°C. However incubation temperatures of 36°C or 37°C may be used depending upon regional environmental conditions.)

Figure 3

FLOW DIAGRAM FOR THE ANAEROBIC CULTURAL EXAMINATION
OF LOW-ACID CANNED FOODS FOR SPOILAGE AND DIAGNOSIS OF RESULTS

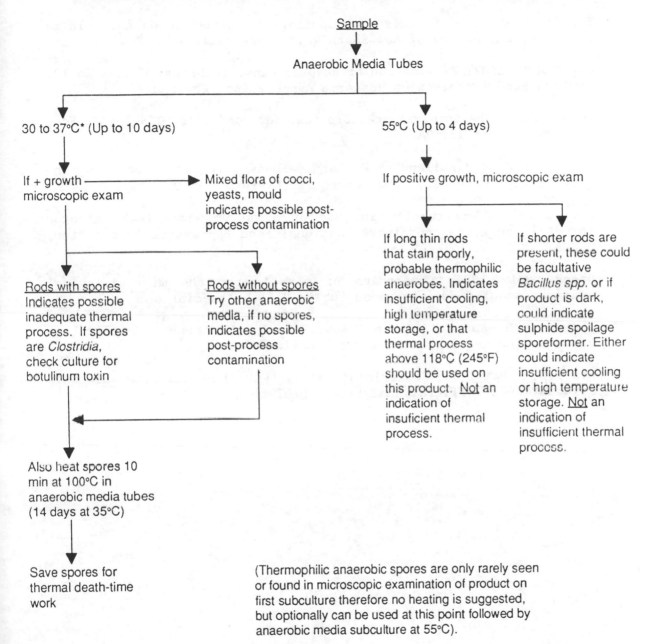

(* Conditions for microbial growth are optimal at 30 to 35°C. However, incubation temperatures of 36°C or 37°C may be used depending upon regional environmental conditions.)

8.   <u>REFERENCES</u>

1.   AFNOR-CNERNA 1982. Expertise des conserves appertisées: Aspectstechniques et microbiologiques, France.

2.   Buckle, K.A. 1985. Diagnosis of spoilage in canned foods and related products, University of New South Wales, Australia.

3.   C.F.P.R.A. 1987. Examination of suspect cans. Technical Manual No.18. Campden Food Preservation Research Association, England.

4.   Empey, W.A., The internal pressure test for food cans, C.S.I.R.O. Food Preserv. Q. 4:8-13;1944.

5.   Hersom, A.C. and Hulland, E.D. Canned Foods: thermal processing and microbiology, 7th ed., 1980, Churchill Livingstone, Edinburgh.

6.   N.C.A. 1972. Construction and use of a vacuum micro-leak detector formetal and glass containers. National Food Processors Association, U.S.A.

7.   Speck, M.L. 1984. Compendium of methods for the microbiological examination of foods. American Public Health Association.

8.   Thorpe, R.H. and P.M. Baker. 1984. Visual can defects. Campden Food Preservation Research Association, England.

9.   U.S.F.D.A. BAM 1984. Bacteriological Analytical Manual (6th edition). Association of Official Analytical Chemists.

Appendix 1

An Example of

A PRODUCT IDENTIFICATION AND HISTORY ENQUIRY FORM[*]

Date:............   Enquiry No...............

Compiled by.................................

1. **REASONS FOR INVESTIGATION**

   1. Spoilage

      1. How detected (consumer complaint, warehouse inspection, incubation study etc.)
      2. Date when problem first became known
      3. Nature of problem
      4. Extent of the problem (incidence of affected and non-affected containers)
      5. Number of burst, swollen or leaking containers observed.

   2. Illness

      (A more complete list of essential information for the investigation of foodborne illness can be found in the Procedures to Investigate Foodborne Illness, 4th Edition, 1986, International Milk, Food and Environmental Sanitarians Inc., P.O. 701, Ames, Iowa, 50010, U.S.A. The 3rd edition, published in 1976 is available in French and Spanish.)

      1. Number of persons affected
      2. Symptoms
      3. Time of last meal or snack
      4. Time elapsed before onset of symptoms
      5. What other foods and beverages were also ingested for up to 4 days before onset of symptoms?
      6. Number of containers of canned food involved
      7. Identity of product, including codes
      8. Complainant product and/or container available for analysis
      9. Were other samples of product having same code taken?
      10. How and where were samples sent for analysis?

2. **PRODUCT DESCRIPTION AND IDENTIFICATION**

   1. Product name and type
   2. Container type and size
   3. Identification of code lot(s) involved

---

[*]   This form is only intended to be an example and may require modification for a specific investigation. For instance, the data to be collected and Section 1.2 (illness) should be expanded if food poisoning is suspected.

4. Date of thermal processing
5. Processing establishment
6. Supplier/importer - if imported, date of entry into country
7. Sizes(s) of implicated lot(s)
8. Location of lot(s)

3. ## PRODUCT HISTORY RELATING TO SUSPECT CODE LOT(S)

1. Product composition
2. Container supplier and specifications

3. Production data (scheduled process) and records
    a. Product preparation
    b. Filling
    c. Sealing

4. Equipment used in thermal processing
    a. Thermal processing
    b. Cooling
    c. Additional quality control and assurance records

5. Storage and transportation
6. Current status of lot(s) under examination - if product not under direct control, describe area of distribution

4. ## SAMPLE DESCRIPTION AND HISTORY

1. Where, when and how was sample obtained
2. Sample size - number of containers
3. Total number of containers at the sample site
4. Number of containers having defects in the sample
5. List defects for each container
6. Describe conditions of storage and transportation
7. Sample identification (laboratory number assigned)

Appendix 2

PROCEDURES FOR MICROBIOLOGICAL ANALYSIS OF THE ANALYTICAL SAMPLE

A.   Mesophiles

1. Media and Incubation Conditions

	Low-Acid Foods (pH > 4.6)				Acidified Low-Acid Foods (pH =< 4.6)	
1. Incubation Conditions	Aerobic		Anaerobic		Aerobic	
2. Media (2)	Liquid DTB PE2	Solid PCA DTA NAMn	Liquid PE2 CMM LB RCM	Solid LVA PIA RCA BA	Liquid OSB TJB APTB APT	Solid PDA TJA SDA
3. Quantity of medium	15 ml/tube	15 ml/tube	15 ml/ tube	15 ml/ tube	15 ml/ tube for APTB 200 ml/flask	15 ml/ tube
4. Replication	=> 2 tubes	=> 2 plates	=> 2 tubes	=> 2 plates	=> 2 tubes for APTB => 3/flask	=> 2 plates
5. Incubation Temperature (3)	30°C	30°C	30°C	30°C	30°C (1)	30°C (1)
6. Incubation Time (4)	to 14 days	to 5 days	to 14 days	to 5 days	to 14 days	to 5 - 10 days

Use at least one medium for each series of solid and liquid media incubated aerobically and anaerobically.

Notes

(1)   Lower temperature, i.e., 20°C or 25°C may be appropriate in some instances, for example, for yeasts.

(2)   Abbreviations used for media

PCA - Plate count agar   OSB - Orange serum broth   DTA - Dextrose tryptone agar

CMM - Cooked meat medium   APTB - Acid products test broth   NAMn - Nutrient agar plus manganese

LB - Liver broth   APT - All purpose tween   DTB - Dextrose tryptone broth

RCM - Reinforced clostridial   PDA - Potato dextrose agar   RCA - Reinforced clostridial agar
medium

LVA - Liver veal agar   SDA - Sabourad dextrose agar   BA - Blood Agar

PIA - Pork infusion agar   TJB - Tomato juice broth   TJA - Tomato juice agar

PE2 - Peptone, yeast extract medium, Folinazzo (1954)

(3)   A temperature of 35°C or 37°C may be used in addition or when ambient (room) temperature is near to or greater than 30°C or when specific organisms of concern have higher optimal growth temperatures.

(4)   Examine tubes and plates periodically, e.g., at least every two days. Incubation is terminated when positive growth is observed.

2.   Verification of suspect positive tubes

All suspect positive tubes should be examined as follows:

1.   Carry out direct microscopic examination of suitably prepared and
      stained smears.

2.   Inoculate at least duplicate plates or slants, and incubate
      aerobically and anaerobically for up to 5 days. For suitable media
      see above.

(Note: If only one tube of each series of tubes inoculated is positive it
is recommended that the above procedure be repeated using analytical units
drawn from the reference sample. Further information with respect to
interpretation of single tube results is discussed in the section on
interpretation.)

3.   Identification of isolates

Facultative thermophiles can grow in cultures at 30°C to 37°C and hence be
mistaken for mesophiles. Positive isolates from cultures grown at these
temperatures must always be confirmed as true mesophiles by demonstrating that they
will not grow at thermophilic temperatures, 55°C.

To assist in identifying the cause of spoilage it is useful to identify
isolates. For this purpose standard microbiological procedures should be used (See
Speck, (1984); ICMSF, (1980); US FDA BAM, (1984)).

B.   Thermophiles

If circumstances suggest thermophilic spoilage, e.g., history of problem,
lowered pH of product, no growth occurring below 37°C (product liquified or not
obviously spoiled), culturing at 55°C on the following media is suggested.

Incubate for up to 10 days.

Thermophilic aerobes (flat sour) - Dextrose tryptone broth

B. coagulans (thermoacidurans) - Proteose peptone acid medium* at pH 5.0 (may
grow at 37°C)

Anaerobes not producing H_2S - Corn liver medium*

C. thermosaccharolyticum - Liver broth*

Anaerobes producing H_2S - Sulphite agar* + reduced iron or iron citrate

* (Hersom and Holland, 1980)

C.   Acid tolerant

It is preferable that all media used should be buffered to a pH value between
4.2 and 4.5.

1.   Liquid

   a)   Acid broth (AB) - (See US FDA BAM, 1984)

   b)   MRS broth, (de Man, Rogosa and Sharpe, 1960)

2.   Incubation

   30°C for up to 14 days.

SECTION 8

<u>**CODEX GENERAL STANDARD FOR IRRADIATED FOODS**</u>
(World-wide Standard)

CODEX STAN 106-1983

INTRODUCTION

The Codex General Standard for Irradiated Foods was adopted by the Codex Alimentarius Commission at its 13th Session in 1979 and was subsequently revised in 1983 by the 15th Session. This Standard has been submitted to all Member Nations and Associate Members of FAO and WHO for **acceptance** in accordance with the General Principles of the Codex Alimentarius.

CODEX GENERAL STANDARD FOR IRRADIATED FOODS[1]
(World-wide Standard)
CODEX STAN 106-1983

1.   <u>SCOPE</u>

      This standard applies to foods processed by irradiation. It does not apply to foods exposed to doses imparted by measuring instruments used for inspection purposes.

2.   <u>GENERAL REQUIREMENTS FOR THE PROCESS</u>

2.1   <u>Radiation Sources</u>

      The following types of ionizing radiation may be used:

(a)   Gamma rays from the radionuclides ^{60}Co or ^{137}Cs;

(b)   X-rays generated from machine sources operated at or below an energy level of 5 MeV.

(c)   Electrons generated from machine sources operated at or below an energy level of 10 MeV.

2.2   <u>Absorbed Dose</u>

      The overall average dose absorbed by a food subjected to radiation processing should not exceed 10 kGy[2] [3].

2.3   <u>Facilities and Control of the Process</u>

2.3.1   Radiation treatment of foods shall be carried out in facilities licensed and registered for this purpose by the competent national authority.

2.3.2   The facilities shall be designed to meet the requirements of safety, efficacy and good hygienic practices of food processing.

2.3.3   The facilities shall be staffed by adequate, trained and competent personnel.

---

[1] Revised version of the Recommended International General Standard for Irradiated Foods (CAC/RS 106-1979).

[2] For measurement and calculation of overall average dose absorbed, see Annex A of the Recommended International Code of Practice for the Operation of Radiation Facilities Used for Treatment of Foods (CAC/RCP 19-1979, Rev. 1)

[3] The wholesomeness of foods, irradiated so as to have absorbed an overall average dose of up to 10 kGy, is not impaired. In this context the term "wholesomeness" refers to safety for consumption of irradiated foods from the toxicological point of view. The irradiation of foods up to an overall average dose of 10 kGy introduces no special nutritional or microbiological problems (Wholesomeness of Irradiated Foods, Report of a Joint FAO/IAEA/WHO Expert Committee, Technical Report Series 659, WHO, Geneva, 1981).

2.3.4   Control of the process within the facility shall include the keeping of adequate records including quantitative dosimetry.

2.3.5   Premises and records shall be open to inspection by appropriate national authorities.

2.3.6   Control should be carried out in accordance with the Recommended International Code of Practice for the Operation of Radiation Facilities Used for the Treatment of Foods (CAC/RCP 19-1979, Rev. 1).

3.   **HYGIENE OF IRRADIATED FOODS**

3.1   The food should comply with the provisions of the Recommended International Code of Practice - General Principles of Food Hygiene (Ref. No.: CAC/RCP 1-1969,

3.2   Any relevant national public health requirement affecting microbiological safety and nutritional adequacy applicable in the country in which the food is sold should be observed.

4.   **TECHNOLOGICAL REQUIREMENTS**

4.1   Conditions for Irradiation

         The irradiation of food is justified only when it fulfils a technological need or where it serves a food hygiene purpose[1] and should not be used as a substitute for good manufacturing practices.

4.2   Food Quality and Packaging Requirements

         The doses applied shall be commensurate with the technological and public health purposes to be achieved and shall be in accordance with good radiation processing practice. Foods to be irradiated and their packaging materials shall be of suitable quality, acceptable hygienic condition and appropriate for this purpose and shall be handled, before and after irradiation, according to good manufacturing practices taking into account the particular requirements of the technology of the process.

5.   **RE-IRRADIATION**

5.1   Except for foods with low moisture content (cereals, pulses, dehydrated foods and other such commodities) irradiated for the purpose of controlling insect reinfestation, foods irradiated in accordance with Sections 2 and 4 of this standard shall not be re-irradiated.

5.2   For the purpose of this standard food is not considered as having been re-irradiated when: (a)   the food prepared from materials which have been irradiated at low dose levels, e.g., about 1 kGy, is irradiated for another technological purpose;   (b)   the food, containing less than 5% of irradiated ingredient, is irradiated, or when   (c)   the full dose of ionizing radiation required to achieve the desired effect is applied to the food in more than one instalment as part of processing for a specific technological purpose.

---

         [1] The utility of the irradiation process has been demonstrated for a number of food items listed in Annex B to the Recommended International Code of Practice for the Operation of Radiation Facilities Used for the Treatment of Foods.

5.3   The cumulative overall average dose absorbed should not exceed 10 kGy as a result of re-irradiation.

6.   **LABELLING**

6.1   Inventory Control

For irradiated foods, whether prepackaged or not, the relevant shipping documents shall give appropriate information to identify the registered facility which has irradiated the food, the date(s) of treatment and lot identification.

6.2   Prepackaged Foods Intended for Direct Consumption

The labelling of prepackaged irradiated foods shall be in accordance with the relevant provisions of the Codex General Standard for the Labelling of Prepackaged Foods.

6.3   Foods in Bulk Containers

The declaration of the fact or irradiation shall be made clear on the relevant shipping documents.

SECTION 8.1

RECOMMENDED INTERNATIONAL CODE OF PRACTICE FOR THE OPERATION OF IRRADIATION FACILITIES USED FOR THE TREATMENT OF FOODS

CAC/RCP 19-1979 (Rev. 1)

INTRODUCTION

The Recommended International Code of Practice for the Operation of Irradiation Facilities Used for the Treatment of Foods was adopted by the Codex Alimentarius Commission at its 13th Session, 1979 and subsequently revised in 1983 by the 15th Session. It has been sent to all Member Nations and Associate Members of FAO and WHO as an advisory text, and it is for individual governments to decide what use they wish to make of the Code. The Commission has expressed the view that codes of practice might provide useful checklists of requirements for national food control or enforcement authorities.

RECOMMENDED INTERNATIONAL CODE OF PRACTICE FOR THE OPERATION OF IRRADIATION FACILITIES USED FOR THE TREATMENT OF FOODS[1]

CAC/RCP 19-1979 (Rev. 1)

1.   ## INTRODUCTION

        This Code refers to the operation of irradiation facilities based on the use of either a radionuclide source (^{60}Co or ^{137}Cs) or X-rays and electrons generated from machine sources. The irradiation facility may be of two designs, either "continuous" or "batch" type. Control of the food irradiation process in all types of facility involves the use of accepted methods of measuring the absorbed radiation dose and of the monitoring of the physical parameters of the process. The operation of these facilities for the irradiation of food must comply with the Codex recommendations on food hygiene.

2.   ## IRRADIATION PLANTS

2.1   ## Parameters

        For all types of facility the doses absorbed by the product depend on the radiation parameter, the dwell time or the transportation speed of the product, and the bulk density of the material to be irradiated. Source-product geometry, especially distance of the product from the source and measures to increase the efficiency of radiation utilization, will influence the absorbed dose and the homogeneity of dose distribution.

2.1.1   ### Radionuclide sources

        Radionuclides used for food irradiation emit photons of characteristic energies. The statement of the source material completely determines the penetration of the emitted radiation. The source activity is measured in Becquerel (Bq) and should be stated by the supplying organization. The actual activity of the source (as well as any return or replenishment of radionuclide material) shall be recorded. The recorded activity should take into account the natural decay rate of the source and should be accompanied by a record of the date of measurement or recalculation. Radionuclide irradiators will usually have a well separated and shielded depository for the source elements and a treatment area which can be entered when the source is in the safe position. There should be a positive indication of the correct operational and of the correct safe position of the source which should be interlocked with the product movement system.

2.1.2   ### Machine sources

        A beam of electrons generated by a suitable accelerator, or after being converted to X-rays, can be used. The penetration of the radiation is governed by the energy of the electrons. Average beam power shall be adequately recorded. There should be a positive indication of the correct setting of all machine parameters which should be interlocked with the product movement system. Usually a beam scanner or a scattering device (e.g., the converting target) is incorporated in a machine source to obtain an even distribution of the radiation over the surface of the product. The product movement, the width and speed of the scan and

---

[1] Revised version of the Recommended International Code of Practice for the Operation of Radiation Facilities Used for the Treatment of Foods.

the beam pulse frequency (if applicable) should be adjusted to ensure a uniform surface dose.

2.2   Dosimetry and Process Control

          Prior to the irradiation of any foodstuff certain dosimetry measurements[1] should be made, which demonstrate that the process will satisfy the regulatory requirements. Various techniques for dosimetry pertinent to radionuclide and machine sources are available for measuring absorbed dose in a quantitative manner[2].

          Dosimetry commissioning measurements should be made for each new food, irradiation process and whenever modifications are made to source strength or type and to the source product geometry.

          Routine dosimetry should be made during operation and records kept of such measurement. In addition, regular measurements of facility parameters governing the process, such as transportation speed, dwell time, source exposure time, machine beam parameters, can be made during the facility operation. The records of these measurements can be used as supporting evidence that the process satisfies the regulatory requirements.

3.   **GOOD RADIATION PROCESSING PRACTICE**

          Facility design should attempt to optimize the dose uniformity ratio, to ensure appropriate dose rates and, where necessary, to permit temperature control during irradiation (e.g., for the treatment of frozen food) and also control of the atmosphere. It is also often necessary to minimize mechanical damage to the product during transportation irradiation and storage, and desirable to ensure the maximum efficiency in the use of the irradiator. Where the food to be irradiated is subject to special standards for hygiene or temperature control, the facility must permit compliance with these standards.

4.   **PRODUCT AND INVENTORY CONTROL**

4.1   The incoming product should be physically separated from the outgoing irradiated products.

4.2   Where appropriate, a visual colour change radiation indicator should be affixed to each product pack for ready identification of irradiated and non-irradiated products.

4.3   Records should be kept in the facility record book which show the nature and kind of the product being treated, its identifying marks if packed or, if not, the shipping details, its bulk density, the type of source or electron machine, the dosimetry, the dosimeters used and details of their calibration, and the date of treatment.

4.4   All products shall be handled, before and after irradiation, according to accepted good manufacturing practices taking into account the particular

---

          [1] See Annex A to this Code. 1/

          [2] Detailed in the Manual of Food Irradiation Dosimetry, IAEA, Vienna, 1977, Technical Report Series No. 178.

requirements of the technology of the process[1]. Suitable facilities for refrigerated storage may be required.

---

[1] See Annex B to this Code.

DOSIMETRY

1.   **The Overall Average Absorbed Dose**

It can be assumed for the purpose of the determination of the wholesomeness of food treated with an overall average dose of 10 kGy or less, that all radiation chemical effects in that particular dose range are proportional to dose.

The overall average dose, D, is defined by the following integral over the total volume of the goods

$$D + \frac{1}{M} \int \rho\ (x,\ y,\ z)\ .\ d\ (x,\ y,\ z)\ .\ dV$$

where

M	=	the total mass of the treated sample
ρ	=	the local density at the point (x, y, z)
d	=	the local absorbed dose at the point (x, y, z)
dV	=	dx dy dz the infinitesimal volume element which in real cases is represented by the volume fractions.

The overall average absorbed dose can be determined directly for homogeneous products or for bulk goods of homogeneous bulk density by distributing an adequate number of dose meters strategically and at random throughout the volume of the goods. From the dose distribution determined in this manner an average can be calculated which is the overall average absorbed dose.

If the shape of the dose distribution curve through the product is well determined the positions of minimum and maximum dose are known. Measurements of the distribution of dose in these two positions in a series of samples of the product can be used to give an estimate of the overall average dose. In some cases the mean value of the average values of the minimum (Dmin) and maximum (Dmax) dose will be a good estimate of the overall average dose.

i.e. in these cases:

overall average dose $\approx$ $\dfrac{Dmax + Dmin}{2}$

2.   **Effective and Limiting Dose Values**

Some effective treatment, e.g. the elimination of harmful microorganisms, or a particular shelflife extension, or a disinfestation, requires a minimum absorbed dose. For other applications too high an absorbed dose may cause undesirable effects or an impairment of the quality of the product.

The design of the facility and the operational parameters have to take into account minimum and maximum dose values required by the process. In some low dose applications it will be possible within the terms of Section 3 on Good Radiation Processing Practice to allow a ratio of maximum to minimum dose of greater than 3.

With regards to the maximum dose value under acceptable wholesomeness considerations and because of the statistical distribution of the dose a mass fraction of product of at least 97.5% should receive an absorbed dose of less than 15 kGy when the overall average dose is 10 kGy.

3.   Routine Dosimetry

Measurements of the dose in a reference position can be made occasionally throughout the process. The association between the dose in the reference position and the overall average dose must be known. These measurements should be used to ensure the correct operation of the process. A recognized and calibrated system of dosimetry should be used.

A complete record of all dosimetry measurements including calibration must be kept.

4.   Process Control

In the case of a continuous radionuclide facility it will be possible to make automatically a record of transportation speed or dwell time together with indications of source and product positioning. These measurements can be used to provide a continuous control of the process in support of routine dosimetry measurements.

In a batch operated radionuclide facility automatic recording of source exposure time can be made and a record of product movement and placement can be kept to provide a control of the process in support of routine dosimetry measurements.

In a machine facility a continuous record of beam parameters, e.g. voltage, current, scan speed, scan width, pulse repetition and a record of transportation speed through the beam can be used to provide a continuous control of the process in support of routine dosimetry measurements.

ANNEX B

EXAMPLES OF TECHNOLOGICAL CONDITIONS FOR THE IRRADIATION OF SOME INDIVIDUAL FOOD ITEMS SPECIFICALLY EXAMINED BY THE JOINT FAO/IAEA/WHO EXPERT COMMITTEE

This information is taken from the Reports of the Joint FAO/IAEA/WHO Expert Committees on Food Irradiation (WHO Technical Report Series, 604, 1977 and 659, 1981) and illustrates the utility of the irradiation process. It also describes the technological conditions for achieving the purpose of the irradiation process safely and economically.

1.   **CHICKEN (*Gallus domesticus*)**

1.1   Purposes of the Process

The purposes of irradiating chicken are:

(a)   to prolong storage life, and/or
(b)   to reduce the number of certain pathogenic microorganisms, such as *Salmonella* from eviscerated chicken.

1.2   Specific Requirements

Average dose: for (a) and (b), up to 7 kGy.

2.   **COCOA BEANS (*Theobroma cacao*)**

2.1   Purposes of the Process

The purposes of irradiating cocoa beans are:

(a)   to control insect infestation in storage,
(b)   to reduce microbial load of fermented beans with or without heat treatment.

2.2   Specific Requirements

2.2.1   Average dose: for (a) up to 1 kGy
                         for (b) up to 5 kGy

2.2.2   Prevention of Reinfestation: Cocoa beans whether prepackaged or handled in bulk, should be stored as far as possible, under such conditions as will prevent reinfestation and microbial recontamination and spoilage.

3.   **DATES (*Phoenix dactylifera*)**

3.1   Purpose of the Process

The purpose of irradiating prepackaged dried dates is to control insect infestation during storage.

3.2   Specific Requirements

3.2.1   Average dose: up to 1 kGy.

3.2.2   Prevention of Reinfestation: Prepackaged dried dates should be stored
under such conditions as will prevent reinfestation.

4.   MANGOES (Mangifera indica)

4.1   Purposes of the Process

             The purposes of irradiating mangoes are:

    (a)   to control insect infestation,
    (b)   to improve keeping quality by delaying ripening,
    (c)   to reduce microbial load by combining irradiation and heat treatment.

4.2   Specific Requirements

             Average dose: up to 1 kGy.

5.   ONIONS (Allium cepa)

5.1   Purpose of the Process

             The purpose of irradiating onions is to inhibit sprouting during
storage.

5.2   Specific Requirement

             Average dose: up to 0.15 kGy.

6.   PAPAYA (Carica papaya L.)

6.1   Purpose of the Process

             The purpose of irradiating papaya is to control insect infestation and
to improve its keeping quality by delaying ripening.

6.2   Specific Requirements

6.2.1   Average dose: up to 1 kGy.

6.2.2   Source of Radiation: The source of radiation should be such as will
provide adequate penetration.

7.   POTATOES (Solanum tuberosum L.)

7.1   Purpose of the process

             The purpose of irradiating potatoes is to inhibit sprouting during
storage.

7.2   Specific Requirement

             Average dose: up to 0.15 kGy.

8.   **PULSES**

8.1   Purpose of the Process

          The purpose of irradiating pulses is to control insect infestation in
storage.

8.2   Specific Requirement

          Average dose: up to 1 kGy.

9.   **RICE (*Oryza species*)**

9.1   Purpose of the Process

          The purpose of irradiating rice is to control insect infestation in
storage.

9.2   Specific Requirements

9.2.1   Average dose: up to 1 kGy.

9.2.2   Prevention of Reinfestation: Rice, whether pre-packaged or handled in
bulk, should be stored as far as possible, under such conditions as will prevent
reinfestation.

10.   **SPICES AND CONDIMENTS, DEHYDRATED ONIONS, ONION POWDER**

10.1   Purposes of the Process

          The purposes of irradiating spices, condiments, dehydrated onions and
onion powder are:

          (a)   to control insect infestation
          (b)   to reduce microbial load
          (c)   to reduce the number of pathogenic microorganisms.

10.2   Specific Requirement

          Average dose: for (a) up to 1 kGy
                         for (b) and (c) up to 10 kGy.

11.   **STRAWBERRY (*Fragaria species*)**

11.1   Purpose of the Process

          The purpose of irradiating fresh strawberries is to prolong the storage
life by partial elimination of spoilage organisms.

11.2   Specific Requirement

          Average dose: up to 3 kGy.

12.   **TELEOST FISH AND FISH PRODUCTS**

12.1   Purposes of the Process

           The purposes of irradiating teleost fish and fish products are:

   (a)   to control insect infestation of dried fish during storage and
           marketing;
   (b)   to reduce microbial load of the packaged or unpackaged fish and fish
           products;
   (c)   to reduce the number of certain pathogenic microorganisms in packaged
           or unpackaged fish and fish products.

12.2   Specific Requirements

12.2.1   Average dose: for (a) up to 1kGy
                          for (b) and (c) up to 2.2 kGy.

12.2.2   Temperature Requirement: During irradiation and storage the fish and
fish products referred to in (b) and (c) should be kept at the temperature of
melting ice.

13.   **WHEAT AND GROUND WHEAT PRODUCTS (*Triticum Species*)**

13.1   Purpose of the Process

           The purpose of irradiating wheat and ground wheat products is to
control insect infestation in the stored product.

13.2   Specific Requirements

13.2.1   Average dose: up to 1 kGy.

13.2.2   Prevention of Reinfestation: These products, whether prepackaged or
handled in bulk, should be stored as far as possible under such conditions as will
prevent reinfestation.

LIST OF STANDARDS, CODES OF PRACTICE AND OTHER TEXTS
ADOPTED BY THE CODEX ALIMENTARIUS COMMISSION

Standard or Other Text	Reference	Type
Labelling of Prepackaged Foods	CODEX STAN 001	Standard
Canned Pacific Salmon	CODEX STAN 003	Standard
White Sugar	CODEX STAN 004	Standard
Powdered Sugar (Icing Sugar)	CODEX STAN 005	Standard
Soft Sugars	CODEX STAN 006	Standard
Dextrose, Anhydrous	CODEX STAN 007	Standard
Dextrose, Monohydrate	CODEX STAN 008	Standard
Glucose Syrup	CODEX STAN 009	Standard
Dried Glucose Syrup	CODEX STAN 010	Standard
Lactose	CODEX STAN 011	Standard
Honey	CODEX STAN 012	Standard
Canned Tomatoes	CODEX STAN 013	Standard
Canned Peaches	CODEX STAN 014	Standard
Canned Grapefruit	CODEX STAN 015	Standard
Canned Green Beans & Canned Wax Beans	CODEX STAN 016	Standard
Canned Applesauce	CODEX STAN 017	Standard
Canned Sweet Corn	CODEX STAN 018	Standard
General Standard for Fats & Oils	CODEX STAN 019	Standard
Edible Soya Bean Oil	CODEX STAN 020	Standard
Edible Arachis Oil	CODEX STAN 021	Standard
Edible Cottonseed Oil	CODEX STAN 022	Standard
Edlible Sunflowerseed Oil	CODEX STAN 023	Standard
Edible Rapeseed Oil	CODEX STAN 024	Standard
Edible Maize Oil	CODEX STAN 025	Standard
Edible Sesameseed Oil	CODEX STAN 026	Standard
Edible Safflowerseed Oil	CODEX STAN 027	Standard
Lard	CODEX STAN 028	Standard
Rendered Pork Fat	CODEX STAN 029	Standard
Premier Jus	CODEX STAN 030	Standard
Edible Tallow	CODEX STAN 031	Standard
Margarine	CODEX STAN 032	Standard
Olive Oil	CODEX STAN 033	Standard
Mustardseed Oil	CODEX STAN 034	Standard

Standard or Other Text	Reference	Type
Quick-Frozen Gutted Pacific Salmon	CODEX STAN 036	Standard
Canned Shrimps or Prawns	CODEX STAN 037	Standard
Edible Fungi & Fungus Products	CODEX STAN 038	Standard
Dried Edible Fungi	CODEX STAN 039	Standard
Fresh Fungus "Chanterelle"	CODEX STAN 040	Standard
Quick Frozen Peas	CODEX STAN 041	Standard
Canned Pineapple	CODEX STAN 042	Standard
Apricot, Peach & Pear Nectars	CODEX STAN 044	Standard
Orange Juice	CODEX STAN 045	Standard
Grapefruit Juice	CODEX STAN 046	Standard
Lemon Juice	CODEX STAN 047	Standard
Apple Juice	CODEX STAN 048	Standard
Tomato Juice	CODEX STAN 049	Standard
Quick Frozen Fillets of Cod & Haddock	CODEX STAN 050	Standard
Quick Frozen Fillets of Ocean Perch	CODEX STAN 051	Standard
Quick Frozen Strawberries	CODEX STAN 052	Standard
Foods with Low-Sodium Content	CODEX STAN 053	Standard
Powdered Dextrose (Icing Dextrose)	CODEX STAN 054	Standard
Canned Mushrooms	CODEX STAN 055	Standard
Canned Asparagus	CODEX STAN 056	Standard
Processed Tomato Concentrates	CODEX STAN 057	Standard
Canned Green Peas	CODEX STAN 058	Standard
Canned Plums	CODEX STAN 059	Standard
Canned Raspberries	CODEX STAN 060	Standard
Canned Pears	CODEX STAN 061	Standard
Canned Strawberries	CODEX STAN 062	Standard
Concentrated Apple Juice	CODEX STAN 063	Standard
Concentrated Orange Juice	CODEX STAN 064	Standard
Table Olives	CODEX STAN 066	Standard
Raisins	CODEX STAN 067	Standard
Canned Mandarin Oranges	CODEX STAN 068	Standard
Quick Frozen Raspberries	CODEX STAN 069	Standard
Canned Tuna & Bonito in Water or Oil	CODEX STAN 070	Standard
Infant Formula	CODEX STAN 072	Standard

Standard or Other Text	Reference	Type
Canned Baby Foods	CODEX STAN 073	Standard
Processed Cereal—Based Foods for Infants & Children	CODEX STAN 074	Standard
Quick Frozen Peaches	CODEX STAN 075	Standard
Quick Frozen Bilberries	CODEX STAN 076	Standard
Quick Frozen Spinach	CODEX STAN 077	Standard
Canned Fruit Cocktail	CODEX STAN 078	Standard
Jams (Fruit Preserves) & Jellies	CODEX STAN 079	Standard
Citrus Marmalade	CODEX STAN 080	Standard
Canned Mature Processed Peas	CODEX STAN 081	Standard
Grape Juice	CODEX STAN 082	Standard
Concentrated Grape Juice	CODEX STAN 083	Standard
Sweetened Concentrated Labrusca Type Grape Juice	CODEX STAN 084	Standard
Pineapple Juice	CODEX STAN 085	Standard
Cocoa Butters	CODEX STAN 086	Standard
Chocolate	CODEX STAN 087	Standard
Canned Corned Beef	CODEX STAN 088	Standard
Luncheon Meat	CODEX STAN 089	Standard
Canned Crab Meat	CODEX STAN 090	Standard
Quick Frozen Fillets of Flat Fish	CODEX STAN 091	Standard
Quick Frozen Shrimps or Prawns	CODEX STAN 092	Standard
Quick Frozen Fillets of Hake	CODEX STAN 093	Standard
Canned Sardines & Sardine—Type Products	CODEX STAN 094	Standard
Quick Frozen Lobsters	CODEX STAN 095	Standard
Cooked Cured Ham	CODEX STAN 096	Standard
Cooked Cured Pork Shoulder	CODEX STAN 097	Standard
Cooked Cured Chopped Meat	CODEX STAN 098	Standard
Canned Tropical Fruit Salad	CODEX STAN 099	Standard
Non—Pulpy Blackcurrant Nectar	CODEX STAN 101	Standard
Fructose	CODEX STAN 102	Standard
Quick Frozen Blueberries	CODEX STAN 103	Standard
Quick Frozen Leek	CODEX STAN 104	Standard
Cocoa Powders (Cocoa) & Dry Cocoa Sugar Mixtures	CODEX STAN 105	Standard
Irradiated Foods	CODEX STAN 106	Standard

Standard or Other Text	Reference	Type
Labelling of Food Additives When Sold as Such	CODEX STAN 107	Standard
Natural Mineral Waters	CODEX STAN 108	Standard
Quick Frozen Broccoli	CODEX STAN 110	Standard
Quick Frozen Cauliflower	CODEX STAN 111	Standard
Quick Frozen Brussels Sprouts	CODEX STAN 112	Standard
Quick Frozen Green & Wax Beans	CODEX STAN 113	Standard
Quick Frozen French-Fried Potatoes	CODEX STAN 114	Standard
Pickled Cucumbers (Cucumber Pickles)	CODEX STAN 115	Standard
Canned Carrots	CODEX STAN 116	Standard
Bouillons & Consommés	CODEX STAN 117	Standard
Gluten-Free Foods	CODEX STAN 118	Standard
Canned Mackerel & Jack Mackerel	CODEX STAN 119	Standard
Blackcurrant Juice	CODEX STAN 120	Standard
Concentrated Blackcurrant Juice	CODEX STAN 121	Standard
Pulpy Nectars of Certain Small Fruits	CODEX STAN 122	Standard
Edible Low Erucic Acid Rapeseed Oil	CODEX STAN 123	Standard
Edible Coconut Oil	CODEX STAN 124	Standard
Edible Palm Oil	CODEX STAN 125	Standard
Edible Palm Kernel Oil	CODEX STAN 126	Standard
Edible Grapeseed Oil	CODEX STAN 127	Standard
Edible Babassu Oil	CODEX STAN 128	Standard
Canned Apricots	CODEX STAN 129	Standard
Dried Apricots	CODEX STAN 130	Standard
Unshelled Pistachio Nuts	CODEX STAN 131	Standard
Quick Frozen Whole Kernel Corn	CODEX STAN 132	Standard
Quick Frozen Corn-on-the-Cob	CODEX STAN 133	Standard
Nectars of Certain Citrus Fruits	CODEX STAN 134	Standard
Minarine	CODEX STAN 135	Standard
Edible Ices	CODEX STAN 137	Standard
Concentrated Pineapple Juice	CODEX STAN 138	Standard
Concentrated Pineapple Juice with Preservatives for Manufacturing	CODEX STAN 139	Standard
Quick Frozen Carrots	CODEX STAN 140	Standard

Standard or Other Text	Reference	Type
Cocoa (Cocao) Nib, Cocoa (Cocao) Mass, Cocoa Press Cake and Cocoa Dust (Cocoa Fines), for use in the manufacturing of Cocoa and Chocolate Products	CODEX STAN 141	Standard
Composite & Filled Chocolate	CODEX STAN 142	Standard
Canned Palmito	CODEX STAN 143	Standard
Dates	CODEX STAN 144	Standard
Canned Chestnuts & Chestnut Purée	CODEX STAN 145	Standard
Labelling of and Claims for Foods for Special Dietary Uses	CODEX STAN 146	Standard
Cocoa Butter Confectionery	CODEX STAN 147	Standard
Guava Nectar	CODEX STAN 148	Standard
Liquid Pulpy Mango products	CODE STAN 149	Standard
Food Grade Salt	CODE STAN 150	Standard
Gari	CODEX STAN 151	Standard
Wheat Flour	CODEX STAN 152	Standard
Maize (Corn)	CODEX STAN 153	Standard
Whole Maize (Corn) Meal	CODEX STAN 154	Standard
Degermed Maize (Corn) Meal & Maize (Corn) Grits	CODEX STAN 155	Standard
Follow−Up Formula	CODEX STAN 156	Standard
Specified Vegetable Fat Products	CODEX STAN 157	Standard
Specified Animal or Mixed Animal & Vegetable Fat Products	CODEX STAN 158	Standard
Canned Mangoes	CODEX STAN 159	Standard
Mango Chutney	CODEX STAN 160	Standard
General Standard for Fruit Nectars	CODEX STAN 161	Standard
Vinegar	CODEX STAN 162	Standard
Wheat Gluten	CODEX STAN 163	Standard
General Standard for Fruit Juices	CODEX STAN 164	Standard
Quick Frozen Blocks of Fish Fillet, Minced Fish Flesh and Mixtures of Fillets and Minced Fish Flesh	CODEX STAN 165	Standard
Quick Frozen Fish Sticks (Fish Fingers) and Fish Portions − Breaded or in Batter	CODEX STAN 166	Standard
Dried Salted Fish (Klippfish) of the Gadidae Family	CODEX STAN 167	Standard
Mayonnaise	CODEX STAN 168	Standard
Pearl Millet Grains	CODEX STAN 169	Standard

Standard or Other Text	Reference	Type
Pearl Millet Flour	CODEX STAN 170	Standard
Certain Pulses	CODEX STAN 171	Standard
Sorghum Grains	CODEX STAN 172	Standard
Sorghum Flour	CODEX STAN 173	Standard
Vegetable Protein Products	CODEX STAN 174	Standard
Soy Protein Products	CODEX STAN 175	Standard
Edible Cassava Flour	CODEX STAN 176	Standard
Grated Desiccated Coconut	CODEX STAN 177	Standard
Durum Wheat Semolina & Durum Wheat Flour	CODEX STAN 178	Standard
Vegetable Juices	CODEX STAN 179	Standard
Foods for Special Medical Purposes; Labelling & Claims	CODEX STAN 180	Standard
Formula Foods for Use in Weight-Control Diets	CODEX STAN 181	Standard
Evaporated Milk & Evaporated Skim Milk	A-03	Standard
Sweetened Condensed Milk and Skimmed Sweetened Condensed Milk	A-04	Standard
Whole Milk Powder, Partly Skimmed Milk Powder & Skimmed Milk Powder	A-05	Standard
Cheese, General Standard	A-06	Standard
Whey Cheese, General Standard	A-07	Standard
General Standard for Named Variety Process(ed) Cheese & Spreadable Process(ed) Cheese	A-08a	Standard
General Standard for Process(ed) Cheese & Spreadable Process(ed) Cheese	A-08b	Standard
General Standard for Process(ed) Cheese Preparations	A-08c	Standard
Cream for Direct Consumption	A-09	Standard
Cream Powder, Half Cream Powder & High Fat Milk Powder	A-10	Standard
Yoghurt & Sweetened Yoghurt	A-11a	Standard
Flavoured Yoghurt & Products Heat-Treated after Fermentation	A-11b	Standard
Edible Acid Casein	A-12	Standard
Edible Caseinates	A-13	Standard
Cheddar	C-01	Standard
Danablu	C-02	Standard

Standard or Other Text	Reference	Type
Danbo	C—03	Standard
Edam	C—04	Standard
Gouda	C—05	Standard
Havarti	C—06	Standard
Samsoe	C—07	Standard
Cheshire	C—08	Standard
Emmentaler	C—09	Standard
Gruyère	C—10	Standard
Tilsiter	C—11	Standard
Limburger	C—12	Standard
Saint—Paulin	C—13	Standard
Svecia	C—14	Standard
Provolone	C—15	Standard
Cottage Cheese, including Creamed Cottage Cheese	C—16	Standard
Butterkase	C—17	Standard
Coulommiers	C—18	Standard
Gudbrandsalsost (Whey Cheese)	C—19	Standard
Harzer Kase	C—20	Standard
Herrgardsost	C—21	Standard
Husallsost	C—22	Standard
Norvegia	C—23	Standard
Maribo	C—24	Standard
Fynbo	C—25	Standard
Esrom	C—26	Standard
Romadur	C—27	Standard
Amsterdam	C—28	Standard
Leidse (Leyden)	C—29	Standard
Friese (Frisian)	C—30	Standard
Cream Cheese (Rahmfrischkase)	C—31	Standard
Blue—Veined Cheeses	C—32	Standard
Camembert	C—33	Standard
Brie	C—34	Standard
Extra Hard Grating Cheese	C—35	Standard
Guidelines on Claims	GL 1	Guidelines

Standard or Other Text	Reference	Type
Guidelines on Nutrition Labelling	GL 2	Guidelines
Evaluation of Food Additive Intake	GL 3	Guidelines
Utilization of Vegetable Protein Products in Foods	GL 4	Guidelines
Radionuclides in Foods	GL 5	Guidelines
Acrylontrile/Vinyl Chloride Monomer	GL 6	Guidelines
Methyl Mercury in Fish	GL 7	Guidelines
Formulated Supplementary Foods for Older Infants and Young Children	GL 8	Guidelines
Addition of Essential Nutrients to Foods	GL 9	Principles
Vitamin Compounds & Mineral Salts; List of	GL 10	Advisory
Mixed Fruit Juices	GL 11	Guidelines
Mixed Fruit Nectars	GL 12	Guidelines
Preservation of Raw Milk by Lactoperoxidase System	GL 13	Guidelines
Spices and Herbs Used in Processed Meat and Poultry Products; Microbiological Quality	GL 14	Guidelines
Standardized Non-Meat Protein Products in Processed Meat and Poultry Products	GL 15	Guidelines
General Principles of Food Hygiene	RCP 01	Code
Canned Fruit & Vegetable Products	RCP 02	Code
Dried Fruits	RCP 03	Code
Dessicated Coconut	RCP 04	Code
Dehydrated Fruits & Vegetables including Fungi	RCP 05	Code
Tree Nuts	RCP 06	Code
International System for Description of Carcasses	RCP 07	Code
Quick Frozen Foods	RCP 08	Code
Fresh Fish	RCP 09	Code
Canned Fish	RCP 10	Code
Fresh Meat	RCP 11	Code
Processed Meat & Poultry Products	RCP 13	Code
Poultry Processing	RCP 14	Code
Egg Products	RCP 15	Code
Frozen Fish	RCP 16	Code
Shrimps & Prawns	RCP 17	Code

Standard or Other Text	Reference	Type
Molluscan Shellfish	RCP 18	Code
Irradiation Facilities used for the Treatment of Foods	RCP 19	Code
Code of Ethics for International Trade in Foods	RCP 20	Code
Foods for Infants & Children	RCP 21	Code
Groundnuts	RCP 22	Code
Low-Acid & Acidified Low-Acid Canned Foods	RCP 23	Code
Lobsters	RCP 24	Code
Smoked Fish	RCP 25	Code
Salted Fish	RCP 26	Code
Minced Fish prepared by Mechanical Separation	RCP 27	Code
Crabs	RCP 28	Code
Game	RCP 29	Code
Frog Legs	RCP 30	Code
Dried Milk	RCP 31	Code
Mechanically Separated Meat & Poultry Meat	RCP 32	Code
Natural Mineral Waters	RCP 33	Code
Ante-Mortem & Post-Mortem Judgement of Slaughter Animals & Meat	RCP 34	Code
Frozen Battered and/or Breaded Fishery Products	RCP 35	Code
Storage & Transport of Edible Oils & Fats in Bulk	RCP 36	Code
Cephalpods	RCP 37	Code
International Numbering System for Food Additives		Advisory
Natural Flavorings		Advisory
Mineral Salts & Vitamin Compounds for use in Foods for Infants and Children		Advisory
Information on the Use of Food Additives	CAC Misc-1	Advisory